THE CONSTITUTION IN A HALL OF MIRRORS

Canada at 150

D1568916

Whether it's the first-past-the-post electoral system or partisan government appointees to the Senate, Canadians want better representation and accountability from the federal government. Before reforms can be enacted, however, it is important to explore and clarify the relationships among Canada's three parliamentary institutions: Crown, Senate, and Commons.

In *The Constitution in a Hall of Mirrors*, David E. Smith presents a learned but accessible analysis of the interconnectedness of Canada's parliamentary institutions. Smith argues that Parliament is a unity comprised of three parts, and any reforms made to one branch will, whether intended or not, affect the other branches. Through a timely, nuanced, and comprehensive examination of parliamentary debates, committee reports, legal scholarship, and comparative analysis of developments in the United Kingdom, Smith uncovers the substantial degree of ambiguity that exists among Canadians and their calls for structural and operational reforms. By illuminating the symbiotic relationship between the Crown, Senate, and Commons, *The Constitution in a Hall of Mirrors* brings government reform closer to reality.

DAVID E. SMITH is Distinguished Visiting Professor in Politics and Public Administration at Ryerson University.

DAVID E. SMITH

The Constitution in a Hall of Mirrors

Canada at 150

UNIVERSITY OF TORONTO PRESS
Toronto Buffalo London

© University of Toronto Press 2017
Toronto Buffalo London
www.utppublishing.com
Printed in Canada

ISBN 978-1-4875-0247-8 (cloth)   ISBN 978-1-4875-2198-1 (paper)

♾ Printed on acid-free, 100% post-consumer recycled paper with vegetable-based inks.

Library and Archives Canada Cataloguing in Publication

Smith, David E., 1936–, author
The constitution in a hall of mirrors : Canada at
150 / David E. Smith.

Includes bibliographical references and index.
ISBN 978-1-4875-0247-8 (cloth). – ISBN 978-1-4875-2198-1 (paper)

1. Canada. Parliament – Reform.   2. Canada – Politics and
government.   I. Title.

JL136.S65 2017   328.71   C2017-901920-1

This book has been published with the help of a grant from the Federation
for the Humanities and Social Sciences, through the Awards to Scholarly
Publications Program, using funds provided by the Social Sciences and
Humanities Research Council of Canada.

University of Toronto Press acknowledges the financial assistance to its
publishing program of the Canada Council for the Arts and the Ontario
Arts Council, an agency of the Government of Ontario.

 Canada Council   Conseil des Arts
for the Arts   du Canada

 ONTARIO ARTS COUNCIL
CONSEIL DES ARTS DE L'ONTARIO
an Ontario government agency
un organisme du gouvernement de l'Ontario

Funded by the   Financé par le
Government   gouvernement
of Canada   du Canada

 Canadä

Dedicated to senators and members of the House of Commons,
Parliament of Canada

Contents

Preface   ix

1 Reflections   3

2 Refraction: The Crown   26

3 Redefinition: The Senate of Canada   49

4 Readjustment: The House of Commons   87

5 Reconsideration   112

6 Recapitulation   134

Notes   143
Bibliography   169
Index   189

Preface

Few phrases have had more influence on political and legal conscious-ness in Canada than that found in the first sentence of the Preamble to the Constitution Act, 1867, which speaks of the desire of the British North American colonies "to be federally united ... with a Constitution similar in Principle to that of the United Kingdom." As the following chapters will illustrate, the ambition of realizing, within a very un-British system of divided jurisdiction, a constitution by association – a constitution of a constitution, one could say – proved more malleable in definition than in achievement. Doubtless, the phrase embraced the three parts of Parliament: Crown, Commons, and a second chamber, in the case of Canada, the Senate. Arguably, it encompassed as well the "ways" of parliamentary government inherited from the United Kingdom: custom, convention, common law, in short, continuity itself. But what adaptation and at what pace?

As the country celebrates the sesquicentennial of its founding, there can be few of its citizens (the daily irritants of democratic governing aside) who would dissent from the proposition that Canada has one of the world's most enduring and successful constitutions. It is among a handful of countries that existed in 1914 and retain the same form of government as then. Peaceful constitutional evolution is the accepted Canadian way, to such a degree that the political system too often is thought to be unchanging and unchangeable. Of course, this is a false impression. The adoption in 1982 of the Canadian Charter of Rights and Freedoms, a domestic amending formula for the constitution (after decades of lack of agreement), and recognition, in section 35, of existing Aboriginal and treaty rights, offer contrary evidence to the sense of sta-sis that critics claim. It would reveal much about the political system's elasticity if the exceptional conditions of three decades ago that made such change acceptable and achievable were closely scrutinized. Yet aside from the details of the federal-provincial negotiations in the early 1980s, the larger influences leading to and the implications of agreement then have gone unstudied. Nor is this the purpose of the present analysis, whose concern is less with the past than it is change of systemic magnitude now underway in Canadian politics.

Such a proposition challenges long-held assumptions about political institutions in Canada, assumptions that originate in the assertion that the constitution on this side of the Atlantic is "similar in Principle" to that on the other side, even though it has always been open to question how similar the political experience of a historic, imperial, unitary, island-state might be to that of a New World, continent-wide, bilingual federation of settlement among Indigenous peoples. Nonetheless, the endurance of British institutions has shrunk Canadian imaginations about politics and democracy itself. Of Parliament's three parts, the Crown and the second chamber in Canada have suffered most from myopia – the Crown indelibly tied to royalty and the unelected Senate equated with the aristocratic House of Lords, although the replacement of hereditary with appointed peers today has – from the perspective of personnel, at least – made the original at Westminster resemble its colonial imitation rather than the opposite.

Too often the images Canadians perceive in their looking glass are not the institutions that actually serve them. Instead, the Crown is viewed as "British," and the Senate a flawed imitation of the Lords as well as a failed federal second chamber, when measured against the upper houses of the United States Congress and Australian Parliament. What should be seen as distinctively Canadian is dismissed and, in the case of the Senate, disparaged. The House of Commons too is labelled a failure, less however because of distortion in reflecting an original concept than in its own right as a representative institution that fails to exercise effective control over government. In short, a squandering of understanding of the Canadian constitution results from external criticism based on the model of another country, criticism that has reinforced the system being criticized but has failed to bring about change. The proposal for a Triple-E Senate, as well as the serial attempts by the government of Stephen Harper over the last decade or so to introduce an indirect electoral component in the selection of nominees for appointment to the Senate, did not succeed because they were devoid of a coherent theory of the constitution. Paradoxically, they did have one lasting effect: to raise the prominence of bicameralism as an essential feature of parliamentary government in the federation – a prominence that is confirmed by the ruling of the Supreme Court of Canada on Senate Reform (2014 SCC 32) and that guarantees a transformation in the governing practices of Canada.

Decades of talk about, but no action on, Senate reform or a more effective House of Commons – but significantly not of the Crown, monarchy, or republicanism, where the predominant sound remains silence – have accustomed Canadians to constitutional and political inertia. It has also dulled their recognition of change when it happens. Another reason for the astigmatism is that change of this order in Canada usually comes from above – which was true of the federal-provincial conferences that over time led to the Constitution Act, 1982. In Canada, there is no constituent power, such as "the people," outside of Parliament, with the result that direct democratic mechanisms, referenda and plebiscites for example, have proved frail weapons in the arsenal of popular opposition to government. Social media and modern electronic communications generally may permanently breach Parliament's defences, but that is in the future.

The purpose of the present study is to assess the significance of constitutional change currently underway or about to begin in the three parts of Parliament. These include the transposition of a Canadian Crown in place of a vestigial monarchy; the rehabilitation of the Senate of Canada in a Parliament where bicameralism has recently been granted unprecedented meaning by the Supreme Court of Canada; and the exploration by Parliament of the new political world that proportional representation purports to offer the House of Commons and the electorate. Having "a Constitution similar in Principle to that of the United Kingdom" has meant that Canada inherited not just institutions but also interpretations of how those institutions worked. Illustrative of that statement is Walter Bagehot's book *The English Constitution*, wherein the author categorizes Crown and Lords as "dignified" parts of the constitution, as compared to its "efficient" parts, cabinet and Commons. Thus in Canada, Crown and Senate lived in the shadows that Bagehot's taxonomy cast until the Supreme Court was called upon to give meaning to section 41(a) of the Constitution Act, 1982, which requires unanimous consent of all legislative bodies in Canada to amend, among other matters, the "office" of the Queen, the governor general and the lieutenant governor of a province, as well as the composition of the Supreme Court of Canada.

Parliament today is a very different institution from what it was not only in 1867 but in 1982. The changes that are underway, their implication for the constitution, and consequent ramification for the political system are the subject of the chapters that follow. The "Hall of Mirrors" reference in the book's title is a metaphor for the uncertainty, confusion, and contradiction that so often accompany discussion of politics in Canada. The analysis that follows is directed towards finding a solution to the puzzle that Canadians believe their political system presents. At one time, a royal commission might have offered a possible exit from the tangled skein of constitutional conundrums. In light of the pace of institutional change already underway in all parts of Parliament, that remedy – if such it might be – no longer appears either realistic or serviceable.

Not so many decades ago, it used to be said that Canadians must be the only people whose airport bookstores prominently carried publications devoted to the subject of federalism. While less true today than a quarter century ago, in part because the moment of federal tension seems to have passed, the observation warrants consideration, because it underlines the sense in Canada that governing the federation may be deemed a challenge. Yet that has never been the view of the conduct of parliamentary government. When reform of the Senate rises as an issue, as it frequently has, the subject has been treated as a matter of the Senate only. To the extent that the Crown or the Commons entered the picture, they too have been viewed as separate entities. Invariably, the larger and more complicated constitutional picture has been ignored.

The present book adopts a different perspective, arguing that in the matter of specific institutional reform it is necessary to evaluate the interrelationship of all parts of Parliament. In short, none can be understood clearly when treated in isolation. This is a major reason why reform – of the Senate, for example – has proven so difficult. On the one hand, an elected upper house poses a challenge to the elected lower house, while on the other, a chamber appointed by the governor general on recommendation of the prime minister is irrevocably tied to the prerogative of the Crown. How to make each compatible with its partners, and how to assure that each, in its distinctive manner, serves the public interest? Absent understanding of these interrelationships, change to any of Parliament's parts is most difficult to achieve.

The book is composed of six substantive chapters. Chapter One, "Reflections," examines the multiple and conflicting interpretations of parliamentary and popular government in twenty-first-century

Canada, and the influence these assessments exert on understanding of the role of Crown, Senate, and Commons. Chapter Two, "Refraction," borrows a term from physics that indicates the deflection light or radio waves experience when they pass between one medium and another. The subject of the chapter is the Crown, more particularly the Crown in Canada, and the emerging distinction between it and "the monarchy" – no longer is it enough to say of the first that it is "a reflection" of the second. Chapter Three is titled "Redefinition," a reference to the importance awarded by the Supreme Court of Canada to bicameralism as a principle of parliamentary government in Canada and to the consequences for the operation of the Senate that follow this rehabilitation. Chapter Four, which focuses on the House of Commons, has the title "Readjustment," a description that takes into account not only an altered relationship with the upper chamber in consequence of the Supreme Court's elevation of the importance of bicameralism but also an acknowledgment of the change latent in an alteration to the system of plurality elections that has prevailed since Confederation. Chapter Five, "Reconsideration," examines the interrelationship of the developments discussed earlier in the book. Among its themes are whether a new constitutional settlement between the Houses of Parliament may be necessary in order to reflect the enhanced legitimacy the Senate carries as a result of the Court's 2014 ruling; as well, there is the question of "the people," and whether, as many voters increasingly believe to be true, they fit in the scheme of parliamentary government, and if so, how; finally, there is the ever mutable, adaptable, intangible Crown – is it still the keystone of the constitutional architecture that grows more visible as Canada enters the second half of its second century? The last chapter, "Recapitulation," underlines the importance of the changes underway with regard to the constitution in Canada. Rather than being seen as a historical residue, the Crown and its prerogative are protected and, one may argue, thereby extended; the Senate, as one chamber of a bicameral Parliament, has been pronounced an equal partner (with the caveat about appropriations understood) in the legislative process; and the House of Commons, whether or not electoral reform of whatever manner is achieved, will necessarily find its relations with the other two parts of Parliament transformed.

As a Distinguished Visiting Scholar, I am indebted to Ryerson University for its support of my research and writing. I particularly wish to acknowledge the generosity of Jean-Paul Boudreau, dean of arts, and

Sorpong Peou, chair of the Department of Politics and Public Administration. Many individuals helped in this research, among whom I would like to thank Aram Adjemian, Richard Berthelsen, David Brock, Karen Dancy, Nathan Elliott, Senator Serge Joyal, Nicholas MacDonald, Eleni Nicolaides, Gary O'Brien, Sébastien Payet, and Neil Thomlinson. Part of chapter three originally appeared as a report titled "Coming to Terms: An Analysis of the Supreme Court Ruling on the Senate, 2014," prepared for a special committee of the upper house established to study renewal of the Senate. I am grateful to the committee for granting me permission to use that research in the context of the present book.

Ursula Acton, who on past occasions has successfully deciphered my handwriting, has more recently mastered the inexpertly typed draft of the manuscript I have presented her. Once more, I am in her debt. Equally, I wish to acknowledge the attentive but calm editorial guidance of Daniel Quinlan.

In April 1660, as he was about to depart France, where for nearly a decade he had sought refuge during the Interregnum, Charles II proclaimed his faith in parliamentary government. A wise commitment in light of past events, the king's pronouncement signalled more than self-interest, for it acknowledged the central importance of the Crown and Parliament – even more, the Crown-in-Parliament – to the future governing of the United Kingdom and, as was to transpire, the settler colonies, including Canada. "We do assure you ... that none of our predecessors have had a greater esteem of parliaments than we have ... we do believe them to be so vital a part of the constitution of the kingdom and so necessary for the government of it that we ever know neither prince nor people can be in any tolerable degree happy without them."[1]

Echoing that royal testament, I have dedicated this book to senators and members of Parliament, upon whose support and service the people of Canada depend in the era of politics now unfolding.

Niagara-on-the-Lake, Ontario, 2016

THE CONSTITUTION IN A HALL OF MIRRORS

Canada at 150

Reflections

In the beginning, this book was to be titled *Counterfeit Constitution*. Yet as appealing as brevity and alliteration were, veracity won the day. *Counterfeit* implies deception and fraud, and however much Canadians think their democracy is less than it should or could be, few believe it a scam. Nor was that the intent of the foregone title, which was to underline how far Canada's constitution is from being what its citizens think it is. Even this less malevolent distinction demands explanation, for in the world of constitutions and countries, Canada is among the blessed. According to the United Nations Human Development Index for 2016, which measures happiness in different countries on the basis of such factors as income, education, health, life expectancy, economy, gender equality, and sustainability, Canada ranks sixth of 157 nations.[1] Moreover, long before well-being became the sophisticated standard of international comparison, Canada's reputation as a politically stable democracy, committed to upholding minority rights and the rule of law, assured pre-eminence as a favoured country. The adjective *counterfeit* really did not apply where such exemplary conditions prevailed.

Nonetheless, the meaning of the term *Canadian constitution* is elusive on several fronts, beginning with the question: "Who is in charge?"

"Grandad, who is the president?"

"Canada does not have a president, Ryder; we have a prime minister."

"Did you vote for him?"

"No, only the people in the constituency where he lives have that choice. Governments in Canada are not elected. The leader of the party that commands the support of the House of Commons is the person who becomes prime minister and plays the role of president – more or less."

"When are we going to eat?"

Perhaps not verbatim, but the sentiment informing that exchange (with my nine-year-old grandson) remains true, and has been repeated over time – his father asked the same question thirty-five years before. Nor is it only the young who have difficulty comprehending the root of constitutional legitimacy in Canada. A senior editor (not with the University of Toronto Press), commenting on this point on the occasion of another constitutional exegesis, replied, "Surely, our government *is* 'democratically elected' and that's what gives it its 'legitimacy,' no?" On occasion, governments themselves may misspeak. In the case *Saskatchewan Federation of Labour v Saskatchewan (Attorney General)*, in reference to an order-in-council that used the phrase "on the day the Executive Council is first installed following a general election," the Saskatchewan Court of Appeal observed, "The 'Executive Council' is not 'installed' following every general election, but only a general election in which the party in power is defeated and another asked to form a government. The rationale for this lies in some of the basic elements of the structure of government, elements which tend to get obscured when addressed in the vernacular of practical politics."[2]

And not only in Canada is there mystification. When Malcolm Fraser – the man appointed prime minister in 1975 by Australia's governor general to replace Gough Whitlam, whom the governor general had dismissed – died in 2015, the *New York Times* News Service noted that "many Australians ... had no idea that, more than 70 years after the country gained independence from Britain, a representative of a British monarch could remove a democratically elected prime minister from office."[3]

And this mystery does not even extend to the imponderables associated with forming a coalition government, such as: "Is coalition legitimate?" At the time of the aborted Liberal-NDP coalition in 2008 – two months after a general election that saw the Conservatives under Stephen Harper continue in power although without a majority – opposition to the proposal, which in this instance was led by the government, fulminated that "[Dion] thinks he can take power without asking you, the voter."[4] The crux of the complaint, said historian Michael Bliss, was that the opposition might "legally succeed in what millions of Canadians see as the overturning of the outcome of the democratic election, and do it without giving Canadians the ultimate say in the matter."[5] Here the Crown, in the person of the governor general, is identified with the law or constitution but *not* with democracy: the precept of this interpretation being that in an election it is voters who choose a government (and by default an opposition) rather than a Parliament from whose ranks these formations emerge. Again, if coalition is legitimate, must the party that won the most votes in the most recent election be a member of the coalition? In 2014, Michael Adams, president of the Environics Institute for Survey Research, reported that "a small majority of Canadians say a coalition should only be permitted if it includes the party that holds the most seats after an election."[6]

Nothing in the Constitution Act, 1867, says that this is the rule, because much of the constitution – as it relates to government – rests outside that Act. In fact, there is a kaleidoscope of patterns in the matter of government formation. Following the 1929 provincial election in Saskatchewan, the Cooperative government comprised parties that stood second and third in number of seats and votes won at the election (Liberal Party twenty-six seats vs Conservative twenty-four, Progressive five, and Independent six; while the Liberal Party won 44 per cent of the vote vs Conservative 36, Progressive 7, and Independent 9). The Liberals had more of each but went into opposition (after being defeated in the new legislature following the speech from the throne), as their federal brethren were to do following the 1957 election, when they won more votes (42 per cent to the Progressive Conservatives' 38.5 per cent) but not seats, or again in 1979, when the same result happened, this time Trudeau Liberals at 40 per cent vacating office for Joe Clark's Progressive Conservatives coming in at 35.8 per cent. It should be noted, because there will be need to refer to the period again, that in 1921 Mackenzie King formed his first government, with the slimmest majority support in the House of Commons, lost that majority in the election of 1925 but continued to govern with support of the Progressives until the 1926 election, when his party again won a majority of seats in Parliament.[7]

Against this shifting scene, it is a challenge to be categorical in pronouncing about the conventions, that is to say, the informal and uncodified procedures, of government formation. It would be more accurate to say that, when it comes to interpreting election returns, Canadian constitutional practice is less about counting than it is about weighing the meaning of the result. In the examples noted in the preceding paragraph, who were the electoral "losers"? In this respect Canadians are unlike Americans, whom one scholar has described as "a calculating people"[8] – a contrast that goes some way to explain why the former, more than the latter, accept a higher degree of non-partisanship in the conduct of elections, such as in the compilation of voters lists, the drawing of electoral boundaries by independent commissions, and the imposition of electoral expense regimes. These characteristics, it is important to observe, apply to Canadian provincial as well as federal jurisdictions.[9]

Here is the explanation for the predictable uncertainty in Ottawa and the provincial capitals on election night if, after the votes are counted, no party has a clear majority of seats. This would not be the case – certainly it would not be feasible – if Canada were not a constitutional monarchy where the Crown's representative selects his or her ministers on the basis of an interpretation of the meaning of the election results. And it is the need to interpret that leads in systems such as Canada's to the presence of advisers to the Crown. They occupy a constitutional penumbra that separates governors from the governed, a shadow world where the unknown – when explained – is accepted as more real than the visible.

At the same time, it is the recurring instances of political discretion at work in the twenty-first century that increasingly feeds a search for certainty. In the first sentence of their book, *Democratizing the Constitution: Reforming Responsible Government*, the authors lament how the prime ministers seem able "to undermine parliamentary democracy."[10] Prompted by the controversies that accompanied the call of the federal election in 2008 and the prorogation of Parliament later that year and in the following year, the authors pose a "four-part reform to address the constitutional dimensions of our democracy problem."[11] It is not the intent of the present discussion to assess the utility of the proposed reforms, but rather to note that each shares one feature in common, a feature that sets the reforms apart from present practice in calling elections and forming governments – they all involve numbers or thresholds: Parliament must be summoned within thirty days after the date of an election; elections would occur every four years on a specific date unless a two-thirds majority of MPs approved a motion to dissolve earlier; a constructive vote of non-confidence (one that identified who would be the new prime minister and form a government with the support of a majority of MPs in the House) would itself require support of a simple majority of MPs; consent of the House of Commons would be required before proroguing Parliament, and where there was a majority government, the consent of two-thirds of the chamber would be required.[12]

There is a leaning away from reliance on the understandings of parliamentary monarchy and towards an inclination to establish laws, or at least practices, of calculable precision and predictable consequences.

No longer are reflections of the past sufficient authority to offer guidance for the future.

Eugene Forsey and Sir John George Bourinot (one-time clerk of the House of Commons) in Canada, H.V. Evatt in Australia, and A.V. Dicey and Walter Bagehot (pre-eminently) in the United Kingdom are distinguished representatives of the class of constitutional interpreters.[13] Bagehot came first, but because his chief work, *The English Constitution*, appeared in the year of Confederation, it was not known to the framers of the Constitution Act, 1867. Of longer-term significance, it appeared in the year the male franchise in Great Britain doubled and at the end of the classic period of the House of Commons, when henceforth the prime minister, cabinet, and political parties were to dominate British politics.[14] Age notwithstanding, the clarity of Bagehot's commentary for a long time provided a dependable analysis for a constitution that was not easily summarized, comprising, as it did to a large extent, unwritten conventions, rules, and understandings, whose coherence was overseen by a sovereign, or in the case of Canada, a surrogate sovereign, whose behaviour in turn was guided by Bagehot's famous treatise.[15]

One of the few other Canadians from the Confederation period to refer to Bagehot was Alexander Campbell, himself a Father of Confederation, who, in a letter to Sir John A. Macdonald, succinctly summarized his opinion of the work: "You must have experience in a colony to enable you fully to appreciate the inapplicability of much of the book."[16] While Campbell offered no explanation for this opinion, it is intriguing to speculate whether he shared the view of a recent scholar that "the efficient part could, in theory be exported, but the dignified part could not ... In other words a non-presidential form of republicanism – cabinet government – was possible and potentially available to new polities."[17]

Bagehot, it could be said, embalmed a constitution already experiencing unacknowledged – certainly in the colonies – transformation, and continued for another century to be a misleading measure of modern British monarchical and parliamentary government, until Richard Crossman, academic and Labour Party cabinet minister, critically revised the account.[18] A journalist by profession and skilled at communicating complex ideas in economical language, Bagehot had famously divided parliamentary institutions into two categories: efficient and dignified – Commons and cabinet in the first, Crown and Lords the second. Crossman demonstrated that the Commons belonged – and had for a long time – in the second category. Forty years after the publication of Crossman's diaries, the placement of Canada's Commons is still a live subject for debate, the sardonic tone of which is captured in the title of a newspaper article by Andrew Coyne, in 2015, "Canada's Potemkin Parliament: On the Surface, It Looks Almost like Westminster."[19] As in so much commentary on Canadian politics – federalism, for example – there is in Bagehot, and in Coyne, an inescapable dualism that arises either from making outright comparisons of political systems (a favourite "other" being the United States, but depending on the subject sometimes the United Kingdom or Australia), or by invoking through linear, temporal analysis the evolving Anglo-Canadian monarchy and Parliament – king following king, prime minister prime minister, precedent precedent.

It is a signal feature of constitutional monarchies of the British model that they depend historically, politically, and morally upon the advice and guidance of individuals who themselves hold no public or accountable office but who are in intimate contact with those who do. The reason why is that "ornamentalism" aside (the word is David Cannadine's), the relationship of Crown *to* Parliament, as well as the internal workings of the Crown *and* Parliament, depend upon conventional behaviour and an unwritten constitution whose appreciation requires extensive study.[20] As regards Canada, however, that statement demands major qualification after passage of the Constitution Act, 1982, section 41(a), which requires unanimous consent of the two houses of Parliament and all provincial legislative assemblies to amend the constitution in relation to "the office of the Queen, the Governor General and the Lieutenant Governor of a province." Contrary to adjectives like "dignified" and "ornamental" associated with them, the offices of Queen, governor general and lieutenant governor increasingly have significant constitutional substance attributed to them.

While the implications of having entrenched the Crown in the written constitution are gradually becoming evident, one immediate consequence is that matters affecting the prerogative are potentially more justiciable in Canada than they are in the United Kingdom. For instance, on the matter of the prerogative of dissolution, Britain has had an uncontentious Fixed-Term Parliaments Act since 2011 – a distinction, it should be said, that moves Canada some distance from having, as the Preamble to the Constitution Act, 1867, states, "a Constitution similar in Principle to that of the United Kingdom." Consider, for example, an application for judicial review in 2014, in respect of the decision of the prime minister "not to advise the Governor General to summon fit and qualified Persons to fill existing Vacancies in the Senate." In declining a request from the government that the application be rejected, Mr Justice Harrington, of the Federal Court of Canada, pointedly summarized the issue when he posed the following question: "If the Constitution requires something to be done promptly ... can the law be flouted by convention?"[21]

Another illustration lies in the following set of facts. In 2007, the Harper government introduced and Parliament passed an amendment (Bill C-16) to the Canada Elections Act establishing a fixed date for elections. Although the amended law provided for a dissolution of Parliament at a time other than the "fixed date" – that is, following a vote indicating loss of confidence in the government – Mr Harper requested (and received from the governor general) a dissolution of Parliament in 2008, at a time when his government still commanded the confidence of the House of Commons. This action was challenged by Duff Conacher of the advocacy organization Democracy Watch on the grounds that a general election at this time violated the terms of the "fixed date election law," which, he argued, had established a new constitutional convention that prohibited the prime minister from exercising his discretion to advise the governor general to dissolve Parliament except as envisioned in the amendment. Both the Federal Court of Canada and the Federal Court of Appeal rejected his suit, for reasons relevant to the topic at hand. While much was said at the time and subsequently as to whether (and by what means) a new convention limiting the prerogative had been established, the core of the decision may be found in the following passage from the judgment:

> It is important to examine the constitutional context because Canada has a system of constitutional supremacy that lays out the boundaries of Parliament's power. In this case, the constitutional context is that the Governor General has discretion to dissolve Parliament pursuant to Crown prerogative and section 50 of the *Constitution Act, 1867*. Any tampering with this discretion may not be done with ordinary statute, but requires a constitutional amendment under section 41 of the *Constitution Act, 1982*, which requires unanimous consent of all provincial governments as well as the federal government before a change can be made to the "office of the Governor General." Subsection 56.1(1) explicitly leaves the Governor General's discretion untouched.[22]

From the perspective of the present discussion, the import of the judgment in *Conacher* lies not in the governor general's discretion remaining untouched by the fixed-election-date amendment to the Canada Elections Act, but in the judicial finding that a constitutional amendment under section 41 of the Constitution Act, 1982, was required to limit the exercise of the Crown's prerogative of dissolution on advice of the prime minister. More than that, as Aucoin et al. write, the action of the prime minister (Stephen Harper) in ignoring the fixed-term election legislation his government had introduced and the decision of the Court that the powers of the governor general were unaffected by the amendment "*reinforced* the prime minister's virtual right to a dissolution."[23] Here is an instance where the interrelationship of pre-rogative and statutory power has been essentially altered by the adop-tion of a constitutional amending formula that subjects amendments in relation to "the office of Queen, the Governor General and the Lieuten-ant Governor of a Province" to the requirement of unanimous approval of Parliament and the legislative assemblies of each province. Here also is an instance that distinguishes Canada from the United Kingdom, where in 2011 the Westminster Parliament passed the Fixed-Term Parlia-ments Act, which provides for parliamentary elections every five years, beginning in 2015. Exceptions to that term allow for a dissolution of Parliament if the House of Commons resolves that it has no confidence in the government, or if the Commons, by a two-thirds vote of its total membership, resolves that there shall be an early parliamentary elec-tion. The contrast in the provisions of the two pieces of legislation and in their history highlights the constitutional separation that now exists between the two countries.

Although the cause and details of the ruling may be different, there is a parallel to be drawn between the preceding argument and the opinion of the Supreme Court of Canada in *Reference re Senate Reform*.[24] Here, the government of Stephen Harper sought a ruling on the constitutional-ity of legislation that would have introduced a system of consultative elections (in the provinces) for the selection of nominees whose names would then be recommended by the prime minister to the governor general for appointment to the Senate of Canada. Analysis of the rul-ing is found in chapter three. For the moment, and in the context of the larger subject of the constitution and the Crown, it is important to cite the following passages from the Supreme Court ruling. First, "The framers of the *Constitution Act, 1867* deliberately chose execu-tive appointment of senators to allow the Senate to play the specific role of a complementary legislative body of 'sober second thought'" (para. 56); and second, "The proposed consultative elections would fundamentally modify the constitutional architecture ... and would constitute an amendment to the Constitution. They would weaken the Senate's role of sober second thought and would give it the democratic legitimacy to systematically block the House of Commons, contrary to its constitutional design" (para. 60).

The role of the Crown in the selection of senators is now determined to be far more central to realizing the function of the upper chamber of Canada's Parliament as envisioned by the framers of the Constitution Act, 1867, than had previously been understood. At the same time, the architectural imagery – with Senate, Commons, and Crown portrayed as structural elements – poses a challenge to constitutional amendment as set down in Part V (Procedure for Amending the Constitution of Canada) of the Constitution of Canada, 1982. How might change to one essential feature be accomplished without threatening the stability of the others or, indeed, without endangering the whole? As with fixed election dates that appeared to limit the prerogative, the outcome once more was the reverse of what was anticipated: no change of the order attempted by statute was deemed possible. Here again, the prerogative appears stronger after the aborted reform than before. Furthermore, the Court deemed consultative senatorial elections, absent a constitutional amendment, a threat to the essential features of the constitution. On the eve of the sesquicentennial of Confederation, the Senate, as designed by the political architects who met at Quebec in 1864, emerged stronger and more secure in its relationship to the House of Commons, and to the government, than any critic might have anticipated. The implications of the Supreme Court's opinion for the conduct of parliamentary government in Canada are impossible to specify at this early date, but that they will be wide-ranging seems indisputable.

To repeat, the Constitution Act, 1982, Part V of which set down the "procedure for amending the Constitution of Canada," established "a system of constitutional supremacy" as well as "boundaries of Parliament's powers," one part of which is the Crown represented in Canada by the governor general. As fundamental as that legal and political truth may be, it nonetheless requires reaffirmation, for it is too easily forgotten that until the Constitution Act, 1982, Part I of which is the Canadian Charter of Rights and Freedoms, there was in Canada – as in Great Britain – no conception of a constitution, in the sense that Americans use that term, or of limits to state power. The sole purpose of the Constitution Act, 1867, had been to divide and distribute legislative power to constitute a federal system in Canada. W.P.M. Kennedy went so far as to maintain that "what a Canadian legislature, acting within its proper ambit, does no power save itself can undo."[25] In this maxim, it might be said, is found the source of the restriction in Canada on inter-delegation of legislative power; the reason constitutional disputes in the nineteenth century turned so much on the distribution of legislative power between the two levels of government; the explanation for why Canadians think of federalism almost exclusively in centralizing and decentralizing terms; and the impetus that drove the provinces to seek executive power commensurate with the legislative power conferred upon them in *Liquidators of the Maritime Bank* case, where the Judicial Committee of the Privy Council found the provinces, under the 1867 Act, in possession of "all powers executive and legislative ... necessary for the due performance of [their] constitutional functions."[26]

The Crown in right of each individual province, that is to say each political executive, was the principal beneficiary of this impetus to self-government. More than that, within the expanding provincial universe, the executive faced no rivals, for, unlike their state counterparts in Australia, who among parliamentary democracies had "the strongest upper house system," Canada's provincial second chambers were weak or non-existent.[27] Against this constellation of power, neither the people nor a piece of parchment might stand as obstacles to realizing legislative will that was *intra vires*.

Nor should the jurisdictional component of Canadian federalism be undervalued when seeking to understand Canadian politics. In the words of H. McD. Clokie, "The political nature of Canadian federalism shines out through every aspect of its structure," pre-eminently, although not always acknowledged, through the role political parties play in the other organs of government.[28] Paradoxically, federalism does not "shine" through Parliament in Canada! It is in the executive part of the constitution, either by way of allocating cabinet portfolios or convening first ministers' conferences, where federalism shows its face. By contrast, in the United States, federalism is entrenched, not in the White House, but in the legislative part of the constitution, most particularly the upper chamber of Congress, the Senate. The critique that Canadian federalism is not just different from its neighbour – the author of the world's first federal system – but deficient, originates in this contrast, whose theoretical veracity is attributable to the claim by the Australian-born federalism scholar K.C. Wheare that "the federal principle has come to mean what it does because the United States has come to be what it is" and, for that reason "justifiable to conclude that although the Canadian Constitution is quasi-federal in law, it is predominantly federal in practice."[29]

It is open to examination whether these two statements are reconcilable. The unsuccessful advocacy of a Triple-E Senate casts doubt on how federal, in Whearean terms, Canada actually was or is. It is a condition Eugene Forsey once emphatically summarized: "All references to other federations or to the nature of federalism in general are beside the point. The Canadian federation is in some respects sui generis, and ... efforts to force it into an American, Australian, Swiss, or logical straightjacket [sic] are just tiresome: bad law, bad constitutionalism, bad political science."[30] By coincidence, another Australian federalism scholar, Preston King, speaks more directly to the condition of Canada's federal arrangement: "Federation generically conceived has less to do strictly speaking with the dispersal of power than with the designation of local agents to represent regional or territorial units at the federal centre."[31]

Jurisdiction or not, less than two decades after Confederation, Goldwin Smith detected an emerging Canadian practice: "From the composition of a cabinet to the composition of a rifle team, sectionalism is the rule."[32] Arguably, federations inhabit parallel worlds where comparison is ripe while unitary systems stand alone, a contrast itself that makes comparison of Canadian and British political practices suspect.

The challenge posed by resorting to referential measures – "a Constitution similar to that of the United Kingdom" – is that Canada is not the United Kingdom. Over time the evolving and maturing constitution, which ultimately united a transcontinental, three-ocean state, deviated from the model offered by the island kingdom it was said to resemble. The reference undervalued what was happening in Canada: through federalism, Canadians made a country – in the view of Harold Innis, "too far and too fast" – but nonetheless, in the process rescued and reconstituted French-English relations, as well as the unity of the heartland.[33] With this history as backdrop, it is misleading and detrimental to self-knowledge for Canadians to continue to interpret their constitution in borrowed terms. It is time, one could say, that they were at the heart of their own history.

Federalism distorted and exhausted Canadians' understanding of their constitution. The school and language conflicts that roiled Canadian politics in the late nineteenth and early twentieth centuries were interpreted through the prism of federalism, a focus that had disappeared by the 1980s, when Manitoba's language law (upheld nearly a century earlier) was found to conflict with guarantees inscribed in the

Manitoba Act, 1870. If, at the beginning, federal questions overshadowed constitutional ones, that relationship had, by the centennial of Confederation, been reversed. The implications of the reversal were to be far-ranging, but nowhere more so than in recognizing that Confederation marked the birth of a double federation. Writing in 1960, on the eve of the Quiet Revolution and a decade before the Official Languages Act, Quebec sociologist Jean-Charles Falardeau observed, "The BNA Act ... is not only a juridical act of the Imperial government creating Canadian provinces and binding them into a federal unit. It is a covenant between the English-speaking majority and the French-speaking cultural minority of the Canadian nation. It is a pact according to which French-speaking Canadians obtained the recognition of a status of partners in the government and in the life of the whole nation."[34]

A feature of the double image of federalism is that one part may reinforce the other, as occurred in 2006, when the House of Commons passed a motion that "recognizes that the Québécois form a nation within a united Canada." Two years later at celebrations to mark the four hundredth anniversary of Quebec City, the prime minister, Stephen Harper, elaborated on his government's understanding of the significance of the motion: "Passing the Quebec nation resolution was an act of recognition and reconciliation."[35]

Enough has been said to indicate that a prime feature of parliamentary monarchy, and even more of parliamentary monarchy in a federation, is the difficulty it presents when the subject at hand is "the constitution." The very nature of conventions is that they are unwritten and are subject to (often conflicting) interpretation. More than that, according to Michael James, "a complacent reliance on convention has helped dissipate in Britain any understanding of the distinction between constitutional and political matters,"[36] a distinction that, by contrast, is growing in Canada. But the Crown is not the only enigmatic element to the constitution. Another is parliamentary privilege, which is commonly thought to include the rights of individual parliamentarians to freedom of speech in Parliament, as well as the collective rights of the chambers of Parliament to regulate their own affairs. In *New Brunswick Broadcasting v Nova Scotia* (1993), the Supreme Court of Canada found that parliamentary privilege should be considered part of "the Constitution of Canada" on the basis that the preamble to the Constitution Act, 1867, proclaims the intention to establish "a Constitution similar in Principle to that of the United Kingdom," where privilege was deeply rooted.[37]

Parliamentary privilege, an essential component of parliamentary democracy, exists to enable Parliament to function effectively and efficiently without undue impediment. Originally developed in Westminster as a means of preventing interference by the sovereign in the workings of Parliament, it has developed in parliaments throughout the British Commonwealth. In Canada, it is enshrined in the Constitution Act, 1867, at section 18 and through its preamble, and is further confirmed in section 4 of the Parliament of Canada Act ... No longer are concerns about privilege centred on the relationship between Parliament and the Crown. Rather, in the late 20th and now in the 21st century discourse about parliamentary privilege centres on how privilege should function in a rights-based legal system exemplified here in Canada by the Canadian Charter of Rights and Freedoms and where the public expects increased transparency and accountability for the decisions made by parliamentarians.[38]

In the controversies over the proposed coalition and then prorogation in 2008, the argument was advanced that the people, not Parliament, should make and unmake governments. Another way of phrasing that sentiment, which would convey its true revolutionary meaning, is to say, "take the executive out of Parliament." Loss of confidence in the government may be the ultimate test of accountability, but how does the popular sentiment implicit in that principle apply in other instances of accountability traditionally considered the preserve of Parliament? Indeed, how far can the chambers be masters of their own proceedings, and to what extent might statute law limit their right to regulate their internal affairs? In *Canada (House of Commons) v Vaid*, the Supreme Court of Canada found that parliamentary privilege did not extend to the power of the Speaker of the House of Commons to hire, manage, or dismiss employees. In unprecedented fashion, the Court spoke directly to the "legislative assembly's work in holding the government to account for the conduct of the country's business."[39] Note that the primary reason for this power is not *because* it is a representative body with legislative functions.[40] This was the first time that the concept of keeping government accountable was recognized by the Supreme Court as a foundational function for the privileges of Parliament. The ambit of the decision is broad and, presumably, might be argued to encompass officers of Parliament, such as the auditor general, the official languages commissioner, the access to information commissioner, the privacy commissioner, and the chief electoral office, whose privileges are protected when they exercise functions that are "essential" (part of the constitution's "architecture," perhaps) for members and senators to hold the government and administration to account.

The question of what are the limits to parliamentary privilege is anything but esoteric or hypothetical. After the terrorist attack on Parliament Hill in October 2014, it was the government – and not the houses of Parliament – that took initiative to alter the policing arrangements of the precinct.[41] Does this initiative trespass on parliamentary privilege? Or, in the Senate expenses controversy that began in 2013 – following an investigation that found thirty instances of questionable spending; after having invited the auditor general to investigate expenses of individual senators; and in light of his recommendation for "transformational change," namely the creation of a new independent body to scrutinize the expenditures of senators – what should be the Senate's response? Would such a "new independent body" limit parliamentary privilege? As with fixed election-date legislation, as with consultative elections for the Senate, so too with this recommendation: in each instance the "reform" is the same – to move from privilege and prerogative to a shelter of rules. Again, the point at issue is not whether these proposals are desirable or otherwise, but to underline the fundamental shift in constitutional tradition and practice they embody. In each instance the value they espouse is not the independence of Parliament, the historic centrepiece of the history of Westminster and, indeed, of colonial legislatures in Canada and elsewhere in the British Empire, but rather the accountability of parliamentarians to others, and not just voters. A transformation in the idea of what constitutes rules appears to be underway.

The decline of deference, a phrase in vogue twenty years ago, has been supplanted in political debate by references to the "democratic deficit," usually supported with statistics showing a decline in voter turnout, especially among younger voters. The terminological sequence is illuminating when the subject is Canada, because the hierarchy in question has been sustained by political and not, as in the United Kingdom, social deference. Legitimacy in Canada, federally and in the provinces, has always come via the electoral route. The Senate of Canada is no exception to that statement, for while social deference is the historic root that feeds the House of Lords, in Canada it is the country's distinctive form of federalism that explains the character of the upper chamber.[42]

Illustrative of the perspective of twenty-first-century analysis of Parliament, in this instance based on interviews with former (since 2009)

MPs, is *Tragedy of the Commons: Former Members of Parliament Speak Out about Canada's Failing Democracy*. Here the authors, Alison Loat and Michael MacMillan, criticize the extent of party discipline in Canada and argue that political parties need to operate in a more open and transparent way. There is so much unhappiness, they say, that "MPs liked to say they were not politicians."[43] "They're trashing their own species and that is very close to trashing the ideas of politics and political leadership. We think those are really, really, really important things and we would prefer if our leaders weren't sort of downplaying and decrying, to do, to lead ... and if they sort of paint it in those terms, why would we be surprised if most Canadians had their impression reinforced that that doesn't matter?"[44]

Criticism of party discipline is hardly new, although it is less common to hear it coming so unapologetically from partisans. In this context it should be recalled that there has never been a taste for direct democracy in Canada, and on the rare occasion when it did appear, according to W.L. Morton, it came from the provinces: "Democracy, as a popular sentiment, was local in its origins and attachments."[45] Infrequent exceptions to that generalization – campaigns to institute the plebiscite, or referendum, or even (rarely) party primaries as political instruments – may be said to support its validity. Nevertheless, it is relevant to the present discussion that provincial legislation providing for initiative and referendum in Manitoba was found ultra vires by the Judicial Committee of the Privy Council (when that body was still Canada's final court of appeal) on the grounds that

> the Lieutenant-Governor is as much the representative of His Majesty for all purposes of Provincial Government as is the Governor General for all purposes of Dominion Government ... The analogy of the British Constitution is that on which the entire scheme is founded, and that analogy points to the impropriety, in the absence of clear and unmistakable language, of construing section 92 as permitting the abrogation of any power which the Crown possesses through a person who directly represents it.[46]

An early Canadian legal commentator, A.H.F. Lefroy, brings the issue sharply into focus: "Laws [may not] be made or repealed by direct vote of the people, for this is to give the law-making powers of the legislature to others, and to substitute a new Constitution founded on new principles, and to interfere with the office of Lieutenant-Governor."[47] In a federal system where there are no provincial constitutions as there are state constitutions in the United States, and where there is a common root to the Crown in Ottawa and each provincial capital, the implications of constitutional monarchy for the operation of Canadian federalism are great indeed – so much so, it might be said, as to determine its development.

Canada is unlike Australia, where mechanisms of direct democracy predate the founding of the Commonwealth and are components of Australia's distinctive electoral heritage still. The poverty of examples of direct democracy in Canada are matched only by lack of scholarly interest in their infrequent appearance. To *that* generalization, exception must be made for the work of S.D. Clark, most particularly *Movements of Social Protest in Canada, 1640–1840*, in which he aphoristically captured Canada's distinction: "Responsible government developed in reaction rather than in response to a true democratic spirit of the Canadian people."[48] What is unusual in the Loat and MacMillan study, cited earlier, is the evident desire of the speakers who were quoted to take party out of Parliament. While more will be said of this subject in chapter four, the quotation is relevant here because it echoes the theme of control discussed above – control of the prerogative, of privilege, and now of parties. One cannot help but wonder what, if any, connection there may be between the strength of partisan sentiment in the past – when compared to the present decline in voter turnout and changing voter loyalty at elections – and the historic reluctance to contemplate strategies of coalition. In this last respect, the contrast with Australia, again, is striking. The contribution of the plurality electoral system to partisan attitudes generally, and to suspicion of coalition in particular, demands examination. It is a requirement that the Liberal government – which came to power in 2015 on a pledge to reform the electoral system – will initiate by embarking on a study of electoral reform.

The disposition to favour elections (direct or indirect) to the upper chamber of Parliament, to deny the lower chamber its traditional right to determine who should form a government (and leave that for the electorate to decide), to limit the exercise of Crown prerogatives (with regard to Parliament and also to the conduct of foreign affairs) is occasionally attributed to what is loosely labelled an "Americanization" of Canadian politics.[49] Inevitably, the adoption of the Canadian Charter of Rights and Freedoms a quarter century ago has been added to the list of supporting evidence. The growing presence of the Prime Minister's Office in the affairs of the two houses of Parliament is regularly cited as well. It could be said that the paper "President and Parliament: The

Transformation of Parliamentary Government in Canada" by Denis Smith, presented to the Priorities for Canada Conference (an event organized by a political party – the Progressive Conservative, following Robert Stanfield's succession to its leadership) as long ago as 1969, launched the argument about the decline of Parliament and the rise of the political executive that continues to the present day.[50]

The easy analysis that Americanization is underway is just that – easy, but it is not informative. It would be difficult to point to a period in Canadian history when the spectre of Americanization was not on offer, be it concern about, among other topics, the Canadian economy (reciprocity before the First World War or foreign investment after the Second World War), Canadian culture (print media or radio and television),[51] or national defence (BOMARC and cruise missiles). Compared to these subjects, American influence on Canadian politics is far less easy to isolate. Leadership conventions, which are a well-known feature of politics in the United States, were introduced into national politics by the Liberals in 1919 as a means of reunifying the party following Sir Wilfrid Laurier's death and after the party had split at the time of the formation of the Union government in 1917. They had no American provenance or feature (for instance, they never displayed the federal complexion of their U.S. counterparts: delegates from "the great province of Nova Scotia," and all others, voted individually and secretly). It is true that during the Pearson years the Liberals became enamoured of the organizational practices of the Kennedy Democrats in the United States at the time, but with disappointing results, especially in western Canada.[52] More would be learned about Canadian politics if the perspective on putative American influences were turned around: that is, how, and how greatly, does Canadian practice or experiment with entrenched rights, delegate leadership conventions, and elections for the upper chamber of Parliament, for instance, differ from experience in the United States?

The hallmarks of constitutional monarchy are confidence, discretion, and privacy, features displayed on the infrequent occasions when public attention is paid to its operation, such as when Mr Harper met Michaëlle Jean, the governor general, in 2008, to request that she prorogue Parliament. Revealed yes, but subject to appeal, no. The suggestion has been made that a governor general should provide reasons for the decision she or he makes when exercising the prerogative. The consequence of offering reasons is that counter-reasons will inevitably be forthcoming, and the governor general would then be involved in a difference of opinion demanding a taking of positions. The argument advanced for offering reasons – that they would inform the public about the operation of constitutional monarchy and clarify otherwise confidential actions – is open to strong doubt.[53] Certainly, the position of constitutional interpreters or advisers like Bagehot and Forsey, not to speak of their modern equivalents, would be vulnerable, since confidence, discretion, and privacy are essential if their role, as well as that of the Crown's representative, is to be faithfully performed.[54]

It is at moments like this when the duality of the constitution – that is, its political and legal face – is most clearly evident. The government-of-the-day is no mere executive. The words of section 9 of the Constitution Act, 1867, are extraordinarily economical in their description of executive power: "The Executive Government and Authority of and over Canada is hereby declared to continue and be vested in the Queen." The executive (federally and in the provinces, where there are no constitution acts), is not elected, and it is more than misleading – it is false – to suggest that the relationship between the political and the legal executives is devoid of significance: "The Fathers of Confederation would say that a good constitution makes a distinction between 'head of state' and 'head of government.' The 'head of state/head of government' provision is what entitles us to think of ourselves as a free country. It's the device that ensures that Prime Ministers and governing parties can be turfed out."[55]

Turfed by whom, the people or Parliament? If the answer is "the people," then, in 2008, that proved possible only with the acquiescence of the Crown. Had the governor general not acquiesced in the request, what then would be the interpretation of the roles of the respective principals? In any case, this homily says less than meets the eye about parliamentary government, for it confuses rather than clarifies the situation: monarchical power increases, not decreases, the power of the political executive. It was written in response to a review of *The People's House of Commons: Theories of Democracy in Contention* by Christopher Moore.[56] Moore disagreed with the book's thesis that popular sovereignty is incompatible with parliamentary government in a constitutional monarchy and argued that "constitutionally speaking," the thesis led to the conclusion that the people seemed not to exist – the Crown, in short, keeps the people out. Disagreement and rejection are different responses, however, and parallels drawn with unitary Great Britain – which does not have an amending formula for its "unwritten" constitution or any provision such as 41(a), but rather a Parliament, which for all intents and purposes is "the constitution" – do nothing to clarify Canada's unique situation. Nor does invoking the word *republicanism* to mean "popular sovereignty," achieved through a government "constantly accountable to parliament representing the people," further understanding of the application of these thoughts to federal Canada. Could a province maintain its links to the Crown within a Canadian republic? Where is there a federal republic with a government "constantly accountable to parliament"? What does that word *parliament* mean as used here; where does bicameralism, more particularly the upper house (selected by whatever means), fit in this scheme? The policy implications of the criticism are left unexplored.

Presumably, since Moore has elsewhere described the appointed Senate designed by the Fathers of Confederation as "infamous," the upper chamber of this proposal must be elected.[57] Republicanism and representation are concepts more usually joined than are republicanism and accountability. In any case, the subject of republicanism is for later discussion. It arises in the present context, although significantly so, because of the historic powers that still reside in the Crown and are normally exercised on advice of the prime minister. How, indeed, are they to be reconciled, since any assertion of popular sovereignty must collide with the sovereignty of the Crown-in-Parliament, which under the principle of responsible government concentrates rather than diffuses power?

To the extent that the tendency in twenty-first-century politics is towards transparency, then constitutional monarchy faces a dilemma, especially in Canada where the Crown is locally worn not by the sovereign but by her representative who, unlike the sovereign, possesses no source of personal or familial authority, and who occupies Rideau Hall for a period of time shorter than the appointed term of some officers of Parliament. Indeed, the office of governor general was not established by the Constitution Act, 1867, although it was referred to; not until 1878 was it created by Letters Patent through exercise of the prerogative. Still, if monarchy in Canada faces a dilemma, it does not face a challenge. The aesthetic political preference in Canada has always been for strong government, and monarchy, subjected to the discipline of responsible government, provides that strength. The intellectual or literary appeal of republicanism (in other words, where the people are the "complete" nation) has never vanquished the attraction of the Crown-in-Parliament. The Maritime colonies had governments derived from the British model before 1867 and their constitutions did not change at Confederation. American state constitutions originated in a vote of the people of the state on a document, and in most cases shortly after adoption of the United States Constitution. Thus the constitutions of the republic and the states were coterminous.[58] In Canada, constitutions never came from the people but from above, and in the case of eight of the provinces (all but Ontario and Quebec), rest outside the founding Act. As regards the Maritime colonial legislatures, the Constitution Act, 1867, transferred certain powers from those legislatures to the new federal Parliament: "They were already, as separate colonies, under the Crown, and federation would leave them there, but instead of remaining in direct relation with the Colonial Office they would now occupy an analogous position towards the new federal government."[59]

There was another attraction of monarchy for Canadians: it meant that they were part of a larger whole, the empire, and later Commonwealth, and never just a local culture. It was a whole in which Canada sought to assert its distinctiveness, because a colony that has achieved independence through legislative action of the Parliament at Westminster faces the conundrum implicit in the doctrine of imperial sovereignty: how to cut the imperial cord?[60] The obverse side of that condition was that Canada did not have a full constitution. It might be (and indeed, was) argued (in the same vein as W.P.M. Kennedy's previously cited maxim on legislative sovereignty) that what the British Parliament did, it could undo, and thus, despite Canada's pretension to autonomy, a statute of this origin was not a real constitution. A variation on the theme of the 1867 Act's inadequate provenance could be found in the long quest for a domestic amending formula. For much of the last century, the attention of the federal (usually Liberal) government was devoted to promoting Canadian nationalism, which "most frequently ... meant constitutional development towards increased autonomy, culminating in independence and the acquisition of the symbols of sovereignty."[61] When the subject touched economics and when the perspective was either east or west of the St Lawrence heartland, nationalism sometimes was viewed as domestic imperialism.

In the years before 1939, "the Crown was crucial to Canadian self-identity because it provided ballast," a theme elevated to a political tenet during the royal visit of 1939, in contrast to much of the post–Second World War period, when there was a sense of attenuation of the Crown.[62] For a long time, Canadians abetted the perception that they were not fully autonomous in their relations with the United Kingdom by employing what might be called the language of a borrowed constitution, whether found in the Preamble to the Constitution Act, 1867 – where the founding provinces "expressed their Desire to be federally united into One Dominion under the Crown of the United Kingdom ... with a Constitution similar in Principle to that of the United Kingdom," or, earlier still, in Governor Simcoe's description of the Constitutional Act, 1791, as "a perfect image and transcript of the British Government and Constitution."[63] It should be noted that the object of Simcoe's admiration was the constitution, made possible by the Glorious Revolution of 1688, whose principle of harmony among its parts was far different from the fusion of powers that later sustained the principle of responsible government.[64] Evidence to support Simcoe's claim came to hand the following year, when the first statute to be passed by the new legislature of Upper Canada incorporated English common law into colonial law. Like privilege and prerogative, the common law depended upon being discovered and not found in a text. The mimicry and symmetry of the Canadian and British constitutions may be pressed too far, however. In 1930, Frank Underhill accused his fellow countrymen of "suffering from a literary theory of our constitution," a disposition that was not calculated to clarify the policy implications of its object, whether that be, for instance, strengthening or supplanting constitutional monarchy. More benignly, James Mallory professed that while the seed of the constitution may have originated in Great Britain, it had germinated on this side of the Atlantic and had produced "a distinctly Canadian tree."[65]

The French philosopher Paul Valéry once wrote, "In the past, almost all the (novelties) which had successively appeared were solutions or answers to very old, almost immemorial problems and questions. The novelty which confronts us, modern men, consists in this that the questions themselves are unheard of, and not the solutions; it is the problems which are new and not the answers."[66]

A less elegantly phrased but comparable piece of social science advice says that the prize goes to the scholar who asks the best question and not the one who gives the best answer. Is it possible then, in the matter of the Crown or the Senate of Canada, that there have been too many answers to too few questions? For example, with regard to reform of the upper house, what is being sought: enhanced representation, a stronger check on the government in the lower house, or improved performance of responsible government? Lack of precision in defining the problem contributes to lack of progress in achieving change. The Valéry observation goes deeper still when applied to current debates on the Canadian constitution. Parliamentary responsible government appears in disrepute, particularly the Crown as the source of political legitimacy. Canada may not yet be a republic, either parliamentary or pure, but the personhood of constitutional monarchy, where there is a surrogate sovereign, grows fainter in consequence of judicial interpretation and protection provided by section 41(a) of the Constitution Act, 1982. The prorogation controversy and the sense that the Crown in Canada was subjected to unconventional pressure in 2008 for partisan benefit existed at the same time as there was promotion of the Crown in the image of the Queen and in company with enhanced royal nomenclature – entombing the substance while memorializing the surface, one could say. In this context, it surely deepens the puzzle and confounds solutions to it to promote as Parliament's goal "a republican forum rooted in the sovereignty of the people."[67] There are so many more, subtle constitutional mirrors than the one that reflects the simple republican self. In such a formulation, the dualism of the Canada's federation in addition to its compound Crown, along with the institutional complexity each embodies, are conveniently ignored.

There are many differences that may be cited between British and Canadian politics, but one that speaks directly to monarchy and its political advisers (in both countries) is the following:

> The fact that acute controversy concerning the role of the Crown has consistently been avoided in the United Kingdom for more than a century is evidence, not that the Sovereign has been bound by convention invariably to follow advice of a government to dissolve Parliament, instead of seeking an alternative ministry, but that … all ministers have been particularly scrupulous to shield the Sovereign from the necessity of making any debatable use of the royal discretion.[68]

Such cannot be said of ministers to the Crown in Canada. When the distinct and distant attitude started may be debated, but Mackenzie King's relationship with Viscount Byng is one, if not the first, indisputable example. Of more relevance to the present discussion is the reason for the separation. Personal differences and colonial-imperial tension no doubt played some part, but the major explanation, and the one that the following chapters will explore, is related to a more general thesis: for the governments of Canada, the most important impetus always was to seek and secure self-government. This ambition motivated every politician, regardless of period, language, religion, region, or party. It explains hostility to second chambers, today and a century ago; it explains antipathy to electoral reform, of whatever variety, at least until the election of the government led by Justin Trudeau; it informs the long indifference to republicanism of any type, because self-government benefits from the concentrated power of constitutional monarchy rather than the diffusion of power that accompanies a republican constitution. It should also be said that responsible self-government accommodated more expeditiously than any other form of government the prominent dualities of Canadian life – among which were language, religion, empire-colony, hinterland-heartland, and relations with the United States and the United Kingdom. It also provided, through the Crown, a modus vivendi with Indigenous peoples, one whose meaning, while still incomplete, cannot be denied.[69]

Canada's vast terrain provides geographical explanation for Northrop Frye's characterization of the country's "longitudinal mentality";[70] yet at the centre, high above the Ottawa River, stand perpendicular Gothic structures, in architectural echo to nineteenth-century Westminster, but unique in Canada, where Georgian legislatures prevail to the east, Beaux Arts to the west, with Romanesque and Second Empire counterparts in Toronto and Quebec City, respectively. At one time politics played out almost exclusively within these parliamentary precincts. This is no longer the case, as modern electronic media challenge the prerogative of political parties. Nonetheless, it is through senators and members of Parliament that the will of the people must still be expressed for law to be made or changed. There is a strain to living simultaneously in two different historical periods, one that celebrates the parliamentary system and the other that laments a democratic deficit and disdains parliamentary and procedural norms. A sign of the times is that today's constitution cannot be summarized adequately through a metaphor – no longer is it a reflection, if it ever was, of something else; no longer is its meaning derivative. Instead, it is a constitution of importance, in and of itself. Today, Crown, Senate, and Commons are experiencing rapid transformation with unpredictable consequences for the interrelationship of the three parts, except that the accumulated effect will be to make the country and its politics even more distinctly Canadian.

Chapter Two

Refraction: The Crown

In the matter of the Crown, and to employ the metaphor used by the Supreme Court of Canada in the Senate reference of 2014, there is too much "constitutional architecture." To be precise, it is necessary to distinguish between the Crown, on one hand, and monarchy, on the other. In twenty-first-century Canada they are not the same thing, and the distance that separates them is growing. Significantly, and it is a subject to which the discussion will return later in the book, no discernible republican sentiment has arisen to fill this space. Nonetheless, monarchy is becoming a receding star, which requires a telescope of reinterpretation to be artificially brought near. Forty years ago, Frank MacKinnon in his study *The Crown in Canada*, made a comparable astronomical allusion, only at that time in reverse and in reference to Canada's emerging autonomy in its relations with the United Kingdom: "The Crown ultimately took a new position, in a kind of outer political space."[1] The process of Canadianizing the Crown, to which the MacKinnon statement refers, was long ago achieved. More relevantly, as a result of the amending provision found in section 41 of the Constitution Act, 1982, the trajectories of Crown and monarchy over the last quarter-century have diverged at an accelerating rate. It is important to be clear on this last point, for in the period since MacKinnon wrote his book, the concept of the Crown as a model of the nation has eclipsed the concept of the Crown as a model of autonomy.

For this reason, and despite admirable scholarship, past literature on the Crown in Canada says little of matters that now dominate discussion of the subject. Examples are always invidious and often unfair, yet consider the following passage from an essay by historian John Conway, written in 1969:

Although constitutional monarchy may be a form of government best suited to Canadian needs, the present-day concept of the Crown as sovereign in Canada must be judged dysfunctional both as a political and as a cultural symbol. To be sure, in Quebec the Crown evokes polite dissent ... without dampening creativity in music, art, or literature. But in English Canada the Crown has had a crippling effect, contributing to a state of psychic confusion that is termed an "identity crisis" in an individual ... [Royal] visits ... accent achievements of another society at the expense of our own. In this way, heroic episodes in our history, by being absorbed into the British myth, provide no colour or vitalizing function for our own society.[2]

While in no respect a universal sentiment, still the theme of monarchy as an influence that diminished Canadian national identity was abroad in the decade of the centenary of Confederation. It would be difficult a half-century later to cite a similar attitude. Content analysis of news reports and of scholarly publications would be necessary to provide empirical evidence to substantiate the claim that interest in the monarchy is in retreat. Yet the impression is strong that interest in monarchy today is far over-shadowed by study of the Canadian Crown, its constitutional powers, and the implications both have for modern understanding of the distinction between the constitution and political matters. Prorogation of Parliament in 2008 and in 2009, a prerogative power of the Crown exercised by the governor general (in this instance, Michaëlle Jean) on the advice of the prime minister (here Stephen Harper), is the most-frequently cited instance. Still, it is far from being an isolated one. Speaking of the federal government only, it is the prerogative that gives the federal executive (prime minister and ministers) control over foreign affairs, defence and war, national security, and public order. In fact,

royal prerogative powers are very much part of modern Canadian government. They include orders-in-council, writs, proclamations, and warrants signed by the Queen's representative, preparation of budgets and legislation, the prerogative of mercy, a myriad of administrative decisions, and a vast range of appointments, ranging from deputy ministers and diplomats to judges, lieutenant governors, and members of boards, commissions and agencies.[3]

More important, it is the opinion of one scholar that the predominant understanding of these powers, which stresses their vestigial status, "fails to account for the actual power and discretion they afford the Canadian executive."[4] A primary reason for this misunderstanding lies in the emphasis scholars have given to the reserve powers of the Crown, such as prorogation, dissolution, and dismissal, rather than to the workaday activities of the political executive, which originate in constitutionalized monarchy.

Unlike past grants of prorogation, of which there have been a number in the Parliament and legislatures of Canada, the acquiescence of Michaëlle Jean in the requests by Stephen Harper in 2008 and 2009 occasioned extensive commentary. For an office and a constitution moulded by precedent, the volume of response to these events proved unprecedented.[5] It was the strength of that response – fed by arguments associated with coterminous events such as a proposed coalition of parties opposed to the governing Conservatives and rejection of that proposal by Conservative supporters on the grounds that "gross violations of democratic principles would be involved in handing government over to the coalition without getting approval from voters" – that removed the Canadian Crown from its customary immunity to public scrutiny.[6] Here, too, however, there was a precedent – the King-Byng controversy in 1926, when the governor general (Lord Byng) refused the request from Mackenzie King, then prime minister, for a dissolution of Parliament but later granted the same request to Arthur Meighen, who had become prime minister when King resigned following viceregal rejection of his advice. There are more details to that story, but in the context of the present discussion the fact worth noting is that there is only the *one* story, later given exceeding prominence by the scholarship of Eugene Forsey.[7] A useful digest of the general subject, as well as comprehensive summary of the particular event, may be found in a more recent article by Peter Neary.[8]

Through his book, articles, and especially letters to editors, Forsey reigned supreme as *the* interpreter of the constitution, especially in matters touching on the Crown. While supreme, he was not alone; other advisory voices were heard, but like him, these more often than not came from historians, political scientists, even journalists, although seldom from those trained in the law. The contrast between then and now, for example the period prior to the 2015 general election – when at the outset of the campaign there was the possibility that no party would secure a majority of seats in the new House of Commons and thus a minority government appeared probable, with the accompanying uncertainty as to whom the governor general might call upon to assume that task of leadership – is striking.

The singular directness that characterized past analysis of the prerogative is being transformed into subtle, and sometimes not so subtle, dialogue. An example of the latter was the proposal by Elizabeth May, leader of the Green Party in Canada, during the campaign period in 2015:

> It's the overlay of the power of well-organized political parties that makes it appear that the party that has the most seats has somehow won the election. But our constitutional reality is still that members of Parliament can go to the Governor General and say, "Wait, we need to have a party and a government that holds the confidence of the House." In a scenario where the Tories emerge with the most seats, May said she would, as Green leader, act as "mediator" or "matchmaker" to get Trudeau and Mulcair working together.[9]

Extensive commentary prevailed during the campaign period, and contrary to the past a significant component of it came from academics trained in constitutional law.[10] To be clear, the distinction being drawn here should not be treated as defensive criticism from a non-legal provenance but as a comment that notes a shift in perspective and emphasis. Arguably, in this and other respects – for instance court cases since 2013 dealing with the oath of allegiance, succession to the throne, and the appointment of senators – the Crown is being encased by a legal and thus textual framework that is public and distinct from its oral traditions, which are by custom private.[11]

If a legal perspective on the Crown in Canada has assumed greater prominence than in the past, it is not at the expense of non-legal commentators. In 2012, 2013, and 2015, edited volumes on the subject were published: Jennifer Smith and D. Michael Jackson, *The Evolving Canadian Crown*; D. Michael Jackson and Philippe Lagassé, *Canada and the Crown: Essays on Constitutional Monarchy*; and Michel Bédard and Philippe Lagassé, *The Crown and Parliament*.[12] While there is some double counting among the contributors to the three volumes, a total of fifty-two authors appear, of whom eighteen were educated in or practised law. In the forty-four chapters that comprise the three volumes, the monarchy in the person of the sovereign, present or past, makes scarcely an appearance, despite the fact that sixteen glossy coloured prints of every monarch since George III, as well as six of kings of France (François I to Louis XV), and Henry VII may be found in the volume of Jackson and Smith. The criterion of the selection, of course, is the monarch, French or English, coincident to colonization of New France and Canada. Visually attractive and historically accurate, the volume's text makes no reference to the plates, a silence that itself speaks to the place of monarchy, as opposed to the Crown, in twenty-first-century Canada.

Each of the edited collections of papers followed a conference, two in Ottawa and one in Regina. (A fourth conference "The Crown in the 21st Century: Deference or Drift?" took place in Victoria in 2016, but the seventeen presentations are, as yet, not in print.) While the number of registrants averaged approximately eighty persons, the composition of the audience became more "official" over time, as the proportion of individuals associated with viceregal offices (federal and provincial) and with the political executive in both jurisdictions increased. The point of this observation lies less in the numbers of participants in the meetings than in the conferences themselves. Arguably, by 2010 the constitutional setting of the Crown in Canada – but not the monarchy – had become a subject of national interest. If so, it would be understandable to attribute this development to the prorogation controversies of 2008 and 2009 – monarchy in the person of the Queen was noticeably absent from the discussion – and yet the word *prorogation* appears no more frequently in the forty-four chapter titles than such subjects as reserve powers, the prerogative, First Nations, and succession. The act of prorogation and the facts of prorogation may be important and of continuing interest, but it is the memory of prorogation associated with the Crown – in the person of the governor general, and not the sovereign – that is of permanent significance. Prorogation in the first decade of the present century has suffused public knowledge of the office of governor general to the same extent as the refusal of dissolution to Mackenzie King did in the third decade of the last century.

In this respect, the events of 2008 and 2009 are a repetition – one might say, a continuation – of the King-Byng conflict of 1926. It would be difficult to find an analysis of 2008 that did not cite, and often begin with, a recitation of the election outcomes of 1921, 1925, and 1926, and in the course of that account detail the succession of audiences between prime minister and governor general that preceded the dissolution of Parliament in 1926. As an aside, it might be said that private meetings of public figures (especially when there are two of them) provides riveting material for exploration – or entertainment, as Peter Morgan demonstrated in his National Theatre production of *The Audience*, in which the Queen (played by Helen Mirren) receives eight of the twelve prime ministers who have served her since 1952. When Morgan was interviewed during the intermission of a televised production of the play, he said that while he could not vouch for the accuracy of each dialogue, he was confident that the accounts were "true." Such a theatrical interpretation of sovereign–first-minister relations would not be possible to duplicate in Canada, for in the same period (since 1952), there have been eleven governors general and eleven prime ministers.[13] The dramatic tension in the two-character play lies in the continuity of one protagonist but serial change of the other. *The Audience* portrays a relationship that does not exist in Ottawa, for if continuity is found in the Canadian system it lies with long-lived politicians. Indeed, today even governors general whose appointments are extended serve shorter terms than most officers of Parliament, and fewer years than the first "Canadian" governors general (Vincent Massey, Georges Vanier, and Roland Michener). The length of the Queen's reign, which now surpasses that of all her predecessors, envelopes the institution to such a degree that it has established the norm for how sovereigns (in the British mode) are expected to act. Nor in the matter of longevity is Elizabeth II a historical anomaly. Together, George III, who became King a year after the Battle of the Plains of Abraham; Victoria; and Elizabeth II have (as of 2017), ruled for 190 years of Canada's 258-year history.

Canadian study of the Crown has no counterpart in the United Kingdom, even though organized research on constitutional reform extends back more than twenty years. In its own words, the Constitution Unit, created in 1995 at the University of London, has "helped the UK navigate an extraordinary period of constitutional reform." At the same time, while the source of many highly regarded publications, the Unit admits that it "has done little work on the Monarchy, because it does not feature on the constitutional reform agenda of any of the main political parties."[14] The same could be said of Canadian political parties past and present, who are mute about republicanism as well, unlike some of their counterparts in Australia. Partisan silence on the matter of monarchy is noteworthy in itself and, when placed alongside claims about the Americanization of Canadian politics, inexplicable[15] – unless, perhaps, there is no connection. For the reason offered more than sixty-five years ago by Gordon Robertson – then a member of the Cabinet Secretariat, in reply to the "Twenty-Four Point Draft Programme for the Abolition of the Vestigial Remnants of Canada's Former Status of Colonial Subordination and for the Creation of Appropriate Symbols of Canadian Nationhood," authored by Escott Reid, at that time a junior officer in External Affairs – "Whatever the legal facts are, most Canadians ... have not thought of themselves as citizens of either a republic or a monarchy."[16]

Robertson did not offer evidence to support his surmise, although later elaboration of the theory of "institutionalized ambivalence," which, it should be said, did not speak specifically to the question of monarchy, lent credit to the contradiction he observed.[17] A thesis could be written on Canada as a country of double images, beginning with its being a federation of cultures and of territory, with two official languages. Crown and monarchy offer another duality with similar though less frequently acknowledged accompanying tension in the relationship of empire and colony/dominion; formal and political executive; executive and legislative powers; partisan versus independent leaning of public servants, and more. While the federation is in fact a compound monarchy, it should be said that the subject of this discussion is mainly the federal arrangement. Nonetheless, lieutenant governors are federal appointees, a condition that historically has brought its own set of tensions, usually of a partisan political nature, though more recently concerning status: "There was ... a regrettable dimension to both tenures [those of Adrienne Clarkson and Michaëlle Jean] at Rideau Hall: the persistent drive to promote the governor general as head of state and downplay the sovereign (and the lieutenant governors) as somehow discordant with the institution of the Canadian Crown."[18] Elsewhere, John Fraser elaborated on this point: "Adrienne Clarkson ... rarely hesitated to push an agenda to promote the role of the governor general of Canada as the actual (rather than de facto) head of state in public consciousness. She pushed it like it never had been pushed before."[19]

Among the sovereign, the governor general, and lieutenant governors, there is no question who comes out on top in a contest of status. When the subject is jurisdiction, it is equally clear, and has been since the Statute of Westminster, 1931, that Canadian legislatures are in no way inferior to the Parliament at Westminster in any aspect of internal or external policy that falls within jurisdiction assigned by the Constitution Act, 1867, and its amendments. After 1931, common allegiance to the Crown and not statutory pre-eminence of the imperial Parliament served as the bond of the new British Commonwealth of Nations. At the same time, however, the Crown underwent division, with the effect that the sovereign who resided at Buckingham Palace became the sovereign of the other realms: Canada, Australia, and New Zealand, for example. In a book with the subtitle *Model Governor General*, John Buchan's most recent biographer, J. William Galbraith, has written that the royal tour of 1939 "breathed life into the Statute of Westminster."[20] Turning that observation around, it might then be said that, absent the royal presence, the constitutional position of the Crown's representative in the sovereign's realms other than the United Kingdom is evanescent. The vigour associated with the position depends upon the individual holder's own actions more than it does on regal association.

For a long time in Canada, that reputation was founded on an amalgam of charitable work, geographic exploration (the North, especially), association with Quebec (residence at the Citadel, for example), and being a "repository of responsibility toward aboriginal peoples."[21] Important as these initiatives were, the Crown's place in the community, or better still, the perception of the Crown's place in the community (national or provincial) has changed dramatically in the last fifty years, a period that coincides with the creation of Canadian and provincial honours. The Canadian honours system is well documented elsewhere.[22] The subject of the present discussion is not the history or characteristics of a particular program, but rather to note the association of awards and honours with the developing sense of community within the jurisdiction in question and, more especially, the accompanying public awareness it brings of the respective representative of the Crown. In this regard – and only this regard – honours fall into the same category as prerogative powers like prorogation, that is, drawing attention to and fixing it upon the governor general, or in the case of a province, the lieutenant governor. Here is an illustration of the Crown acting in its capacity to strengthen the model of a nation.

Except for a brief period in the early 1930s, when R.B. Bennett was prime minister, and after a parliamentary resolution in 1919, initiated by a Conservative-Unionist MP (W.F. Nickle) during the period of Union government, the sovereign ceased to give titular honours to Canadians. In this form of self-imposed abstinence, Canada stood apart from other Dominions, and from the Australian Commonwealth and state governments to the present day. For the next half century, until the launch of the Order of Canada, there was no "system" of honours. As a result, Canadian honours today, and the recognition that comes with them, are associated solely with the governor general or, in the case of the provinces, the lieutenant governors. Writing of the Order of Canada, but the assessment could be extended to the provinces, it has been said that "a prime reason for the effectiveness of the new honour was its non-political basis: the order's secretariat was the responsibility of the office of the governor general at Rideau Hall, and the selection of recipients was made by an independent advisory council from among nominations from the public, then ratified by the governor general. This was totally unlike the partisan political appointments of the pre-1919 honours."[23]

This discussion demonstrates the complexity of a relationship that is often described in linear, or Canadianization, terms. Yet a sense of circularity pervades the subject: in Canada there appears to be a double loop – London and Ottawa, Ottawa and the provincial capital. As seen by First Nations, there is even a triple one, when the subject is the Crown and treaty obligations. Arguably, there may be too many Crowns to accommodate a single theory, a pluralism that helps explain the growing prominence of the courts in resolving disputes when they arise. The physicist Niels Bohr once pointed out that anyone who is not perplexed when first encountering quantum mechanics cannot possibly understand quantum mechanics. The same may be said of anyone who does not find constitutional monarchy in Canada "perplexing."[24]

There are many considerations that affect the Crown in Canada, among them jurisdiction, politics (for instance, prime ministerial influence), and the federation, as well as those that are self-imposed. The result is a complicated, multidimensional subject that eludes easy investigation. A common textbook approach, in answer to the democratic challenge posed by the extraordinary prerogative power that lies in the hands of the Crown, is to take comfort in the distinction drawn between head of state and head of government – one matters and the other does not. Except that in English common and statute law the Crown is the state. When applied to Canada or the Queen's other realms, "head of state" is a confusing term in any case, because it distances what is in fact close to hand – the exercise of unaccountable power. In the caustic language of Tony (Anthony Wedgwood) Benn,

> Royal prerogative, exercised not by the Queen but by the prime minister in her name, is seen as the final guarantee that democratic decisions by parliament and the people could never be allowed to undermine the hierarchical and semi-feudal system we have ... The fount of honour has been re-routed from Buckingham Palace and now sprays the holy water of patronage on the chosen few ... Declarations of war and Britain's adherence to treaties such as the new European constitution are exercised under prerogative powers by the prime minister, who may or may not choose to consult the Commons or the electorate in a referendum.[25]

Here, according to Andrew Marr, is "the reality of monarchical power." A reality, as Philippe Lagassé demonstrates in his study of the defence power in Canada, "Accountability for National Defence: Ministerial Responsibility, Military Command and Parliamentary Oversight," that prevails across the Atlantic as well.[26] Sovereign and governor general, governor general and prime minister, prime minister and minister, minister and senior public servant – the chain of legitimacy may become clouded through misunderstanding, from which attempts to escape by injecting Parliament, offer neither clarity nor exit, as the saga to establish fixed dates for federal elections bears witness.

> In Canada, matters of war and peace and decisions relating to the disposition of the armed forces are executive prerogatives of the Crown, the sovereign power that nearly always acts on the advice of those members of Parliament who form the governing cabinet. These prerogative powers have been enshrined in the common law, codified in Canada's Constitution Act, and only partially constrained by statute law. The Crown's prerogative powers for "the defence of the realm" and the use of armed force to preserve the public peace can be traced to the feudal responsibilities of English kings during the Middle Ages ... When the Canadian constitution was written in 1867, the drafters codified this aspect of England's "historical constitution." Section 15 of the Constitution Act states, "The Command-in-Chief of the Land and Naval Militia, and of all Naval and Military Forces, of and in Canada, is hereby declared to continue and be vested in the Queen."[27]

The importance of the quoted study is twofold: it affirms the central position of the Crown in the conduct and administration of defence and military matters and, at the same time, it underscores the fundamental principle of the Canadian constitution – political accountability – even where the subject at issue is exercise of the prerogative. "Holding government to account" is another way of describing responsible government, where the executive must command the support of the popularly elected chamber. As originally expressed by Lord Grey, the colonial secretary, the governor general was "to act generally upon the advice of the executive council, and to receive as members of that body those persons who ... possessed the confidence of the assembly." Grey's words took the form of a royal instruction, not a statute. Accountability then and now is a political not a legal concept, and legal considerations are insufficient justification for ministers to withhold information from Parliament.

As noted earlier, parliamentary privilege protects individual members from legal prosecution, for instance suits of libel, at the same time as it empowers Parliament to use its investigative powers to the full.[28]

The House of Commons is the first, last, and only authoritative voice of the Canadian people. For instance, there is no constitutional provision for instruments of direct democracy. In Lagassé's words, "The Crown's defence minister is individually responsible and accountable for the state of the armed forces and Canada's defence affairs. This convention is the bedrock of responsible government in the Westminster tradition."[29] Any proposal that has as its object the sharing of responsibility, for instance subjecting military or defence decisions to a parliamentary vote, would have a common outcome: weaker and less accountable government. How clearly and widely the parliamentary safeguards necessary to securing the principle are understood will be discussed in chapter four.[30]

For much of the last half of the twentieth century, a prominent theme in Canadian politics was the promotion of "national status" (the Finding Aid to the St Laurent Papers in Libraries and Archives Canada makes use of this phrase). In the realm of the sovereign's representative, the theme appeared in a succession of guises, as, for example: issue of Letters Patent for the Governor General (1947); appointment of the first Canadian governor general (1952); the first state visit of a governor general outside North America (1969); signing by the governor general (and not the sovereign) of Letters of Credence and Commission for Canadian diplomats (1979). The St Laurent years were also identified with grand, national development schemes, such as the St Lawrence Seaway, the building of the Trans-Canada Highway, and the introduction and expansion of a national television network. At the same time, debate about and search for a national anthem, a distinctive flag, and a domestic amending formula accelerated. At least since the First World War, the study of Canadian politics and history is an enterprise studded with dates: 1919 (Versailles), 1927 (Canadian legation in Washington), 1926 (Balfour Declaration on dominion status), 1931 (Statute of Westminster), 1939 (Canadian government's declaration of war and Parliament's vote in support of the declaration), 1947 (Canadian Citizenship Act), and 1952 (change in the Queen's titles so as to include Queen of Canada). More examples might be cited, but the thrust of a common theme is clear: to distance Canadian governmental autonomy from Great Britain. It was this concern for status, and not about monarchy as a form of rule, that motivated Liberal governments. The sense of a received citizenship was being replaced by self-conscious acts of citizenship of both bestower and applicant. In his first public address after the Citizenship Act's passage, Louis St Laurent asserted that "a constructive national consciousness has to be built," and the crucial emphasis in that important announcement lay in its verb. Increasingly, in the decades after the Second World War, the core of that consciousness reflected cultural as much as it did political concerns.[31]

While apprehension at being implicated through British foreign policy decisions, whether Chanak (Turkey) in 1922 or Suez in 1956, influenced the actions of Mackenzie King and Louis St Laurent (and Lester Pearson, then secretary of state for external affairs), it would be a mistake to believe that external concerns directed events by the time Pierre Trudeau was prime minister. By then, national unity and not national status was the issue. Paradoxically, and for a reason that predated the achievement of Confederation, the Crown stood close to the centre of this recast debate. On 19 February 1867, on second reading of the British North America Bill, the Earl of Carnarvon (then colonial secretary) addressed the House of Lords. He reminded his fellow peers that, "unlike every other federation that has existed – [Canada] derives its political existence from an external authority, from that which is the recognized source of power and right – the British Crown. And I cannot but recognize in this some security against those conflicts of State rights and central authority which in other federations have sometimes proved so disastrous."[32]

The compound monarchy that resulted from the divided jurisdiction set down by the 1867 Act established another set of dualities in Canadian life and politics, one that continues to the present day and thwarted the Trudeau government's scheme to Canadianize the Crown through domesticating the office of governor general. In 1978, under Bill C-60 (Constitutional Amendment Bill), the governor general's authority would no longer derive from prerogative instruments but would emanate from the constitution itself. He would possess all the prerogatives, functions, and authority belonging to the Queen in respect of Canada, and laws would be passed in his name, and not the sovereign's. In fact, the Bill provided for the governor general to be known as the "First Canadian." Other details of the proposed legislation may be found elsewhere. Of interest here is that the Bill failed to find favour among provincial premiers, because they (some more than others) saw it as threatening to politicize the governor generalship, an outcome that long-standing rivalry between Canada's federal and provincial governments made it impossible to accept. Significantly, the Queen expressed her approval, because, it was reported, if she was to remain Queen of Canada, "the title must have some meaning to it … The idea of a constitutional monarchy in Canada suffered from the poor standing of the Governor General."[33]

It is germane to the present discussion to note that Bill C-60, though never enacted, was still being invoked in 2015. The explanation lay in British legislation, The Succession to the Crown Act, 2013 (UK), c 20, which abolished two discriminatory rules that limited succession: male primacy and disqualification from the throne of anyone marrying a person of the Roman Catholic faith.[34] The question then became whether Canada, because it shares its monarch with the United Kingdom, needed to enact separate legislation – in fact a constitutional amendment – to incorporate the changes made at Westminster. Was it, in short, a matter of Canadian law? By this time, it should be said, the question of the law of succession had been before the courts for more than a decade, during which the familiar principle of Canada's having a "constitution-by-association" had arisen:

> The adoption of a specific institution or principle of parliamentary government by a written constitution implies the inclusion within the constitution of those parts of British constitutional law "necessary" and "essential" to the "proper functioning" of that institution or principle, an inclusion affirmed by the assertion found in the preamble of the Constitution Act, 1867, that Canada's constitution is "similar in principle" to the United Kingdom constitution.[35]

In *O'Donohue*, "the rules of royal succession … [were found to be] 'essential to the proper functioning of the shared monarchy principle' and so are 'by necessity incorporated into the Constitution of Canada' as part of 'the unwritten and unexpressed constitution.'"[36] A decade later, the Parliament of Canada assented, by means of its own Succession to the Throne Act, 2013, to the changes enacted in Great Britain. As might be expected, dissent arose in Canada from those who believed more was needed than an apparent mirroring of British law to effect change. The point of the present discussion is not to determine the correct response to the dispute (that will come via the judiciary), but to note the conflict of views, even values, at issue. The opening paragraph of this chapter asserted that the concept of the Crown as "a model of the nation" had supplanted an earlier concept of the Crown as "a model of autonomy." The conflict over the law of succession bears out that assertion, for it supports the claim that the new aesthetic, when it comes to the Crown, is domestic and not external. Echoing Kipling, the recessional is at an end. The Crown is the Crown in Canada through identification with and not incorporation of the sovereign of the United Kingdom.[37] Because of existing symmetry, it is unnecessary, indeed it is redundant, to incorporate a change in British succession law through a further Canadianized law. At the time of writing (January 2016), the issue had reached Quebec's Superior Court in a case brought by two Laval University law professors, *Geneviève Motard and Patrick Taillon v Attorney General of Canada*, with the attorney general of Quebec, Canadian Royal Heritage Trust, and the Honourable Serge Joyal as interveners on the side of the defence.[38] In his submission, the last intervener turned to the history of Bill C-60, noting its abandonment by the federal government in the face of strong provincial opposition but emphasizing too that at no time had opponents ever cited as cause for complaint the effect of its provisions on the law of succession to the throne.[39]

When the subject is Canada, its Crown, and the monarchy, there is an inescapable sense of the interpenetration of the real and the invented. Every step on the long road to autonomy, especially where it entered the realm of national iconography, which coincided temporally with the development of federal policies of multiculturalism and bilingualism, distanced both the symbols and citizens' understanding of monarchy. In consequence of the court cases discussed above, and below, the reality of the Crown in Canada has grown increasingly textual at the expense of its historic root, which is personal. To what cause may this change be attributed? While a number may be given, and some have been given, the central, even systemic, explanation lies in the fact that the constitution is not an aggregate but a whole, which for several decades has included the Constitution Act, 1982. That Act, especially Part V (the amending provisions of the Act), has isolated monarchy, as traditionally understood, even though, paradoxically, elevating the Crown.

There is an important exception to this general statement, which is First Nations. Section 35(1) of the Constitution Act, 1982, asserts that "the existing aboriginal and treaty rights of the aboriginal peoples of Canada are hereby recognized and affirmed." In *Delgamuukw* (1997), Chief Justice Antonio Lamer said that "the Crown is under a moral, if not legal, duty to enter into and conduct those negotiations [with Aboriginal peoples] in good faith."[40] It is of intrinsic importance, however, to recall that First Nations have long argued that "the relationship established by treaties was with Britain, not Canada – a position ... Lord Denning (and the other justices) countered [in 1982] by asserting that in English law the Crown, once considered to be a 'unity,' was now understood to be 'divisible.' So that, even though the queen is one person, the term 'the queen' actually refers to separate entities."[41] This complicated – and far from concluded – question is raised only as a reminder that emendations to the thesis advanced in this chapter would be required, if the subject of discussion were, which it is not, the Crown and Indigenous peoples. The longevity of the British monarchy, compared to the monarchies of any past or present European country, and the stability of the aristocracy and society that accompany it, are features of the United Kingdom that set it apart from contemporary European systems but not Indigenous peoples, as Aboriginal leaders remind Canadians. The contrast between such regime hegemony and modern Canada, where for more than half a century no ethnic idea has been sought or claimed as a base for Canadian nationality, is striking indeed. In this respect, Canada has become a country of horizons, not boundaries.

For some years after the Canadian Citizenship Act was passed in 1946, on the inside cover Canadian passports was printed the statement that "Canadian citizens are British subjects." That injunction has disappeared, but to recall it is to be reminded of a time that now seems antique. The scaffolding that undergirds citizenship has been redesigned, with a constitutional – not personal – pillar its principal support. Today, the Crown overshadows monarchy to an unprecedented extent, although Canada remains monarchist in one indisputable sense: there is no republican sentiment. It is also the fact that the governor general, the representative of the sovereign, is no mere figurehead as is, say, the president of Germany. At approximately the same time David Johnston was selected (by a new, non-partisan procedure, which has since been regularized through creation of a committee of the Privy Council for viceregal appointments),[42] Germany chose a new president through a "secret" election by a college of electors composed of members of the federal parliament and of state representatives. Despite the institutional separation intended to discourage partisan influence, the presidential vote, according to the *New York Times*, was a "Test [for] Merkel's Ailing Coalition," one that the coalition survived: "Merkel's Pick Wins German Presidency."[43] No one in Germany appeared to find this manner of selecting the president problematic for the intrusion of partisan politics it permits, but then German presidents possess few of the prerogative powers that rest in the hands of Canada's governors general.

In *McAteer v Canada (Attorney General)*, 2014 ONCA 578 (Docket C57775), the subject in dispute was the oath (or affirmation) of allegiance found in the Citizenship Act, which the appellants in the case argued violated their rights under sections 2(a) freedom of conscience and religion, 2(b) freedom of expression, and 15(1) equality of the Charter of Rights and Freedoms. They sought to make the oath optional. The Court of Appeal of Ontario rejected the appellants' argument, reasoning that

> the oath in the [Citizenship Act] is remarkably similar to the oath required of members of Parliament and the Senate under The Constitution Act, 1867. In that oath, the reference to the Queen is symbolic of our form of government and the unwritten principle of democracy. The harmonization principle of interpretation leads to the conclusion that the oath in the Act should be given the same meaning. (para 6) Moreover, the Court found that the oath is secular and is not an oath to the Queen in her personal capacity but to our form of government of which the Queen is a symbol. (para 7)

Furthermore, citing with approval, as had the lower court, the judgment quotes the Hon. Bora Laskin: "Her Majesty has no personal physical presence in Canada ... [O]nly the legal connotation, the abstraction that Her Majesty or the Crown represents, need be considered for the purposes of Canadian federalism. Giving the term 'Her Majesty' or 'the Crown' a personal meaning is [an] anachronism" (para 52).[44]

How has Canada come to this distinctive position with regard to the Crown and monarchy? Unlike the assessment offered by the British scholar Ben Pimlott, that the republican movement in Australia would result in the Queen's "civic death,"[45] this is neither sought nor probable in Canada. Canada's independent view on monarchy today needs to be placed in the larger context of its independent disposition on imperial and Commonwealth matters in the past, when the country was more closely aligned on imperial matters with South Africa (and sometimes, the Irish Free State) than Australia and New Zealand in the first six decades of the last century. The first two Dominions acted immediately to take advantage of the terms of the Statute of Westminster in 1931; Australia waited until 1942, New Zealand until 1947. Tension associated with national unity in Canada and South Africa, aggravated by domestic disagreement over the extent of military involvement in the European wars, accounted in part for the contrasting alignment. An important point of reference here is that monarchy did not enter into the discussion. For reasons unique to itself, South Africa became a republic in 1961, but that was an option that at no time appealed to Canadians.[46] One reason for disinterest is that while the Fathers of Confederation had expressed a wish to have a *constitution* "similar in Principle to that of the United Kingdom," there was never a counterpart desire to replicate British social or class structure. Canadians – French and English – were settlers in a frontier society. More important than the societal considerations were the political: republicanism languished in Canada not because of insufficient opposition to monarchy but because, as long ago as the 1850s and in the words of Francis Hincks, joint premier (with Augustin-Norbert Morin) of United Canada, "the [republican] scheme of rendering public offices elective [was viewed] as a Conservative measure ... as checks on the popular will expressed through responsible government."[47] Republicanism and responsible government were, and remain, antithetical concepts in the constellation of Canadian political thought.

Thus, while not weightless in Canadian life, monarchy never weighed heavily either. This is why an element of shadow-boxing hovers over defenders of monarchy: who else is in the ring? In *The Secret of the Crown*, John Fraser sees the opponent as something of a tag team: philosophical republicans, such as University of Toronto historian Michael Bliss; personal attackers, with Prince Charles a favourite subject of ridicule; Canadianizers of the Crown, governments (mainly) inspired by the confidence of the 1967 centennial celebrations; prime ministerial betrayers – Paul Martin of Adrienne Clarkson and Stephen Harper of Michaëlle Jean – both of whom placed the Crown's representative in positions demeaning to their person and their office. Defenders of the Crown in Canada, who are not to be confused with apologists, appear to share the fate that Simon Leys, literary critic and author, saw visited on G.K. Chesterton and Rudyard Kipling: "Catholicism has done to Chesterton's reputation what the British empire did to Kipling's: in the eyes of a shallow and ignorant public, it became a liability ... a sectarian pretext for support or rejection."[48] Fraser says that "Canada has been able to transform the British monarchy into the Canadian 'Crown,' and it's about the niftiest constitutional trick we have ever pulled off."[49] But can you be a subject (imperial no longer, of course) and a citizen at the same time? What do the words mean in this context? Is it possible to be both, to be in two places at the same time, although for Canadians place is everything since they are not a folk? Or must a choice be made, with the consequences Goldwin Smith once alluded to: "In Canada, government being parliamentary and 'constitutional,' monarchy is the delegation of a shadow; and any attempt to convert the shadow into a substance ... by reinvesting the viceroy with personal power, would speedily reveal the real nature of the situation."[50] And that – "the real nature of the situation" – is the question, which, while difficult to answer, does not mean it should not continue to be asked.

In his study of British patriotism, Raphael Samuel, the brilliant Marxist historian, observed (in 1989) that "it is the domestic rather than the dynastic preoccupation of monarchy which rivets public attention, the personal rather than the political."[51] The "national idea," Samuel argues, has been "undermined" in consequence of the "decentering" of other basic (and in the main, Protestant) institutions, such as the established church along with non-conformist chapels, and schools in public life. By contrast, it might be said that religion, imperialism, and the rise of national sentiment remain underdeveloped topics of historical study in English Canada.[52] It is worth remembering, because it tends to be forgotten in the New World, that "Britain is an invented nation not much older than the United States," where new unifying allegiances have been superimposed on older loyalties, which have not disappeared, as the devolution campaign in Wales and Scotland four decades ago and the referendum on Scottish independence in 2014 revealed. Relatedly, it should be recalled that Welsh and Scottish nationalism emerged in the last quarter of the nineteenth century, "when the Empire itself became nationalistic."[53]

The triumph of personal over political interest in monarchy owes much to the usual explanatory factors – the invasive and pervasive media, for example – but there is a monarch-centric reason as well. The abdication of Edward VIII in 1936 was probably the most determinative event in Elizabeth II's reign, if only for what that constitutional rupture meant for her father: "Under George VI, royal interventions, even minor ones, diminished. The acceptance of a cypher-monarchy, almost devoid of political independence, began in 1936." Because the Queen was "her father's daughter" and "he ... her model," it was not surprising that "the most striking personal feature of the succession (in 1952) was the sense of continuity from one reign to the next."[54] Advisers are common at court, but where the sovereign is ill-disposed to take initiative, they assume high prominence. The autobiography of

Sir Alan Lascelles, assistant private secretary to four monarchs, including the Queen, ought to be required reading for anyone interested in constitutional monarchy, in Canada as well as Great Britain. Although he says nothing about Rideau Hall and governing, his experience as private secretary to the Earl of Bessborough, governor general (1931–5), brought him into close contact with prominent Canadians, who appear at intervals throughout the memoir.[55] Historical counter-examples to regal passivity are easily found. A neglected aspect in commentary on the 1910 constitutional crisis – when the Asquith government sought to pack the Lords by creating new peers in order to secure passage of financial bills with heavy social consequences – was the reason George V objected to the scheme: the Lords, he believed, was being "destroyed" and he "manipulated," in a procedure that accorded him "neither the confidence nor consideration to which he was entitled."[56]

Although British nobles and aristocrats were appointed governor general in Canada until 1952, a crucial aspect of the King-Byng affair was the defeat it represented for the assumptions underlying gubernatorial appointment. Mackenzie King's barb that royalty and peers could avoid political controversy if "they kept out of politics" – that is, were not appointed as governors general – possessed an element of self-serving logic.[57] Still, it is tempting to compare the events of 1926 in Canada to those of 1909–10 in the United Kingdom in the sense that each marked for its respective country a permanent change in constitutional equilibrium and, essentially, in the same respect – the depreciation of the titled but even more, the Crown in the person of the sovereign. The Balfour Declaration, whose enunciation of dominion autonomy presaged the Statute of Westminster by five years, was adopted in 1926, the same year that Viscount Byng departed Ottawa. When in 1910, George V was resisting Asquith's request to appoint additional peers to the Lords, he asked one of his personal advisers (Lord Knollys), who sided with Asquith and who himself has been an adviser to Edward VII, when the parliamentary crisis first began: "Is this the advice you would have given my father?" Knollys replied, "Yes, and he would have taken it" – as, it might be said, monarchs have done ever since.[58] In the United Kingdom, but not Canada, the Crown is its own referent. The results in Canada, however, have not been that different, except in one crucial respect: the governor general's invariable acquiescence in highly controversial requests of the prime minister to exercise the prerogative to prorogue or dissolve Parliament, for example, has had a secondary (or, some might argue, primary) effect on the perception some Canadians hold of monarchical government. In essence, and whatever the personal qualities of royalty or its representative might be, the abstraction of the Crown has increasingly come to replace the matrix of monarchy as an object of loyalty, a diminuendo in association that has received approval through judicial interpretation of the Canadian Charter of Rights and Freedoms. Crudely phrased, the Crown's utility has come to outlive its wearer.

More than any other component of Canada's similar-in-principle-to-the-United-Kingdom constitution, the Crown has experienced over time an essential change in character as it travelled across the Atlantic. As the next chapter will argue, the Senate of Canada was never the North American imitation of the House of Lords that critics and defenders maintained, if only because it was designed to serve a federation. The House of Commons came closer to the Westminster model, but even then it could not be mistaken for the original; the demands and mechanics of representation in a federal as opposed to a unitary political system are fundamentally different. The Crown was another matter: in no clause or phrase of the eight sections of Part III, whose subject is "Executive Power," of the Constitution Act, 1867, does the word *Crown* appear. Section 9 declares that "the Executive Government and Authority of and over Canada is hereby declared to continue and be vested in the Queen," and that nomenclature does not change. A glance at the Department of Justice publication *A Consolidation of the Constitution Acts, 1867 to 1982* reveals that Part III is the only one of nine original Parts not to have appended to it a change, revision, or amendment.[59]

A constitutional monarchy at its birth, Canada remains one still but in altered form: in the "hall of mirrors" that houses the "constitution" of this book's title, the depersonalized Crown supplants the Queen. The present chapter employs the title "refraction," a term borrowed from physics to signify the change in direction of light when it passes between one medium and another, to signal this changed monarchical condition. Monarchy has become the antecedent to a more national and intellectual interpretation of the constitution. For good or ill, it is scarcely possible to raise such matters without invoking Bagehot once again – his taxonomy of "dignified" and "efficient" parts of the constitution is too seductive to resist. In the present instance, however, Bagehot has been turned on his head, for the Crown with its prerogative powers is as efficient an institution as it is dignified, a duality strongly noted by political observers in the last decade. Canada's surrogate sovereign is the governor general, and it is he or she who exercises the prerogative at the request of the prime minister, the leader of the political executive. David Johnston, the governor general who succeeded Michaëlle Jean, who granted Stephen Harper's highly contentious prorogation request in 2008, has said that "my duty as Governor General is ... to uphold Canada's system of responsible government." Lawrence Martin, writing of this speech, commented that Mr Johnston "repeatedly stressed the great importance of the Crown in the functioning of our democracy, as if to say: 'Don't call me a figurehead.'"[60] On another occasion, Mr Johnston described himself as "the representative of the spirit of the country."[61] In so doing, he evoked Isaiah Berlin's description of royalty, but not dynasty: "an eternal, immutable attribute, unitary and equally accessible to the vision of all men, at all times, everywhere; somewhat like a Platonic 'idea.'"[62]

In the earlier address, the governor general observed that "without healthy and robust national institutions, we can well ask ourselves, 'What is Canada?' Our institutions reflect our national values, values which unite us as Canadians. They are therefore precious beyond measure." This is an observation of great moment, for it draws attention, if obliquely, to the sense many Canadians increasingly voice that their institutions are not healthy, that is, balanced, but rather the opposite, and for the reason that the political executive is too powerful – whether in relations with the Senate or the Commons – in significant part because the extensive prerogative powers that rest with the Crown are exercised on advice of the political executive. No longer is the Crown accepted as a tidy narrative of monarchy but rather is understood to constitute an indispensable armature of government. The long reach of the Prime Minister's Office is too well documented to require substantiation – the scandal over expenses of senators, themselves appointed by the governor general "in the Queen's Name" on advice of the prime minister, confirmed a blurring of executive and legislative responsibility – and too frequently noted to require elaboration.[63]

One might say that the Crown, as opposed to monarchy, has entered the public's consciousness. The Crown matters, and there is general understanding of that truth. The three parts of Parliament have always been linked, an attachment symbolized in the ceremony of royal assent to legislation, either given personally by the governor general in the Senate of Canada, or by declaration notifying agreement by the deputy of the governor general, who is normally the chief justice of the Supreme Court of Canada. Yet royal assent is little publicized. There is another demonstration of linkage of Parliament's parts, and that is in the harmony or disharmony they display in the passage of legislation. While it is infrequent for the Senate to reject a bill coming from the Commons, on occasion it does happen. It is rarer – one might say unheard of today – for the governor general to refuse to sign legislation, which does not mean that he or she may not privately express reservations on the wisdom of the requests. The conditions that have promoted this climate of acquiescence may be about to change, for two reasons. First, there is the prominence the Supreme Court of Canada has awarded bicameralism as an essential character of the legislative process and the complementary role enunciated for the Senate as a result (see chapter three). There is no reason to think that the *Senate Reform Reference* ([2014] 1 SCR 433) will lead the upper house to assert itself as a confidence chamber, but there is reason to expect that the Senate will be less pliant to partisan pressure exerted from the Commons or from the political executive. All the more reason is this to be expected in the immediate future, because the Liberal government elected in 2015 has severed its partisan links to the Senate and has set about establishing an independent advisory committee to propose names of individuals to the prime minister who may, in turn, be recommended to the governor general for appointment.[64] Relations between the two houses of Parliament *in the making of law* are undoubtedly to become more public.

A second reason why the parts of Parliament in the legislative process will rise in visibility lies in the promise the present prime minister, Justin Trudeau, has made to change the First Past the Post (plurality) electoral system, which has historically determined the outcome in constituency contests. A proportional system of election – whether total or in part, alternative or preferential ballot – is less likely to produce governments that command majority support in the House of Commons than is the case under the present system. In that context, the complexities associated with the formation of governments will multiply; the role of the governor general as guardian of the constitution will be reinforced; and the importance of Parliament in the public's mind will increase. The debate preceding the 2015 election, when polls suggested that no party would secure a majority in the Commons, and the conflicting advice offered in the media to the governor general as to his duty in securing or retaining his first minister illustrate the central and un-figurehead role he (or she, since in 2016, Mr Johnston is in the last year of his appointment, and a successor must be appointed) may well be called upon to perform.[65] The vigour of that debate acknowledged a reality about the position of governor general that often goes unremarked: the occupant of the office is non-partisan – never has there been a suggestion of viceregal partisan bias – yet the consequences of his or her actions are far from neutral, particularly would this be true in over-seeing negotiations leading to the formation of a government. Remarked or not, the parliamentary changes underway in Canada have more than the potential – they have the certainty – of raising the visibility and stature of the governor general, beyond being the centre of ceremony and patron of the arts. (An indication of what might be expected may be found in the experience of another Commonwealth constitutional monarchy, New Zealand, after it introduced a mixed-member proportional electoral system in 1996.)[66] With that probability, other considerations follow, which lie outside this discussion. For instance, should the term of appointment be longer than at present; if the electoral system changes and with it the expectation of majority government, would a longer term contribute to the institutional stability Canadians accept as normal but be less common in the future?

There is reason to expect that the character and talents of the governor general will have more potential to influence the composition and practice of government than has been true in the past. To the extent that this occurs, then the governor general will be subject to greater scrutiny than he or she has formerly received, because the fortunes of governments will lie more often, more directly, and more publicly in viceregal hands. If it is true that a "constitution is only effective and legitimate to the extent that it is 'of the people,' that is, to the degree that it accords with the authorized vision such a community has of itself, however variegated its constitutional elements," then the governor general may well come to determine both the strength and reputation of parliamentary government in Canada.[67]

Chapter Three

Redefinition: The Senate of Canada

When it comes to public understanding of its character and function, the part of Parliament most often abused as a result of the constitution-by-association analogy is the Senate of Canada. Section 9 of the Constitution Act, 1867, provides for "executive authority" to continue to be vested in the Queen, while in nomenclature, appearance, and composition the new House of Commons on the right bank of the Ottawa River bears striking resemblance to its namesake at Westminster. By contrast, the Senate was designed to serve the needs of the new federation, a purpose the Fathers of Confederation took seriously, despite depictions of them lounging eternally at Charlottetown and Quebec City. Every account of the Quebec Conference testifies that they spent more time on the plan of the new upper chamber than they did on any other subject, an allocation of interest that signalled the exceptional enterprise underway.

The constitution's Preamble notwithstanding, the Senate was unlike the Lords in almost every respect – except that each was and remains, in contrast to the lower houses of their respective Parliaments, a continuous legislative body. In the words of United Canada's attorney general (Lewis T. Drummond) in 1856, "The attempt to give us a transcript of the constitution of England, in so far as the House of Lords is concerned, is like the attempt which the child makes to build with a few cards a castle to imitate one of the old gothic structures of Europe."[1] The Lords comprised hereditary aristocrats with no fixed upper limit, while senators, originally appointed for life by the Crown, were restricted in number to seventy-two (twenty-four from each of three initial senatorial divisions – Ontario, Quebec, and, at the outset, Nova Scotia and New Brunswick). It should be noted that there were (and still are) senatorial districts within Quebec, in acknowledgment of the province's heritage of linguistic and religious dualism. Canada was the first country in the world to unite federalism with parliamentary government, and no part of its constitution bore the marks of this experiment more than did the upper chamber. Among the most visible indices of union are the senatorial divisions countrywide and senatorial districts within Quebec – a testament to Canada's double federation of provinces and peoples.

The decade of Confederation proved to be a transitional period for the upper houses of the British and Canadian Parliaments, but in contrasting respects. With the Second Reform Act, in 1867, the (male) electorate in Great Britain grew sharply and with it the sense that the Lords, once the premier chamber, was in eclipse. At some point in the future – the Parliament Act of 1911, which introduced a suspensive veto for the Lords, turned out to be the tipping point – the Parliament at Westminster would become in constitutional reality, according to American political scientist William Riker, a unicameral legislature.[2] The political trajectory for the Lords was one of decline. For the Senate, which was a core part of the governing arrangement of 1867, there was no past, only a future – one that a century and a half after its creation, and as a result of the ruling of the Supreme Court of Canada in 2014, appears poised to transform the conduct of parliamentary government in Ottawa. It is the ramification of the ruling for the two halves of Parliament and for the conduct of politics more generally that is the focus of this chapter, with particular attention paid to three topics that the Court emphasized: federalism, bicameralism, and institutional independence.

As with the Crown, the Senate is a continuing subject of confusion and disagreement, although unlike the Crown whose origins are so distant as to have lost modern meaning, the disjunction between the Senate's design and its interpretation is a continuing source of argument. Critics do not like appointment as a method of selection, since it is believed to be overwhelmingly partisan in character, and they do not like an arrangement where senatorial numbers are unrelated to population – Nova Scotia and New Brunswick, for instance, each have ten senators while the four western provinces, each of which is more populous than either of the two Maritime provinces, have only six senators apiece. Seldom, however, is the fixed total size of the Senate an object of complaint, although without that limitation discontent with partisanship in the upper house would doubtless be greater than it is.

Senate criticism is diffuse and episodic, a feature of second-chamber discourse worldwide, it would appear, as documented in a report commissioned by Sir Edward Grey, British foreign secretary in 1907 (in the period leading to the Parliament Act, 1911): "Everywhere there is a Second Chamber problem ... Everywhere there is dissatisfaction and irritation ... This is to enter a field that is peculiarly one of opinion."[3] Here is an assessment borne out over time by literature on the Senate of Canada. While it is a challenge to summarize chronic and disparate criticism, it might be stated as follows: "In composition and operation, the Senate of Canada does not contribute to a sense of constitutional coherence." The nucleus of that coherence lies in the operation of responsible government, and the importance of the Supreme Court's ruling in 2014 is to be measured by the extent it promotes the Senate as a critical ally of responsible government.

Yet to the extent that intention enters into second-chamber discussion in Canada, then the motivation of the architects of the Senate is regularly dismissed out of hand. An example, but not alone, is Patrick Boyer, a former member of Parliament, who has judged that "the greatest single role of the Senate was this, enabling Confederation to take place at all. The day Confederation became a reality on July 1, 1867, the Senate's principal function had been fulfilled." As well, he adds, "regional representation [that is, senatorial divisions] give the appointed chamber an honourable creation story."[4] The thrust of his comment is that the Senate and, for example, section 145 (the pledge to construct the Intercolonial Railway) are of the same order – terms of a deal, a slighting turn of phrase for an agreement on a constitutional enterprise that united much of British North America, for the first time, into one of the world's then-largest countries; that reconstituted French-English relations (for another century and a half) from their near-paralysis in the last years of the United Province of Canada; and that gave birth to a political and economic engine that would in a few decades drive territorial expansion to the Pacific and the Arctic Oceans. It does an injustice to the vision of the men who conceived (and for many of them, carried through) the project to so categorize their achievement. The uniquenesses, exceptions, and anomalies that lie at the core of Canada are waved away in the service of a rootless conceptual principle.

Federalism

Alexander Galt spoke especially for the provinces east of the Ottawa River when, at the Quebec conference, he prophesied, "To the Legislative Council all the Provinces look for protection under the

Federal principle."[5] Quebec and the Maritime Provinces looked to each other for support in balancing their interests alongside those of ever-expanding Ontario, and they had every reason to look to the Senate as a sanctuary, because in that chamber seats were allocated equally among senatorial divisions, of which there were originally three: Ontario, Quebec, and the Maritime Provinces. It should be noted that Galt was not alone when he linked the Legislative Council (the Senate) and federalism. Contrary to the view expressed in the twentieth century that Canada is a second-best or quasi-federal system and that the Senate of Canada falls short of a model federal second chamber, the Fathers of Confederation disagreed.[6] The cry of "Rep-by-pop" heard west of the Ottawa River had no echo to the east, nor would the huge central provinces then (or ever) accept equal membership in the Senate for all provinces. The structure of the Senate, as agreed to at Quebec and incorporated in the founding act of the new Dominion, represented the terms of the federation then, and to come. Even if today there were universal support for abolishing the Senate – which there is not – it is not possible to abolish the reasons why there is a Senate.

To equate the work of the Fathers of Confederation as a deal – and no more – telescopes decades of history into one moment of time and treats the Senate as weightless. Neither the Commons nor the Crown is treated this way. When it comes to examining the Senate, the orientation of critics is always to look at the institution's past – and when it comes to the claim that Confederation was a deal, the orientation is actually to the past's *own* past. That is, how to explain what happened 150 years ago? Never is the perspective reversed, so that the future of the past – its realization or problems encountered in seeking to secure what the founders of modern Canada sought – is examined. Yet history has a future, and modern Canada – warts and all – is the future the Fathers of Confederation set in train.

In that enterprise federalism was a key principle and the Senate central to its realization. No other institution acknowledged federalism: in the minds of the framers, the Crown was indivisible (the Judicial Committee of the Privy Council's revisionist interpretation of the Constitution Act, 1867, was yet to come) and the Commons was about the achievement of the long-sought principle of representation of population, although the chamber's seats were distributed among the provinces using a formula that, until the 1940s, saw Quebec the basis for calculating the allocation of seats to other provinces. In this arrangement, as in the constitution's original recognition of distinctive language, educational, and religious rights, Canada was a federation that from its birth acknowledged distinctions of identity.

It is customary, when referring to federalism in modern Canada, to speak and think of the provinces. The phrase *federal–provincial relations* or *federal–territorial relations* encourages the assumption of a jurisdictional dichotomy – for good reason, because there is such a parallelism. More than that, what might be called the rhythm of federalism sustains that perspective: fourteen budgets, fourteen speeches from the throne, fourteen sets of elections. Provincial or territorial life somewhere in the federation is front-page news every day. But there is more to federalism than its pulse; there is also its sustainability. The continuity of Canadian federalism owes a debt to Canada's national institutions, among them the Senate. If, in the muscular vocabulary of democratic legitimacy, the House of Commons embodies through its elected members the will of the people from coast to coast to coast, the Senate expresses the sum of those other identities the constitutional architects believed essential to acknowledge at the creation of Confederation.

It is a distinctive feature of the constitution in Canada (but not the United States, which is so often cited by critics when indicting the Senate) that it is used to strengthen federalism. Affirmations of identity are but one example. Very different, and specifically related to the Senate, is representation in the Commons. In 1913, the Maritime Provinces sought to stem the rep-by-pop principle in action a half-century after Confederation, first by means of a "Memorandum on Representation" whose object was to restore the "representation of the Maritime Provinces in the House of Commons … to the number allowed upon entering confederation upon terms that the same may not in future be subject to reduction in that number."[7] Later, the Constitution Act, 1915, amended the 1867 Act by the addition of section 51A, which read, "Notwithstanding anything in this Act, a province shall always be entitled to a number of members in the House of Commons not less than the number of senators representing such province." The nexus thus created between a province's Commons and Senate seat allocations has fixed the attention of small provinces in particular upon the guarantee the nexus provides and strengthened their resolve to resist any change that might threaten it. The desire of the Maritime Provinces for predictability in 1913 as to their numbers in Parliament achieved a level of unimagined certainty decades later in the Constitution Act, 1982 (section 41), when one of the four specified matters requiring unanimous consent for their amendment – the Crown, the Supreme Court of

Canada, the use of the English or the French language were the others – was the guarantee that no province should have fewer members of the House of Commons than it had senators.

One other feature of the 1915 Act requires notice: a half-century after Confederation and following a debate in which no member of Parliament dissented from the principle of senatorial regions, the Act reiterated the constitutional logic of the Fathers of Confederation by recognizing the four provinces of Western Canada as the fourth such region. Writing soon afterward, constitutional scholar A.H.F. Lefroy observed that "this Act preserves, or rather restores, the Senate's original quasi-federal aspect which had become impaired, the original idea of the composition of the Senate having been that of affording protection to the smaller provinces which they might not always enjoy in a House when the representation was based on numbers only."[8] Christopher Dunkin, the minister in charge of Canada's first census, described Confederation as the "three kingdoms."[9] The allusion was to the United Kingdom, which encompassed England, Scotland, and Ireland, along with the principality of Wales, and notwithstanding whose diversity appeared to the Fathers of Confederation the paradigm of a successful nation. Lefroy's insight was to appreciate the significance that came with "broadening out," from a trio to a quartet of senatorial regions – although regions still. The addition of territory rather the creation of new provinces helped keep the Senate formula stable, in contrast to the United States, where the creation of new states before 1860 made a series of "compromises" on the slavery question necessary but ultimately futile. Nonetheless, one consequence of Canadian practice was that the "tight" federation Macdonald had been instrumental in creating became less tight. In the Confederation Debates of the Province of United Canada, Macdonald drew a revealing analogy:

> The union [between England and Scotland], in matters of legislation, is of a federal character, because the Act of Union between the two countries provides that Scottish law cannot be altered … No matter … how much it may interfere with the symmetry of the general law of the United Kingdom … that law is not altered except with the consent of the Scottish people, as expressed by their representatives in Parliament. Thus, we have, in Great Britain, to a limited extent, an example of the working effects of a Federal Union, as we might expect to witness in our own Confederation.[10]

The Anglo-Celtic model of this political homily worked – and only worked – in Canada if the members of Parliament of the "third kingdom," the Maritime Provinces, were part of the calculation. Canada East would never have entered Confederation without the Lower Provinces as partners. At one point Macdonald jauntily explained rep-by-pop: "The whole thing is worked by a simple rule of three."[11] By that he meant the ratio of Quebec's population per member determined the number of members each province would have in the new lower chamber. Three was a magic number: four provinces but three senatorial regions – and the regions mattered, then and now. (The redistribution that came into effect in 2015 means that those provinces with the most seats in the House of Commons got more, while the Atlantic Provinces, Saskatchewan, and Manitoba remained as they were – or in proportionate terms, had fewer seats. In consequence and just from the perspective of arithmetic, the rationale for the Senate in the nineteenth century continues and perhaps has grown stronger.)

The fourth senatorial region came into being forty years after two of the four western provinces had been established and after the creation of Alberta and Saskatchewan. The constitutions of three of the western provinces are found in statutes of the Parliament of Canada; British Columbia's is in the form of an imperial order-in-council. The Prairie Provinces were areas of homesteading, with initially slow and then very rapid population growth, so rapid that a quinquennial census had to be introduced (1906) to keep track of the pace of change (until 1936). This was the change that, if there was no constitutional intervention, the Maritime Provinces feared would silence their voice in national politics. The West proved unsettling to the federal government as well, beginning with the uprising at Red River in 1869. When introducing the Manitoba Act in 1870, the prime minister told the House that "it was not a matter of great importance whether the province be called a province or a territory. We have provinces of all sizes, shapes and constitutions ... so that there could not be anything determined by the use of the word."[12] The postage-stamp province of Manitoba that resulted – with its bicameral legislature, official bilingualism, and denominational schools – conformed to no blueprint, past or future. In the words of David Mills, Liberal journalist and later minister in the Mackenzie government, Parliament, but more particularly the Conservatives, had failed to do what "the theory of their system required."[13]

First Nations and explorers notwithstanding, the West was new and the rest of the country old. The national policy, the national railway, a

flood of immigrants, and a sense of grievance against the federal government set the region apart from the centre. The Constitution Act,
1915, incorporated the West as an equal partner in the Senate. Senate
critics would say the amendment was of little importance. In that opinion they are wrong; the 1915 Act reiterated the constitutional logic of
the Fathers of Confederation – without (to repeat) any opposition. In
this regard, it is important to note that at their creation – and constitutional provisions to the contrary – western provinces were not treated
equitably in the allocation of Commons seats. For instance, "Manitoba,
which had an electorate far too small to entitle it to even one member,
was given four; British Columbia, which could muster almost enough
citizens to justify a single representative, was given six." Manitoba's
number was guaranteed only until the census of 1881, when the constitutional formula for seat allocation would come into effect; British
Columbia's number was treated as permanent, in the sense that it could
only increase.[14]

Senatorial regions constituted a rare institutional affirmation of federalism in the Constitution Act, 1867. By contrast, the federalized cabinet, to which attention traditionally is paid, is a creature of convention.
The hallmark of Canada's federal system lies in the division and distribution of legislative power found in the Constitution Act, 1867. It
is these reasons – the absence of federal institutions and the centrality
of jurisdiction – that support W.P.M. Kennedy's claim of long ago that
"the federal idea [in Canada] has sought from, and been granted by,
political parties a place in the other organs of government."[15] Significantly, in the book in which Kennedy's article was reprinted, Dawson
(the editor) gave more space to political parties than he did to federalism; moreover, he believed political parties a fit subject for inclusion
in the "constitutional" category. And it is for these reasons too that the
Senate serves to act as an institutional corrective to the majoritarian
results revealed through a general election.

It is commonly said that Canada is among the world's most decentralized federations,[16] although the exercise of the federal spending power,
a single criminal code, the desire from the outset to make the common
law uniform (section 94), and since 1982 a Canadian Charter of Rights
and Freedoms stand as correctives to that generalization. Nonetheless,
there are grounds for that sentiment, and it is this: there is no model or
template for province-hood. In this regard Canada is unlike the United
States. The United States Constitution did more than provide for the
institutions of the three branches of government; it founded the first

modern federal system and, almost simultaneously, recreated the states of the Union. With no prior claim to recognition based on historic, collective, or popular identity, their security lay through Congress in "the mutual recognition of the legitimacy of statehood."[17] Such was not the case in Canada, where the constitutions of the Maritime Provinces predate Confederation: in Nova Scotia, "the basic components of the constitution were, in fact, two prerogative instruments, the Commission and Instructions to the governors," and in Prince Edward Island, "the British North America Act [section 129] provided for the continuance of existing provincial institutions, principles, and practices, except in so far as they were changed by the Act itself."[18] It surely was with this knowledge in mind that George Étienne Cartier justified equal treatment of the Maritime Provinces with Quebec and Ontario when it came to Senate membership: "It must be recollected that they had been independent provinces, and the count of heads must not always be permitted to out-weigh every other consideration."[19]

Canada's is a double federation – of jurisdictions and cultures, although seldom expressed as directly as found in the Constitution Act, 1867, which on the one hand recognizes Quebec's distinctiveness in its civil law, while on the other hand provides for (section 94) and deeply wishes to see uniformity of the law elsewhere. Nor has the vulnerability of minorities ever been more poignantly expressed than by Archbishop Taché, the ecclesiastical and national leader of French Canadians in Manitoba, on the eve of the creation of Canada's "first" new province: "Number is going to make us weak, and since under our constitutional system number is power, we are going to find ourselves at the mercy of those who do not love us."[20]

Canadian provinces do not have constitutions in the sense that American states do: provincial constitutions do not come from the people – never has there been a vote – but rather from above through prerogative power of the Crown. Even where, as in the case of the Prairie Provinces, there is a statutory component, this hardly begins to tell the constitutional story. Entry into Confederation was subject to negotiation, each set of terms sui generis. Canada never had legislation like the Northwest Ordinance in the United States, passed in 1787 by Congress under the Articles of Confederation, which pledged republican governments and constitutions for the states to be created out of that vast territory beyond the Ohio River. A territory had to have a population of 60,000 people, but once admitted the new state would be treated as an equal to the original thirteen states. The contrast between this regimen and what happened in Canada when provinces were created by Parliament out of Rupert's Land and the Northwestern Territory is central to understanding the different constitutional experiences of the two North American settler democracies. If Americans are a calculating people committed to rule-based behaviour, Canadians appear an accepting people tolerant of constitutional ambiguity. And ambiguity does not lend itself to codification.

Whether it is the amending formula adopted more than a century after Confederation or the composition of the Senate whose lineage originates in the Quebec conference, equality as a federal principle is honoured fitfully. Despite what proponents of a Triple-E Senate once implied, the provision in the United States Constitution of equal representation of each state in the upper house of Congress is by no means uncontroversial.[21] As a value and as a precept, equality underlies Canadian society and law – but not in politics. The baroque history of electoral redistribution in the Commons offers proof enough: whatever the formulae establish, it is not rep-by-pop. That statement should perhaps be written in the past tense, because independent federal electoral boundary commissions increasingly are drawing boundaries in a manner to promote closer population equality among constituencies within each of the provinces. Arithmetic carries more weight today than in the past, and other considerations, language and ethnicity for example, less. Since one of the roles of the Senate is to protect or be alive to the needs of minorities, the consequences of more equitable electoral redistribution in the House of Commons demand a more vigilant Senate. While the occasion for this comment is the subject of federalism, it is important to be aware that the Senate is a second chamber in a bicameral parliament, and that the subject of bicameralism (and the upper chamber's position in that arrangement of legislative power) is central to understanding the Senate and its future. Or, in the words of the Supreme Court of Canada in the *Reference re Senate Reform* [2014] 1 SCR 704, "The Senate's fundamental nature and role [is] as a complementary legislative body of sober second thought" (paragraph 52).

Bicameralism

The Senate and the House of Commons are not autonomous legislative entities but comprise one unity, together with the Queen or her representative – Parliament. Yet the subject of bicameralism has largely been ignored by scholars of Canadian government. Instead, for instance, in his book *The Modern Senate of Canada, 1925–1963: A Re-Appraisal,*[22] F.A. Kunz uses in a chapter title the inadequate phrase "relations between the two houses"; inadequate because, in the words of the Supreme Court of Canada in 2014, the relationship is complementary – the health of each chamber nourishes the other.

Westminster-style systems of government are distinctive on several grounds, one of which (as earlier noted) is their reliance upon constitutional scholars for interpretation. It was Walter Bagehot who characterized British governmental institutions as "dignified" and "efficient," and who placed the Lords in the first category. The accuracy of his perception, then or now, is neither here nor there. What mattered is that from the year his book appeared – the year of Confederation – it was common practice to view Canada's parliamentary system as a reflection of Westminster's (where, after the extension of the franchise in 1867, a House-of-Lords "problem" was emerging) and equally common to depict the Senate in a peripheral relationship with the Commons. This was an analogy whose mistake was to confuse imitation with duplication, and thus to disregard the Senate as a chamber – different from its counterpart in Washington, to be sure – of federalism.

Bagehot alone was not responsible for the denigration of upper chambers in Canada. There was a reason indigenous to colonial government for accepting his assessment uncritically. It originates in the narrative of "the achievement of responsible government," at whose core lies the triumph of the legislative assembly over the legislative council.[23] In the first decades of the nineteenth century, there was a need to distinguish the executive in the assembly and to exclude ex-officio members from the assembly. By contrast, the Supreme Court of Canada ruling (2014) demonstrates that the Senate is not (nor was intended to be) tangential to its surroundings. On the contrary, the stereophonic effect of bicameralism is emphasized – neither chamber is superior or inferior to the other. Instead, the upper chamber is recognized in the following respect: the Senate matters constitutionally, legislatively, and politically.

Placing the Canadian Charter of Rights and Freedoms to one side, governing in Canada has been primarily about power and never about restraint. The conception of a constitution as a limit on state power has been largely absent, no doubt because it took so long to develop a sense that Canada possessed a full constitution. Arguably, the Supreme Court ruling challenges that assertion. The requirement of dual legislative discussion of law and policy matters can no longer be ignored or dismissed. For much of its history, the common attitude was that the

Senate did not matter. The Court says it does. And it matters not for its appearance (i.e., its representative capacity) – which has been the focus for a century or more of criticism and proposed reforms – but for what it does as one part of Parliament. In the words of the Court, "The framers sought to endow the Senate with independence from the electoral process ... in order to remove Senators from a partisan political arena that required unremitting consideration of short-term political objectives" (paragraph 57).

What the Senate does, as a *legislative* body, is complement the House of Commons in several respects:

1 Long tenure in the upper house versus short in the lower, with the result that the Senate has a stronger corporate memory and is not as easily disrupted as the Commons;
2 Another way of saying this, is that the Senate is professional (senators bring and acquire experience and perspective) while the Commons is amateur, "one of the most amateur assemblies among advanced Western nations," according to C.E.S. Franks[24];
3 The chambers have contrasting career paths with different perspectives on the past and future: parliamentary activity occurs at a different time in an individual's career;
4 The contrasting size of the chambers – the Commons is three times the size of the Senate, with the former continuing to grow as larger provinces become more populous and occupy more Commons seats;
5 Senators are equals because, unlike in the Commons, there is less distinction in their ranks: for example, government versus opposition, front versus backbench; indeed, there is no alternative government in the Senate – equal senators give equal weight to matters;
6 Majoritarianism is reconciled with federalism, that is, the symmetry of the Senate (equality among divisions) and the asymmetry of Canadian federalism (the contrasting weight and size of the units of Confederation).

The division calculus is important because Canadians live in a majoritarian polity, which at the same time is a federation. Insufficient attention has been paid to the "act of incorporation" that was Confederation: instead, emphasis is placed on responsible government, the maturing of dominion status (colony to nation), and the subjection of Canada's immense geography – "the national dream," although today the national dream might better be portrayed in terms of the Charter and a rights-based citizenship.[25]

The Fathers of Confederation were committed to creating a federation that would promote unity and combat prejudice by emphasizing and protecting diversity. That was the reason for the fixed total number of senators, as well as their allocation among provinces. Institutionally and constitutionally, the pluralism that defines Canada is founded on and sustained by bicameralism and, more particularly, the distinctively Canadian feature of a fixed number of members in the Senate (never in post-Confederation Canada could there be, as in the United Kingdom, threats from the majority of swamping the upper chamber in order to secure passage of contentious legislation). The unlimited prerogative power of the Crown in the person of the sovereign to name peers had no counterpart in the relationship of the governor general and senators. The measure of the Senate is not to be found, as critics invariably assume, in its history or what it looks like, but rather in the logic of the agreement that produced it: to make modern Canada possible. The year 1867 was not about creating a new political system but about welding existing self-governing colonies into a federation. The Court's ruling in 2014 makes that intention explicit: "The Senate is a core component of the Canadian federal structure of government" (paragraph 77). At the same time it is important to remember that, unlike in many countries, the bonds of Canadian loyalty are essentially political: there was no pre-political community identity on which to erect the federation. Each colonial government had been separate from the other, each totally autonomous. In contrast to the metaphorical "boot" destined to become a unified Italy, Canadian unity defied, first, geography and, second, "manifest destiny" on the part of its powerful neighbour.

Parliament's upper house offered a platform for expressing concerns about the federation and minorities. Unlike members of Parliament, senators were not, in and of themselves, reflections or imitations of "something else": they were not accountable to a constituency, however defined, nor obliged to interpret legislation in any predetermined way. The Senate's is an individual voice – it does not speak for a constituency, or a province, or a government. Two consequences flowed from this feature. Bicameralism assumed fundamental (even existential) importance – the two chambers must work, and they must work in tandem for the benefit of the Canadian people, wherever they might live. At the same time, the second chamber must not rival the first. It must never, in other words, be elected by a constituency, since a democratic vote for the Senate would devalue everything but that vote. If this were to happen, conflict between the chambers would follow and the Senate's function as a moderating and unifying agency would be jeopardized. Senate thought would no longer be sober, that is, contemplative, nor would it logically come second.

Present-day opponents of the upper chamber, Patrick Boyer as well as some historians – Christopher Moore, for instance[26] – share with George Brown a preference for majoritarianism. The difference between them and Brown, who did favour a unicameral Ontario legislature, is that the latter realized federation demanded at the centre what was not required in the parts – a bicameral Parliament to help balance sectional and regional tensions.

It may be an exaggeration – but it is not false – to say that those who share the majoritarian indictment of the upper chamber appear to be committed to the proposition that everyman is, or should be, his own legislator. In consequence, the Senate as an institution is disparaged, its history disregarded. The physics of a unicameral Parliament preoccupy their attention. For instance, according to Boyer, there are "two solitudes of sovereign power – the Crown and the people," even though that last "solitude" does not exist in Canada, where, unlike the United States, there is no theory of popular sovereignty embedded in its constitution.[27] Arguably, in this interpretation, the compact theory of Confederation is not just dead, it never lived.

Boyer employs the word *people* as a synonym for electoral democracy, a usage that delegitimizes the Canadian model of bicameralism. To what extent, one wonders, is this imprecision again attributable to the Canadian practice of claiming a constitution by association, whether in the 1867 Preamble, or even earlier, in Governor Simcoe's description of the Constitutional Act, 1791 (noted in chapter one), "as … a perfect image and transcript of the British Government and Constitution." The British analogy refuses to acknowledge the uniqueness and strength of the Canadian upper house. The test of the Senate lies not in who comprises it but in what it does, usually in concert with the Commons. And what it does, in structure and practice, is to validate Canada's distinctive form of federalism, a subject ignored by those who criticize the Senate on grounds that it is undemocratic. More than that, this charge fails to acknowledge the primacy the Supreme Court of Canada has repeatedly awarded federalism: "The dominant principle of the Canadian constitution is federalism" (Patriation Reference, 821); "One of the constitution's principles is federalism as a system of the country's government" (Secession Reference, 217);

and "the Senate is a core component of the Canadian federal structure of government" (Senate Reference 2014, 745).[28]

Bicameralism was as vital to the peace, order, and good government of the new country as the division of powers was to preserving the federation.

Federalism was about more than resolving the conflicts of United Canada, although political problems in that colony drove the Confederation initiative. The original union comprised three former colonies, then four provinces; Ontario, Quebec, New Brunswick, and Nova Scotia. Though few in number, those provinces were unequal (extremely so) in size and population. The Senate was designed to secure the voice of Maritime interests, and minority interests generally, in a Parliament whose lower house, based on rep-by-pop overwhelmingly advanced the concerns of central Canada.

Patronage, and Senate appointments in particular, as well as appointment over election itself, are regularly cited to disparage the second chamber, as is Macdonald's known preference for legislative over federal union. As an aside, it is ironic that Macdonald, the feigned federalist of this interpretation, should a century and a half later be celebrated as the pre-eminent nation-builder of the world's most extensive federation. Then again, perhaps there is no irony. Perhaps Macdonald, a man who before and after 1867 regularly displayed a talent for vigorous political invention, perceived what theorists have not seen – that parliamentary institutions are extraordinarily adaptive. (Indeed, one might argue that it is their fluidity that makes reform of a concrete nature so elusive.) And in British North America before 1867 there had been a number of occasions to demonstrate that adaptability: St John's Island (Prince Edward Island) separated from Nova Scotia (1769); New Brunswick and Cape Breton Island separated from Nova Scotia (1784); Quebec divided into Upper and Lower Canada (1791); Upper and Lower Canada joined in United Canada (1840). The men who met – in Charlottetown, Quebec, and London – were neither amateurs nor ingenuous when it came to constitutional matters. (It should be noted that after Confederation the boundaries of Ontario, Quebec, and Manitoba were extended northward with the addition of vast northern regions to each province, and that the entry of Newfoundland and Labrador brought further boundary adjustments, this time affecting and aggrieving Quebec. The contrast in practice with Australia, where "the mother colony" of New South Wales bequeathed territory for the creation of sister-states Queensland and Victoria, is striking.)

More than that, and despite the fact that several of their number were prominent members of colonial legislative councils, there was in their discussions, and certainly among colonists generally, strong allegiance to the principle of responsible government. In the study of Canadian political history, it cannot be stressed too often that the achievement of responsible government and of colonial self-government "within the Empire" went hand-in-hand. It was not necessary to be a "firebrand," like William Lyon Mackenzie, to dismiss the pretensions of governors, upper chambers, and colonial cliques of whatever name to interfere with the work of the people's assemblies. Deference was paid to electoral power and not social status. It may be an exaggeration to say that Canadians are a unicameral people, but it is only that – an exaggeration. The link between that attitude and unfavourable opinion of the Senate today is not hard to make. Even though the history concerns colonies and the Senate is the upper house of a bicameral Parliament of a federation, it must be appreciated that negative opinion about the upper chamber is deeply rooted.

The achievement and conduct of responsible government, as far as the legislature was concerned, emerged with the formation of political parties. The principle depends upon more than the legislature for its realization, however.[29] It was political parties that gave coherence to the conduct of government in the legislature and provided the voter with a means of exacting accountability at the polls.[30] For efficient implementation, each of these functions looked to the development of the concept of party discipline. In an unelected upper chamber, where the government does not sit and which is a legislative but *not* a confidence chamber, a comparable rationale for disciplined political parties is less easily advanced.

Historically, there has been more talk than action on the matter of upper chambers in Canada, whether the subject was making the body elected or abolishing it. In the 1850s, colonial legislatures in British North America debated resolutions that would have seen their upper houses become elected. Prince Edward Island and United Canada instituted the change; but at the time of Confederation unicameralism prevailed in the new Ontario legislature, while an appointed upper chamber was established in Quebec. Only five Canadian provinces had second chambers after Confederation; two continued into the twentieth century, with the last (Quebec's) being abolished in 1968.[31] Despite precedents that Senate abolitionists cite, there was no parallel between the vanished provincial houses and the Senate. For example, and as noted earlier, the Maritime Provinces were masters of their own (pre-Confederation) constitutions; more significant, Canada's upper house was a legislative body in a federation whose design rested with the framers of the constitution.

The object of criticism since its birth, the Senate of Canada has never been described as impotent. Indeed, its potential for legislative influence is the factor that traditionally agitates critics. The Senate's powers today are the same as they were at its creation. Indeed, every feature of the upper chamber – except term of appointment, now to age seventy-five but originally for life – is as it was then. It is imperative to be clear as to the Senate's fundamental features. First, as just noted, senators hold their positions until age seventy-five. Second, there is a fixed number of senators (twenty-four per senatorial division, of which there are four, as well as nine add-ons [six from Newfoundland-Labrador – provided for in the Constitution Act, 1915 – and one each from Yukon, Northwest Territories, and Nunavut]; two divisions are single provinces, and the other divisions have three and four provinces respectively). A consequence of this limitation is that the Senate (at 105 members) is less than a third the size of the Commons, almost intimate in atmosphere. Third, to repeat, the number is fixed and it is extremely difficult to add extra senators, a feat done only once. The fourth and last feature is that senators are appointed, on recommendation of the prime minister, by the governor general. Why did the Fathers of Confederation decide upon these particular features for the Senate?

Constitutional monarchy makes explicable – if not acceptable to some – appointment of senators by the Crown on advice of the prime minister. There is no need to rehearse the arguments against an appointed upper house. They are well known. What can be said is that constitutional monarchy offered the Fathers of Confederation a practicable method of selecting senators to the upper house at a time when there were few alternatives. Election was not popular in United Canada after the experiment initiated in the 1850s. More than that, revitalization of the upper house through election relied on the theory of a balanced constitution (which originated in the Glorious Revolution of 1688 in the United Kingdom), where "each branch should be independent of the other" – a theory that was largely destroyed in the early nineteenth century by the rise of responsible government with power concentrated in a political executive that dominated the lower house.[32] At the same time, selection by provincial legislatures of delegates from among their numbers to sit at the centre, as was done in the nineteenth-century

United States, violated the common sense of Parliament as the supreme legislative power (as in the United Kingdom) and the belief British North Americans held that creation of a national parliament marked an important step to constitutional maturity. According to J.G. Bourinot, the only examples in the nineteenth century of unicameral polities were the republics of Central America, the Balkan states, and the Landtags and Diets of the Austrian and German states.[33]

Membership in the upper chamber is by senatorial region. The guarantee of fixed equal (regional but not provincial) representation with the more populous provinces of Ontario and Quebec was responsible for the entry of the Maritime colonies. "On no other condition could we have advanced a step," said George Brown.[34] The Senate was a form of compensation for securing rep-by-pop in the House of Commons: compensation to Quebec for what it had lost (equal representation in the Parliament of United Canada), and compensation for the Maritimes for what areas of growth elsewhere would gain. In this fundamental feature, as in others, can be detected the skeleton beneath the constitution now aged 150 years. For this reason, it is neither possible nor prudent to forget what time has created or abandon what went before.

Independence

The Canadian Senate is not just an upper house in a federation, or a second chamber in an ordinal sense, but rather it is the co-equal legislative partner in the Parliament of a constitutional monarchy. Senators hold their position in the chamber because they were selected ("summoned," section 24, Constitution Act, 1867) by the Sovereign's representative. As with so much about the Senate, this is not as esoteric a point as it sounds, since it is related to the hallmark of the Senate and senators – its (and their) independence. One ingredient of the independence that senators are expected to possess may be said to emanate from their manner of selection, that is to say, selection by the Crown's representative. In a system of parliamentary-cabinet government, the coronation oath of the sovereign to do good becomes the obligation of her ministers, and her judges, to fulfil. And while the logic may at first glance appear circular, the advice that ministers and, in this instance, the first minister, give the sovereign or her representative must itself be good.

Contrarily, what would happen if, following advice, the governor general's action were viewed as not good, but rather prejudicial to constitutional values; or, in the absence of advice, the governor general were unable to perform his or her constitutional duties, such as summon a senator? This is the nub of an undecided issue before the courts in the summer of 2015, where an applicant sought to require the governor general to fill vacancies in the Senate that Stephen Harper, then prime minister, had stated he would not fill. In May 2015, Mr Justice Harrington of the Federal Court summarized the issue by posing the following question: "If the Constitution requires something to be done promptly, i.e. that Senate vacancies be filled, can the law be flouted by convention?" Furthermore, he said, "The Supreme Court made it perfectly clear in the *Reference Re Senate Reform* that significant changes to the Senate ... require a formal constitutional amendment."[35] In fact, as a result of the change in government and the restoration of Senate appointments, the case as regards vacancies was declared moot, "the grounds ... [having] evaporated."[36]

Hypothetical perhaps, but not unimaginable, and clearly of strong constitutional import. The selection of senators by the Crown is a first-order difference between the Senate and the Commons, and one the Fathers of Confederation deliberately chose. The difference may appear obvious enough to be self-evident, but that is a misreading of the situation because the difference is disguised by the partisan cloak that envelopes the appointment process. It is that misreading that encourages a view of the Senate not as a distinctive legislative chamber but as a "weak Commons," principally because the government (and currently, no ministers) sit in the upper chamber. There is no study of the Crown and the Senate, as there is of the Crown and Lords in the United Kingdom.[37] The exceptions are the occasional biography of a governor general, where senators may make a fleeting appearance, and Eugene Forsey's article on section 26, Constitution Act, 1867 (the addition of senators in certain cases).[38]

Yet after 2015, the method of appointing senators became a matter of discussion and change. Mr Trudeau had said that he would retain the prime minister's monopoly on advice to the governor general (short of constitutional amendment, there was nothing else he could do); but he also pledged to seek names of potential nominees from an independent panel, which made its first selection of nominees public in March 2016. In addition to that crucial element in the selection process, there is another, more systemic consideration: the selection of governors general. When Stephen Harper sought a candidate to replace Michaëlle Jean as governor general, he is reported to have established a "secret committee to search for candidates" who would possess constitutional knowledge and be non-partisan. C.E.S. Franks, a constitutional authority, praised the "new" process and "recommended that it be made permanent in law."[39] The procedure followed in 2010 altered existing practice and in so doing increased the space between Canada's first minister and the representative of the Crown. How much space is open to question. In 2015, Mr Harper asked David Johnston (chosen in 2010) to continue in his office until 2017: "I look forward to him continuing his fine work in this critical role."[40]

The fact remains that Canada's first minister selects the representative of the Crown, in that he or she proposes the name of that individual to the sovereign; in the United Kingdom, the sovereign selects the first minister (which actually should be *first ministers*), since sovereigns are on the throne far longer than first ministers are in office. "A successor [to Johnston] ... would [have] little time to prepare for a possible constitutional confrontation [if no party were to secure a majority of seats in the House of Commons at the 2015 election]."[41] Here is an early example of a political calculation (such as discussed in chapter two) that may accompany change in the electoral system.

In light of the unprecedented importance attributed to bicameralism, where the Senate is assigned a complementary legislative role, the mechanics of selection of its members will demand more attention than in the past. And this will be the case irrespective of partisan sentiment. Such a change in attitude is all the more probable because election of senators is not going to happen anytime soon, as nearly a decade of frustrated attempts by the Harper government to achieve that end makes clear. Combined with the decline in public respect for political institutions generally but growing support for the Charter and the values it entrenches in civic life, the partisan monopoly on nominations of senators will certainly be challenged, with ramifications for both the political and formal executive in Canada.

There is historical irony in this approaching transformation, for the Fathers of Confederation could never have anticipated such a development. They lived at a time when democratic values were less discussed than today. It is well known that the men who met at Quebec thought that the constitution of the United States leaned too far in a popular direction – the American was not to be the British North American way. There is another reason, structural but unpredictable, why the constitutional development of Canada would have come as a surprise to its founders. If there is one feature common to every interpretation of the life and times of Confederation, it is the political instability that plagued the Province of United Canada in the late 1850s and early 1860s. By contrast, post-Confederation Canada has only had one coalition (really union) government, that led by Robert Borden after the election of 1917. At the very least, it was unexpected that, given what had happened before 1867, the government of the new federation should be dominated by one man for the next quarter century, and by one party. Macdonald's achievement as the pre-eminent "father" of modern Canada is rivalled by his creation of the first national (i.e., federal) political party in constituencies from coast to coast. Before 1867, governments in Ottawa, much like governments at Westminster, were made and unmade in the House of Commons. After Confederation, and as a result of Macdonald's perception, governments increasingly were made in conformity to the election returns from the constituencies. His successors, regardless of party, sincerely flattered him in seeking to imitate his electoral success.

Shifting political alliances moving back and forth across the legislative assembly of the colony did not prepare politicians after 1867 for the ascendancy of a single individual, and more to the point, one in control of patronage of Senate appointments, as well as of almost all other patronage. Here was a dominance that Mackenzie King, Louis St Laurent, Pierre Trudeau, Brian Mulroney, and Stephen Harper, among others, continued to exercise. The difference between Senate and, say, senior public service patronage, is that senators until 1965 were appointed for life, and since then until age seventy-five. Contrary to the complaint that the major problem with the present-day Senate is the imposition of party discipline, it is the monopoly of appointments over such long periods of time that create parliamentary ruptures and disruptions that emanate from the Senate.

The appointment of senators on recommendation of the prime minister is much criticized although loosely articulated, with the animus directed more towards partisan nomination than gubernatorial appointment. Canadians have long accepted, indeed celebrated, constitutional monarchy and an appointed judiciary. In other words, the principle is not in disrepute. From the point of view of the public, the problem with the conventional mechanism for selecting senators is that it is almost exclusively partisan. Partisanship is unfavourably viewed by the public, particularly for selecting members of a chamber whose primary characteristics are supposed to be independence and sober second thought in the conduct of its work.

Among the major problems with this form of nomination is less political allegiance per se than that the process will lead over time to an upper chamber that is imbalanced in terms of parties. Paradoxically, legislative bodies and political systems need the articulation of conflicting views if they are to be strongly democratic: the law of politics bids debate. The logic of different voices is the sine qua non for fair and competent legislation, and for coherent discussion. In the well-known words of Edmund Burke, "Our antagonist is our helper." In a chamber whose function is to be contemplative, and complementary to the Commons in the exercise of its legislative responsibilities, party sentiment is welcome as an organizing force. But because party discipline silences disparate voices and prevents dissent, it is destructive of the contribution the upper chamber may make to public policy. Where governmental confidence is not an issue, as it is in the lower chamber, discipline subverts the tone and substance of the Senate's work and, at the same time, challenges the cardinal feature assigned it by the constitution – independence.

Political parties comprise a loose aggregate of kindred minds on societal, economical, and personal visions of the world. Party discipline forces senators to abide by a predetermined position, to vote against their own mind, and, at its limits, to be sanctioned or disciplined for a refusal to obey, thus preventing them from using their freedom of expression in the chamber, contrary to parliamentary privilege long established in the Bill of Rights of 1689. Discipline imposed from below vitiates Senate claims to independence, for it puts the Senate in the service of the government. The defence sometimes heard, that party discipline promotes accountability to the public, may apply to the Commons but has no relevance when the subject is the unelected Senate. On the contrary, discipline betrays the purpose of the Senate as set down by the framers of the constitution, because it distorts the regionally and minority-inclined Senate by making it the mirror image of the majoritarian-impelled Commons. Similarly, because the Senate is not a confidence chamber, it is misleading and detrimental to its operation to transfer the government-opposition alignment into the upper chamber, for there is no "opposition" in the House-of-Commons sense of an alternative government.

The legal basis of Senate membership has nothing to do with political parties: there are no writs of election; there is no conventional commitment to an electoral platform. The prime minister who recommends a candidate for appointment will have left the scene before the terms of the senators he or she has recommended are completed. In other words, the *personal* allegiance of the latter to the former is transitory. Most senators serve under different prime ministers of different political parties.

The question then becomes how to promote cross-party cooperation in the legislative process and Senate procedures. Although the Senate cannot defeat the government or withdraw confidence, it has been argued that "the Senate is better equipped to hold executive government accountable for its policies and conduct than is the House of Commons."[42] The commonly held view that government derives its authority and legitimacy from the Commons alone, rather than from Parliament as a whole, is limited and "insidious," because it "subverts the Senate's constitutional role of check and balance."[43] The Senate cannot check the Commons if the Senate merely duplicates the Commons, that is, if it is elected on a partisan base similar to that of the House, or if, as an appointed body, the object of attention as a result of party discipline is the same as the Commons. Duplicating is not complementing.

How far can the Senate disagree with the Commons? The House has public support, demonstrated by the results of the last election, on its side; among the reasons for creating the Senate was to challenge majoritarian rule when that rule conflicted with minority or regional interests. Which majority – that found in the House of Commons or currently among the people – should prevail? How far may the Senate legitimately obstruct the Commons? Is there a clear answer to that question? This is unlikely, since the purpose of a complementary chamber is to force the other chamber to concentrate its attention on what is being said and to reconsider its position in light of what it hears. The upper chamber's constitutional power to veto a bill, which the Senate has exercised infrequently and which has been denied to the Lords for more than a century, is defensible on these grounds: its potential use demands that the government and the Commons pay attention to what is happening in the Senate. Bicameralism is not – nor should it be – a contest of wills. If, as is generally agreed, the Senate should not thwart the will of the Commons as the voice of the people, then the government in the Commons should not, through the extension of party discipline in the upper chamber, thwart the will of the Senate as it exercises its independence to complement the work of the Commons.

Nominations to the Senate have been, and remain, overwhelmingly partisan, since it is the prime minister alone who proposes names to the governor general. Indeed, this practice, as much as any other on the part of all prime ministers, has fed proposals for an elected Senate.

The problem with such an alteration, as the Supreme Court of Canada has noted, is that an elected upper house would jeopardize parliamentary bicameralism where the House of Commons is the confidence chamber. The Senate expense scandal and subsequent investigation by the auditor general of senatorial expenses more generally have raised media and public attention of the upper chamber to unprecedented levels. One consequence of heightened criticism was the decision of the leader of the Liberal Party, Justin Trudeau, to sever Liberal senators from the party caucus and to introduce a new non-partisan means of selecting senators. Such a revolutionary change in selection, with accompanying change in personnel and practices of the Senate, is achievable not by statute or constitutional amendment but by altering the exercise of the practice that guides the selection process.[44]

Sir John A. Macdonald instituted present practice and his successors emulated it, but there is no legal or constitutional reason why another mode of selection might not replace it. Bearing that in mind, there are two provisos to that statement. First, an altered method must respect the Crown's right to appoint (in other words, it must not, as the Supreme Court of Canada said of Senate election legislation, dissimulate by "privileging form over substance" [paragraph 52]). Second, it must respect (and more particularly, avoid) section 41 of the Constitution Act, 1982, which requires unanimous consent of the Senate, House of Commons, and legislative assembly of each province for amendment in relation to "the office of the Queen, the Governor General and the Lieutenant Governor of a province." On this point, as on many others, the accuracy of the preambular phrase in the Constitution Act, 1867 – that Canada should have a constitution "similar in Principle to that of the United Kingdom" – is increasingly cast in doubt. Indeed, the Constitution Act, 1982, with the Canadian Charter of Rights and Freedoms and the amending formulae, should serve to warn that the tradition of viewing Canada's constitution as one of association with that of Great Britain is suspect.

This observation is timely, because the transition of the House of Lords from a hereditary and aristocratic chamber to one where those characteristics are but shadows of the past and a portion of whose members are selected in a non-partisan fashion may offer an attractive model for Canada to emulate. The comparative merits of upper chamber reform at Westminster nonetheless require more study than can be given here. Still, British example should be treated prudently (some might say, sceptically) by Canadians. In 2015, the Lords is more than seven times the size of the Senate, and may grow even more, since there is no upper limit on its numbers. Indeed, the process of institutional evolution is a hallmark of the Lords, although far less so of the Senate. (In 2009, with the establishment of the Supreme Court of the United Kingdom, the Lords ceased to perform their historic judicial function – a function the Senate was never called upon to perform.) The Fathers of Confederation specifically agreed and deliberately acted so as to protect the Senate from being swamped by government appointees. The Lords was an aristocratic chamber, with close ties historically to the established church. In modern Britain, class and religious hierarchy are out of fashion, as witness (regarding the latter) changes made in the Succession to the Crown Act, 2013. The real and property qualifications of section 23 of the Constitution Act, 1867, may be (and have been) cited to support the claim that the Senate exists to protect privilege, although it could also be said that they helped guarantee that appointees would be more financially (and thus, politically) independent than members of the Commons. In any case, there is no hereditary component to membership in the Senate. Macdonald admired the legislative union of Scotland and England, a union less unquestioned than it once was. The argument heard in Great Britain, that the Lords needs to become more territorially and demographically diverse, is not echoed in Canada, where senatorial divisions of equal size help complement the diversity that the federation was intended to accommodate.

To these contrasts should be added what might be called systemic differences between Canada and the United Kingdom. British political parties and the governments they formed in the last two decades of the twentieth century were, by Canadian standards, strongly programmatic in their manner of governing. Margaret Thatcher and Tony Blair held firm and (similarly) negative views of the Lords at the end of the last century. The former ignored them, the latter sought to change them. The mechanism Blair chose at the outset was a royal commission (Mrs Thatcher appointed no royal commission during her years in office, her view of the utility of such bodies being the same as her view of the Lords). There has never been a royal commission on the Senate in Canada, nor a proposal for one, despite continuing criticism of the upper chamber. The reason is that Canadian political parties have not articulated coherent views on Senate reform, and in their absence terms of reference for an inquiry are difficult to draft. More than that, for a long time and unlike the Senate, the Lords had the potential to disrupt. It is worth remembering that the parliamentary crisis of 1910 and

1911, along with near-civil war in Ireland and the rise of the suffragette movement helped destroy the Liberal Party.[45] The Lords posed a threat in British politics then, and one that even a moderate leader like Clement Attlee later, in 1949, recognized when the first Labour government to have a majority in the Commons limited the Lords' suspensive veto even further than that set down in the 1911 legislation.

The majority of Lords are still appointed on recommendation of the prime minister. The "non-party-political peers," who are appointed on recommendation of the Lords Appointments Commission and who number fewer than one hundred, sit as crossbenchers and not with party groups. One may assume that it is this feature of the Lords today that appeals to Canadian advocates of a less-partisan selection process for Canadian senators. The analogy is far from perfect, however. There are no crossbenches in the Senate and, historically, there have been only two party groupings, as opposed to three (now four, with the Scottish Nationalists, SNP) at Westminster (Conservative, Labour, and Liberal-Democrat). In addition, there are sixty-some other peers drawn from bishops of the Church of England, other parties, and non-affiliated members. The comparative merits of the two schemes would require more research than is possible here. What is worth emphasizing is that the schemes differ, with the British arrangement looking more like the Canadian today than in the past. Such convergence as there is results from changes carried out in the United Kingdom and not in Canada. Following the election returns of May 2015, which saw dramatic change in fortune for the SNP, Liberal-Democratic, and Labour Parties, the calculations that underlay a reconstituted Lords a decade ago appear less certain. The attraction of upper chamber reform is related to whether the viewer possesses a majority or minority in the lower chamber. The SNP gained fifty seats but remains without a voice in the Lords; the Liberal-Democrats lost forty-eight seats but retain their 100 peers; Labour lost its stronghold north of the Tweed but still counts 224 (of a total 783) peers among its parliamentary ranks.

The digression into reform of the House of Lords may seem tendentious, but is important because of the historic association drawn between the upper chambers of the two countries and because the parallel relationship each upper house has with its lower, popularly elected chamber. Different premises inspire upper chamber reform. While various reasons may be offered for criticism directed at the Senate, one indisputable source is the partisanship that pervades selection of its members and conduct of its work. The emphasis the Supreme

Court of Canada has placed on the Senate as a complementary house in a bicameral parliament underlines the conundrum when expectation confronts reality. In contrast, the "party question" does not provide momentum to the House of Lords. Debate on the upper chamber in the United Kingdom has touched on many issues, but concern about the level of party influence has not been pivotal. The appointments commission mentioned earlier only vets nominees' qualifications; the majority of persons recommended to the Queen for appointment still hold party affiliation. A more accurate depiction of a paramount issue is the Lords as a representative body. In Canada, and outside of the Triple-E proposal for what might be called structural change, the Senate as a representative body is not the question, since the constitution settles that point by establishing senatorial divisions of equal numbers and, when there is more than one province in a division, allocates senators by province.

A conclusion from the foregoing comments is to exercise caution when using comparative examples. The Fathers of Confederation weighed and – for the purposes of the new Dominion – found wanting on a number of counts the example of the United States Senate. Similarly, Canadian society is different from British society in multiple ways, but relevant to this discussion is the contrasting setting of its politics. Canada is not an island kingdom but a continent-wide political, indeed partisan, construct. This is neither good nor bad, but true. Partisanship is pervasive in Canada and it has been a struggle to tame it – in the bureaucracy for the first half of Confederation and now in Parliament: officers of Parliament, independent electoral boundaries commissions, election finance regimes, and more have the common purpose of limiting its excesses. The search for independence is a hallowed topic.[46]

A second model that recommends itself to some critics of the current practice of senatorial selection is drawn from Canadian experience with the selection of judges. Section 92 court appointments, that is appointments to provincial courts through action by one of the ten respective lieutenant governors, vary according to jurisdiction. This discussion will focus on section 96, or federal, court appointments. The present committee system for federal judicial selection was introduced in the 1980s at the time Brian Mulroney was prime minister. The structure of the scheme reflects the fact that Canada is a federation, as section 96 selection committees typically comprise the chief justice of the province, a person appointed by the federal minister of justice, another appointed by the attorney general of the province, along with two lawyers and two laypersons normally appointed by the vote of the other committee members. Selection committees classify applicants as either highly recommended, recommended, or not recommended.

Compared to past practice of senatorial nomination, where the prime minister has exclusively dominated, the attraction of what may be called the judicial selection model lies in non–prime ministerial vetting of the process. Recommendations for the appointment of judges come to the governor general from the prime minister. Similarly, were this procedure to be copied with regard to senators, those recommendations would follow the same route. Presumably, the broader set of consultations demanded by this proposal would not trespass on the prerogative of the governor general in making the senatorial appointment. Yet even if imitable from this perspective, practical differences exist. The most obvious is a contrast in numbers: 105 senators versus 1118 judges and supernumeraries (as of February 2017).[47] If not full-time, the work of the judicial advisory committees, especially in large provinces like Ontario, is a continuing commitment. In provinces with four or six senators, which is to say half the provinces of Canada, the work of senatorial advisory committees would be discontinuous. It would not be feasible to compile lists of approved candidates for recommendation to the governor general years in advance of the need for action. Nor would individuals wish their expression of interest in the position to languish for an indeterminate time. More than that, law is a profession that, in Canada, is highly provincial in its character – law schools, articles, bar associations (along with judgeships) are examples. By contrast, the collegiality of senators is a post- not pre-selection phenomenon.

In the matter of models, a third, very recent, and in many respects apt precedent is the Advisory Committee on Vice-Regal Appointments: "a non-partisan committee established to provide the Prime Minister with non-binding recommendations on the selection of Governors General, Lieutenant Governors, and Territorial Commissioners." Comprising the Canadian secretary to the Queen, as well as two permanent (one anglophone and one francophone) federal delegates, each serves for a time not exceeding six years. For the appointment of a lieutenant governor or commissioner, two additional members drawn from the relevant province or territory will be temporarily added as members, each is a member for no longer than six months. A representative of the Office of the Prime Minister acts as an observer only.[48]

Irrespective of how applicable they may be in the present situation, these modified selection processes for senators attract little, very little, public interest. The Senate expense scandal and earlier debate over the Triple-E Senate proposal draw attention to the genesis of senators, but to date the attention has been transitory. Proposals for parliamentary participation in the selection of justices of the Supreme Court of Canada, and even precedents of this nature, appear to have no public, as opposed to an academic or specialist, constituency to sustain them. Because populism is not a constitutional principle – or even value – it offers no rationale for direct or indirect participation in appointments. In this regard, Canadian attitudes towards constitutionalism are intimately tied to Canadian attitudes towards the Senate: public ambivalence has serious repercussions for public understanding.

In its introductory comments on "senatorial tenure," the Supreme Court of Canada ruling observed that "security of tenure is intended to allow Senators to function with independence in conducting legislative review … Fixed terms [as set down in the government's impugned legislation] provide for weaker security of tenure." While "independence" may appear a non-controversial term, on reflection its meaning rapidly loses certainty. For instance, the American colonies won their War of Independence by separating from imperial control in Great Britain. On this occasion, independence implied a severing of ties or emancipation. By contrast, Peter C. Oliver concludes his important study, *The Constitution of Independence: The Development of Constitutional Theory in Australia, Canada, and New Zealand*,[49] with a chapter titled "Constitutional Continuity and Constitutional Independence." Here the outcome is the reverse to what happened in the United States: independence and continuity complement each other, with a marriage of apparent opposites – difference and similarity – being achieved.

In the sense in which the Supreme Court ruling in 2014 uses the term, independence cannot mean oversight, or control, or autonomy, for the reason that any of these definitions would vitiate the Court's pronouncement that "the Constitution should be viewed as having an 'internal architecture,' which means the individual elements of the Constitution are linked to the others and must be interpreted by reference to the structure of the Constitution as a whole." What can be said is that independence is an essential element in the Senate's performance of its complementary function in the legislative process. "Performance" and "function" are not structures that can be built; rather they emanate from attitudes and conditions that pervade the legislative process. It is a fallacy to think of bicameralism as a matter of structures, when at its core it is a matter of the mind, or in the words of the Supreme Court

evaluation, "the assumptions that underlie the text" (paragraph 26). It
is this intangible quality that allows the two chambers of a bicameral
legislature to think and work together rather than to think and work
apart or in parallel.

A major criterion of Senate effectiveness lies in its skill at improving legislation, which in light of the chamber's other features depends
upon independence from government and the lower chamber, capacity for contemplative or sober second thought, acuity in revising and
reviewing legislation, the resource of institutional memory, and responsiveness to minority and regional concerns. "A core function of Parliament is debate, and the *process* of debate is as important as the decision
taken."[50] In this activity the Senate plays a major role, because greater
freedom of debate occurs where the confidence question does not prevail. The Senate is better situated than the Commons to connect with
the public. While some senators have held elected office, many have
not, and in that respect they are not professional politicians in the sense
their opposite numbers in the Commons are. Instead of representing
voters, they represent citizens, who also are not elected. In that important regard, senators and Canadians share common ground. When the
Senate turns partisan, it loses public trust in its deliberative capacity –
the quality of the institution Canadians most admire.

In contrast, with lower turnout generally, and especially among
younger Canadians, the ballot has become the equivalent of a ticket
of admission to formal political participation. Canadian polling expert
Michael Adams has demonstrated that the political parties earn the least
respect among political institutions, with only 7 per cent of Canadians
trusting them a lot, compared with 32 per cent not at all.[51] Advocates
of an elected Senate invariably argue that election is a source of legitimacy. This is a disputable claim in light of the strong support Canadians evidence for their appointed judiciary. Assuming for the moment
the validity of the assertion, it needs emphasizing, although the point
is rarely mentioned, that the legitimacy of the electoral system rests
upon the independence of election administration from government
in every jurisdiction in the country. And election administration is a
far more complex process than the two-word phrase suggests, including, as it does, regulations, budgets, enforcement, implementation, and
reporting.[52]

There is nothing to stop the Senate from creating opportunities to
listen to public opinion. To some extent it already does this, and in
some respects its form is better suited than is that of the party-aligned

Commons. Support for the Senate among informed and active Canadians originates in the knowledge of its accessibility – thousands of witnesses over the years cannot be wrong. The 2014 ruling of the Supreme Court of Canada has made clear that independence is a primary characteristic expected of the upper house. Nor is that condition a matter of choice: the constitution requires the Senate to fulfil its fundamental roles and responsibilities. Ignorance, apathy, or a disinclination to act no longer suffice to explain inaction. Relatedly, one might ask, how far may the Senate be impeded by others in the fulfilment of its functions? Too often, or more often than in the past, the problem of the Senate appears to be the House of Commons, or more precisely, the party discipline under which the Commons operates and which makes comity between the chambers difficult.

Comity occurs between equals, and contrary to past attitudes that have assumed a hierarchy of chambers with the Commons above the Senate, that perspective is no longer (if it ever was) theoretically or practically valid. The Supreme Court ruling of 2014 is free of any doubt on this score: the Senate is an independent and complementary legislative body, constitutionally equal to the House of Commons. The upper chamber is not a partisan colony of the lower. A more succinct metaphor would be a swimming pool: in the eyes of all past governments, the Commons has occupied the deep end and the Senate the shallow. The Senate reference alters that assumption. Now the depth is uniform, but the temperature at the lower and upper house "ends" is different.

The House of Commons may appear tangential to the present discussion. And so it is, but it cannot be ignored altogether. Canada is an electoral democracy whose centrepiece is the Commons. Members of Parliament are the one and only national officeholders Canadians have the opportunity to choose. All MPs are members of political parties; "independent" candidates do not get elected. The few MPs who "cross the floor" seldom are re-elected. A strong case can be made that the political history of Canada is the history of its political parties.[53] A consequence of fundamental importance for the political culture of Canada follows from the pivotal position that parties play: partisanship and partisan sentiment pervade public life and debate, and to that extent party politics becomes the measure of Parliament itself.

From one point of view, that comment may appear tautological; still, it is defensible. The shadow of an approaching or departing election always hovers. It is the partisan prism that explains the perpetual distortion of parliamentary life found in the media and public discussion: that governments in Canada are "elected"; that the official opposition lacks credibility because it is not "elected"; that governments have "terms" (this even before the arrival of "fixed-date" election laws); and more. It is by the partisan "measure" – more than by any other – that the Senate is said to fail to meet the test of "legitimacy." Freely invoked, this is a crude standard nonetheless, when only a minority of members of the Commons enjoy the support of a majority of voters in their constituencies. Governments in Canada are appointed, but nobody sees this as a problem, or if they do, they do not see it as significant. Senators are appointed, and many people see this as a problem, but for different reasons: they are not accountable (to the public) or they are partisan, to the extent that the Senate cannot fulfil the complementary role the Fathers of Confederation intended, and the Supreme Court has reiterated, they should play. What is to be done? How to sort out the matter?

What Is to Be Done?

The Senate should democratize its iconography by emphasizing that its rules and procedures are less rigid and more accommodative of public opinion than are those of the Commons. Party discipline is not as oppressive above as it is below. It should be noted too that public perception of the Senate influences how the Senate sees itself. In short, a reciprocal relationship exists between senators and the public, one that is essentially different from that which obtains between MP, as representative, and the constituent, as represented. It needs repeating that senators are not agents of a principal. Absent that connection they are, on the one hand, free of the constituency pressures MPs experience but, on the other hand, they are bereft of the personal, political, and community support that members of the Commons predictably and necessarily attract. It is the absence of that support that explains the isolation senators experience.

Compared to the past, even the recent past, there is more activity and interest today in the Senate. As source of the interest, the critic might cite the trial of Senator Duffy and the report of the auditor general of Canada on senatorial expenses in 2015.[54] While no doubt true as far as it goes, the work and range of Senate activity, especially of its committees, is equally important as an explanation. Although the committee work of the Senate is regularly lauded by media, academics, and the public, the scope of that activity and the sense of access to its proceedings deserve closer study than may be given it here. Indicative of its volume, however, are data in the annual Senate Report on Activities for the periods 2008–9 and 2012–13, which reveal over 2300 committee meetings to have taken place with more than 6000 witnesses in attendance, and that produced roughly 500 committee reports.[55]

The opportunity exists to help empower civil society, for, unelected though it is, the Senate stands as an ally and not an opponent of the popular will. Also, it is more accessible than the House of Commons. Canada is a country of contrasts – big versus little – whether the subject is territory or population; and in either case, the contrast is the bane of each of the ten (federally appointed) provincial independent electoral boundaries commissions appointed following the decennial census. Because the Commons is composed of many small constituencies and the Senate of a few large divisions, one would expect that the focus of Commons business would be on micro matters and the Senate on macro ones. But there is a counterargument to be made to that assumption.

First, there is a very big difference in the size of the two chambers: 105 seats in the upper house versus 338 seats (after the redistribution following the 2011 census) in the lower. And there is a large difference in their contrasting trajectories of growth: in 1917, the Commons had 235 seats; in 1974, the number was 264; and in 2015, 338. In other words, in the last century the House has increased roughly by the size of the Senate. In the same period, the Senate grew by just nine seats. Second, the House of Commons would be expected to represent smallness because of the multitude and variety of its constituencies, but political party discipline obliterates localism – as it always has. The smaller, complementary, but free-of-constituency-accountability Senate is better positioned to articulate specific concerns, whether or not rooted in geography. Third, the Commons is highly polarized in an era when the public is more pluralistic and volatile in party affiliation. Again, according to Michael Adams in the previously cited study *AmericasBarometer*, since 2012 more than half the population have been active in the last year signing petitions, sharing political information online, and participating in demonstrations and protest marches. Political activity on the Internet is growing rapidly, especially on social media, which is most popular among younger Canadians (those under the age of thirty [45 per cent]), who are more than twice as likely to use social media for political expression than those sixty years of age and over (19 per cent).

A number of reasons may be offered for this development. One relevant to the discussion, a heightened belief in the need for real and perceived fairness and a resulting transformation in the sense of what rules should look like, is voiced by Australian Judith Brett – people do not like the tone of parliamentary conflict: "For those experienced with the modern informal meeting and its consensual style of reaching a decision, parliamentary procedure is no longer seen as enabling but as precluding co-operative action."[56] There is a sharp contrast here between what might be termed a permissive view of organizing the public forum and the long, unchallenged authority of *Robert's Rules of Order* and the atmosphere it demanded. An example of the contrast is given by George Ross, premier of Ontario and later a senator, in his autobiography: "[As a young man] I associated myself with a division of the 'Sons of Temperance' ... The business of the division was conducted according to well-defined rules of procedure and debate, which gave it an air of dignity and self-restraint not unlike a parliament in miniature."[57] Adams's research demonstrates that Brett's observation is not confined to Australia: "Half of Canadians (50 per cent) strongly agree with the statement: 'Political parties should allow MPs to vote in Parliament according to what they believe is right, even if it is not consistent with their party's position,' with very few (six per cent) who strongly disagree."[58]

The dominion of the Senate derives from the chamber being accessible and scrupulous in the conduct of its legislative work (consider, and compare to the House of Commons, the breadth of its examination of the Fair Elections Act in 2014). Embracing these qualities, the Senate acts as a bridge to the public, whose concerns most often are not political so much as concerns about the workplace, family, religion, health, diversity, and citizenship. To that list of familiar topics may more recently be added civic issues that defy traditional jurisdictional compartments: science, the environment, and culture. These are not constituency or regional issues as those terms are generally understood. Still, they serve to thicken the network of Canadians interested in the activity of the upper chamber. Like the country it serves, the Senate has demonstrated a capacity for adaptation, and may still do so. Distinctively Canadian at its creation, it remains so 150 years on.

Another dimension of civic empowerment is the representation, promotion, and protection of regional interests. In its ruling in 2014, the Supreme Court of Canada specifically speaks to the "distinct form of representation for the regions" provided by the Senate. This raison d'être is as relevant today as at the drafting of the constitution. Nor should the relevance be assumed to be limited to voice alone, for as the Supreme Court of Canada observed in 1980, "a primary purpose of the creation of the Senate, as part of the federal legislative process, was ... to afford protection to the various sectional interests in Canada *in relation to the enactment of federal legislation*."[59] There is another reason to see the Senate's contribution to bicameralism benignly: regional politics often tells us about ourselves more faithfully and more accurately than do the electoral returns from the constituencies or the nation. This is because region is more than a geographic expression. That is why the Senate is such a useful sounding board for cultural, professional, and social interests, among others, that are not territorially rooted: children, the elderly, the poor (rural and urban), the sick and dying are but examples of the demographic heterogeneity that constituency and even provincial profiles inadequately convey.

Notwithstanding the contrasting total numbers for the Commons and Senate (given above), it is important in this discussion to bear in mind that to talk of the Senate at work is very often to talk of the committees of the Senate at work. Legislative studies, regardless of the country in question, too often adopt a global perspective. This is ironic, since legislative committee work is usually acknowledged to be the site in most political systems of the most productive and least partisan activity. More than that, in Canada the effect of equal senatorial divisions is to defend regional interest against combinations of majorities. It is also the case that the effect of seat redistribution on House of Commons representation of slow- or no-growth provinces is to reduce the potential influence of MPs from those areas, and increase that of senators from the same areas. Might this inter-cameral transference be another aspect of complementarity? Here is an unacknowledged aspect of bicameralism, one that helps explain long-observed reticence of the governments of the Atlantic Provinces to consider proposals for Senate reform of the Triple-E variety. In the same vein, Philippe Couillard, the premier of Quebec in 2015, indicated that he was "unequivocally opposed to the abolition of the Senate. He believes that its core mission of giving Canada's regions a voice in Parliament is more relevant than ever."[60]

A variation on this theme – but one that touches on other minorities – concerns parliamentary representation of official languages: the Senate makes more audible at the centre the voice of French-speaking Canadians from those parts where they do not comprise a majority of the population. In a study commissioned by the Office of the Commissioner of Official Languages (2007), political scientist Louis Massicotte concluded that "official language minority communities have little to gain but much to lose if the selection process for senators is amended [that is, replacing appointment with election]."[61] He noted that "official language minority communities are proportionately *better represented* in the Senate than in the House of Commons."[62] Two reasons explain the contrast between the chambers. First, senators are appointed on the recommendation of prime ministers, who, whether Liberal or Conservative, have treated the appointment of French-speaking senators (and not only from Quebec) as important. Second, MPs are elected, and in the absence of a territorial concentration of French-speaking voters – as occurs in New Brunswick and parts of Manitoba and Ontario – it is unlikely that French-speaking candidates will be elected. Even where such concentrations of population exist, the redistribution principle of one-person, one-vote, one-value (which is becoming more pronounced with each redistribution) may trump the counterclaim of respect for representation of official language minorities.[63]

Is there a place for the alignment of government versus opposition in the Senate? What does the designation "government" signify in a chamber that lacks a means of exacting accountability? The author of a 2015 paper, "Working Together: Improving Canada's Appointed Senate," speaks to this point: "[A] possible initiative, unexplored in debate and the literature so far, would be to move for the conduct of Senate business from a Government/Opposition model to a Majority/Minority model. The Government/Opposition designations are misleading, suggesting as they do that the Senate might have some role, which it doesn't have, in the functioning of responsible government."[64] The ministerial and collective versions of the doctrine of responsibility do not exist in the Senate, and that is a big part of the chamber's attraction. This is a red-flag-to-a-bull statement for its critics but a source of strength too, for absent a personal stake (re-election) in the success of their advocacy, senators are accountable only to the sovereign by whose command they are appointed, and to their personal and fraternal honour. These are essential ingredients if the Senate is to act as a complementary body in a bicameral Parliament. It is no small matter that the reputation of the Senate depends upon the reputation of its least honourable member. This is not true of the Commons, and one reason for the difference, one may surmise, lies in the equality of status of each appointed senator versus an accretion of difference resulting from the individual election over time of more than three hundred MPs. If the public carries a picture of the Senate in its mind, it must be that of the stately "red chamber," the image reproduced to the exclusion of any other by the media. Such static representation discourages making the effort, either to get outside the frame and examine the context of Senate business, or to go inside it and explore the complex layering of Senate activity beneath the surface.

What would be the hallmarks of a more open and democratic Senate? A revised selection process for senators is one, if only because the present (and past) prime-ministerial monopoly on appointments is irreconcilable with any pretence of openness. Adoption of a committee- or commission-style system analogous to that used for judicial appointments in Canada, or for Canadian governors general and lieutenant governors, or for appointments to the House of Lords in the United Kingdom has much in principle to recommend it in the context of this discussion. The details of this altered scheme require study and refinement to accommodate the diversity of the federal system, but the object of the change is clear and the intent lucid. From the standpoint of the ruling of the Supreme Court of Canada in 2014, such a change would reinforce a commitment to the values of bicameralism, independence, sober second thought, fundamental principles of the Constitution such as democracy, constitutionalism, and the rule of law, and perhaps even the guarantee of "a Constitution similar in Principle to that of the United Kingdom." As well, it would address the Court's concern about the integrity of the Constitution's architecture, for it is a fact that overbroad patronage over time has actually been reduced in its exercise in some areas of the public concern, a claim studies of the public service and the judiciary support.

How to create a working relationship between the Senate and the Commons, one that does not at the same time devalue, through the imposition of party discipline, the upper chamber's independence but that, in turn, is an essential element if the Senate is to perform its constitutional role as a complementary legislative chamber? Critics never tire of enjoining the Senate not to thwart the will of the Commons because the Commons embodies the will of the people. Quite right, but challenging is not the same as thwarting; nor does it act in this manner when the will of the people is clear. Equally, the Commons, which under a scheme of responsible government means the government, should not, through the imposition of party discipline, thwart the Senate in the exercise of its constitutional responsibilities to listen, investigate, study, and report upon matters of public import. If it is the function of the Senate to detect and communicate the views and opinions that the representative system in the Commons fails to detect adequately, how may silencing or limiting the upper chamber in the performance of its (non-elected) mandate be defended?

A unique demonstration of the two chambers making their own distinctive contribution to the passage of legislation of major public interest occurred in the spring of 2016, when after strong debate in the Senate (absent party discipline) and the Commons, Parliament passed Bill C-14 (the doctor-assisted dying law). In the eyes of some observers, the Senate's assertion of independence in its deliberations constituted "rebellion," while in the eyes of others, the actions of the two houses brought "new life to Parliament."[65] In a political system that values precedent as much as Canada's does, the influence of the example established by the two chambers in reaching agreement on such a contentious matter of legislation remains (at the time of writing) to be demonstrated.

The need for second chamber independence is pressing. The Senate is a chamber of the people but not a representative body, in the sense of its selection or rendering account. On the contrary, it is a continuous legislative body, whose members address one another and whose primary purpose is to afford protection to the various sectional interests in Canada in relation to enactment of legislation. Politicians carry the story of Canada forward daily. The details may change, their origin does not. The "limited identities" that historians once saw as essential to Canadians' understanding of themselves has disappeared. Not limited but multiple identities (gender, age, occupation, for example), few of which are regionally specific, define Canada today. Adopting Richard Hofstadter's phrase, one could say of north of the forty-ninth parallel what was said of the United States: "Born in the country, [Canada] has moved to the city,"[66] a truth the economy, society, and plural culture verify each day. The Senate is in a better position than the Commons to speak of the common lived experiences of the people of Canada no matter where they reside, because it has the potential and perspective to engage the interests of modern Canadians who are less set than preceding generations in their partisan loyalties. John Stuart Mill argued that people are represented only if they think they are represented. Surveys repeatedly demonstrate that people believe the Commons is ineffective in representing them, particularly in holding government to account. Under a system of parliamentary government, the Senate must never replace the Commons and hold government responsible but it may make government more responsive – and responsible – and, in that respect, help moderate public cynicism about politicians and the constitution.

Chapter Four

Readjustment: The House of Commons

Although the claim runs counter to every political value Canadians hold, the Senate is the core institution of Confederation, for without it there would be no Canada. In this respect the Senate may be designated as original. Indeed, as its critics tirelessly intone, it is unlike any other upper chamber in the world. In contrast, the House of Commons is familiar, similar even (one might say) to its counterpart at Westminster. In this respect the Commons may be described as vestigial. That implicit assumption underlies much of the literature on the lower house of the Canadian Parliament. In the language of this book's title, the British legacy provides one mirror in which to view the federal legislature, but it is not a looking glass free from distortion. Imperfection arises from two contrasts that set these parliamentary democracies apart.

Canada is a federation; the United Kingdom a unitary political system, although with an increasing degree of devolution to the territories peripheral to England. Commons seats are allocated to Canadian provinces so that after each census provinces that have had an increase in population over the preceding decade receive additional seats, while those that have not experienced sufficient growth continue with the same Commons "representation" as before, or in other words, proportionately fewer seats. In this respect, and only this one, federalism is incorporated by constitutional means in the lower chamber. By convention, prime ministers from John A. Macdonald to the present choose members of their cabinets with a view to acknowledging linguistic, religious, and provincial claims to representation in government. Earlier chapters in this book have offered reasons for the (surprisingly) faint impress of federalism on the House of Commons. One is that Canadian federalism is about divided jurisdiction, within whose walls respective federal or provincial governments are sovereign. Another is the Senate, within whose equal senatorial divisions senators are allocated among provinces, if there is more than one province in a division.

Notwithstanding the viewer's perspective on the function and performance of the Senate, there can be no dispute that both chambers of Parliament are expected to advance the interests of Canadians in different regions, constituencies, and provinces of the country. Moreover, the foregoing explanations for the character of legislative federalism reinforce each other: the jurisdictional compartments of one central and ten provincial governments contribute to a peripheralization of the provinces and, in turn, the Senate. Certainly a distinguishing feature of Canadian federalism is the asymmetry between legislative bicameralism at the centre and unicameralism in the parts. It would be a mistake, however, to assume that peripheralization implies weakness. On the contrary, it increases the power of the provincial governments in their relationship with the centre. The principle of representation by population and its realization in Canadian politics will be discussed briefly below (a substantial literature on this subject already exists). The relevance of the topic here lies in the subterranean influence of the Constitution Act, 1915 (i.e., its requirement that no province have fewer members of Parliament than it has senators), which made the principle of "rep-by-pop" subservient to a province's right to *adequate* representation in Parliament, in light of the "surrender of a large measure of self-government" by each colony on joining Canada. While at Quebec City in 1864, Edward Palmer, attorney general of Prince Edward Island, advanced this argument: "Representation by population is not applicable when a certain number of Provinces are throwing their resources into one Confederation, and giving up their own self-government and individuality."[1]

Canada is a federation, and the two chambers of its Parliament are mutually obligated to promote the constitutional goals of peace, order, and good government. As the previous chapter discussed, except for the introduction of a retirement age in place of appointment for life, the Senate in all respects today is the same institution the Fathers of Confederation designed in 1867. The reason for reiterating this point is to underline how different the Canadian situation is from the British in relations between the chambers of the two Parliaments. With each expansion of the franchise in the United Kingdom (1832, 1867, and 1885), the justification for the hereditary upper chamber and its powers grew less clear. The House of Lords "problem," which emerged in the mid-nineteenth century, continues to the present day, since British parliamentary theory treats as foreign the premise of accountability to any domestic external body. (The adverb is crucial, because as a result of obligations associated with entry into the European Communities in the 1970s – and exit, following the 2016 referendum result – the United Kingdom may be held accountable for its actions across the Channel.) For the past century and a quarter, the House of Lords has been deemed to fall into that category: "One of the direct results of the growth of modern political parties [and electoral democracy] in the late nineteenth century was the development of a House of Lords question."[2]

Attempts to deal with the problem have taken two forms: first, weaken the Lords as a legislative body through the introduction of the suspensive (or delaying) veto in 1911 (shortened from two years to one in 1949) and, second, make its membership more diverse and reflective of British society, such as with the introduction in 1958 of appointed peers. It was via that route, and in that year, that women entered the Lords; it was not until 1963 that the first woman peer took a hereditary seat (the Peerages Act of that year also authorized the disclaimer for life of a peerage; the first, and still among the most publicized, disclaimers was by Viscount Stansgate, later Tony Benn, cabinet minister and Labour MP for over fifty years). Historically, the composition of the Lords has been diverse in respects not found in Canada: the inclusion of law lords (removed a decade ago with the creation of the Supreme Court of the United Kingdom) and of archbishops and bishops of the Church of England still. In the period since passage of the House of Lords Act, 1999, and publication of *A House for the Future*, the report of the Royal Commission on the Reform of the House of Lords in 2000, the proportion of hereditary peerages has fallen precipitously, with attention now being paid to non-establishment appointments.[3] Hardly "similar in Principle" to the House of Lords in 1867, the Senate of Canada is even less so today, for as the Supreme Court observed in the Senate reference in 2014, the Senate is an equal and not inferior legislative body to the House of Commons. From the perspective of the upper chamber alone, it is clear that the Westminster model gets in the way of understanding how the parliamentary system in Canada is organized and works.[4] This is an operational contrast as distinct from the political-cultural one usually alluded to in historical analyses: "The much praised balance of the British constitution … could not in any event be exported; the coexistence of realm and dominions at different stages of constitutional development made for confusion; the methods of management and harmony in British politics were too subtle and too secret to be translated easily."[5]

The reason for the preceding comments on the second chamber in a chapter devoted to the first chamber is to underline the parliamentary unity the two houses comprise. Geographically contiguous, nonetheless there is a scholarly tradition in Canada of treating them almost as foreign in their relations to one another. Of three major works written about the Senate in the twentieth century, Robert A. MacKay, *The Unreformed Senate of Canada* (1926); F.A. Kunz, *The Modern Senate of Canada, 1925–1963: A Re-appraisal* (1965); and Colin Campbell, *The Canadian Senate: A Lobby Within* (1978), only Kunz devoted a chapter to the Commons, with the enigmatic phrase in its title, "Relations between the Houses."[6] The primary basis for discrimination lies in the fact that the Commons is elected and the Senate is not, which in the eyes of defenders of the former and critics of the latter is an irremediable contrast. But not always so: the link deemed necessary between population and representation assumed paramount importance only in the last quarter of the nineteenth century. The evolution in attitudes is captured in comments by two prime ministers: the first from Sir John A. Macdonald in 1872: "While the principle of population was considered to a very great extent, other considerations were also held to have weight; so that different interests, classes and localities should be represented, that the principle of numbers should not be the only one"; and the second, twenty years later, from Sir John Thompson: "We have been guided by the principle almost exclusively ... that we should interfere with the representation in those districts where additional representation for increased population had to be provided."[7]

Compared to the past, rep-by-pop assumed inflated importance in the twentieth century to the extent that the twin concerns that had motivated the achievement of responsible government were eclipsed. These were, first, to secure the accountability of the executive, initially in the person of the colonial governor and then embodied in the political executive, to the elected chamber of the legislature; and second, to guarantee the independence of the individual member of the elected assembly and, eventually, of the House of Commons. The first of these objects is more frequently the subject of discussion in parliamentary discourse than the second, but the latter is as vital a feature. The principle of the independent legislator explains why the delegate model of representation is treated as a heresy in parliamentary theory; why recall of an MP is illegal (Canada Elections Act – Statutes of Canada 2000, c 9, s 550); and why initiative and referendum are viewed as much a trespass on the political prerogatives of Parliament as they are on the constitutional prerogatives of the Crown. Legislative bodies alone are masters of their proceedings, including whom they seat: twice elected and twice expelled, Louis Riel never took his place in the Commons. A whole chapter, or more, could be written on this subject, and Norman Ward wrote such a chapter, "The Independence of Parliament," in his book *Representation*. For instance, members may not be in receipt of an emolument, in other words a benefit from the Crown, which would compromise their position. This is why placemen, or office holders such as judges, were eventually excluded from sitting in colonial legislative chambers; that is why until the 1930s, and extending back almost a century, by-elections were statutorily required when sitting members (in Ottawa, the provinces, or the colonies before that) were appointed to cabinet. In the opinion of James Gardiner (reviled or celebrated for his political skills, depending upon which side of the legislative aisle the commentator sat), "No other action taken since responsible government was set up has placed greater power in the hands of a single individual than this has placed with the Premier or Prime Minister."[8] The intricacies and minutiae of the matter may or may not intrigue students of the subject, but the principle that informs the topic lies at the heart of parliamentary government: control of the executive rests with the legislature, which is to say the members who sit in it, and not with the people who are outside its precincts. Control does not mean a veto over governmental actions, in theory or practice; rather it means accountability of the executive to the legislature. This is the justification for the privileges that parliamentarians claim and historically have been granted.

Here is the essence of the constitutional settlement of 1688, traditionally called the Glorious Revolution, which subjected the Crown to the control of Parliament. Historically, it refers to the expulsion of James II, a Roman Catholic, and the invitation by Parliament to William of Orange and Mary (daughter of James II), who were Protestants, to replace him. Hereafter, the Crown (now within Parliament, and financially supported through the annual vote of the Civil List, a practice later emulated in Canada) was the sole source of authority in Great Britain and its colonies. Hereafter, loyal opposition might come solely from within Parliament. Parliament, and not the people, called upon

William and Mary to assume the throne. Unlike the French or American Revolutions, the Glorious Revolution did not create "a people." At most, it could be said that under the conventions of constitutional monarchy, which have their roots in this era, a dissolution of Parliament is in its essence an appeal from the legal to the political sovereign. With this cursory history as backdrop, it is a moot question whether executive power in the Canadian system of government should be viewed as descending from the Crown or flowing up from the people. Moot perhaps but not hypothetical in Canada, where in 2008 during the prorogation controversy Canadians were told, by opponents of the putative Liberal-NDP coalition, that it is only voters who choose governments.

One answer to the question would have to recognize that in Great Britain popular resistance to tyranny is rare and on the one occasion it succeeded, the event was known, retrospectively and revealingly, as the Interregnum. In Canada, the single extra-parliamentary resort to arms took the form of the rebellions of 1837, where the model in the rebels' mind was republican (American rather than French), and it failed to take hold in part because, said a perceptive George Brown fifteen years after the event, "the effect of the elective principle [was] to check the will of the people."[9]

Consequences flow from the premise that the centrepiece of the constitution is the Crown-in-Parliament. Among the most important is to understand that political life in the House of Commons is not a reflection of what happens elsewhere. In other words, it is not a mirror of local opinion – and in any case it would be a strange and inadequate notion of political representation, which says nothing about what representatives actually do. In the parliamentary system, political life is autonomous. This is true whether the subject is Parliament at Westminster, at Ottawa, in the provincial capitals, or in the colonial assemblies once the principle of responsible government had been acknowledged. Confirmation of the sense of obligation that accompanied conferral of the principle is explicit in the passage from a letter written in 1877 by the Alexander Mackenzie, when he was prime minister, to the governor general, Lord Dufferin:

Her Majesty's *Canadian* Government have functions to perform which no other Colonial Government is called upon to discharge ... Canada is a difficult country to govern ... While there are no class interests to consult there are more difficult interests always cropping up in those of Race and

Creed ... It is quite impossible that an English Minister can understand Canadian affairs so well as to undertake without Canadian advice to act.[10]

Three decades earlier, Lord Elgin, governor general of the Province of Canada, had written to Lord Grey, his uncle by marriage, in the same vein but colloquially: "I am disposed to believe that the less you meddle in Canadian appointments ... the better."[11]

The legislative inferiority of Canada, and the other ducal Dominions, ended with the Statute of Westminster, 1931 – or so it was argued (unsuccessfully) by those bringing the Motard-Taillon challenge to the Succession to the Throne Act, 2013 (chapter two, note 38) – but the principle of political autonomy pervaded the conduct of parliamentary government long before that date. In no respect does the assertion of autonomy appear more explicit than when the government, following a defeat in the House, chooses to seek a dissolution of Parliament and go to the electorate. A change in the electoral system – as promised by the Liberal Party in the campaign of 2015 – that would make defeat of the government in the House of Commons more probable where it lacks a majority, elevates the matter of autonomy in bold fashion. This is not a new concern, however. In 1923, William Irvine, at that time Dominion Labour Party member of Parliament for Calgary East, introduced the following motion: "That in the opinion of this House, a defeat of a Government measure should not be considered as a sufficient reason for resignation of the Government, unless followed by a vote of lack of confidence." Both Mackenzie King, prime minister, and Arthur Meighen, leader of the opposition, rejected the motion's premise. In King's words, "The idea that the Ministry should be in any way restricted in its appeal to the people at any time is the very antithesis of democracy," while Meighen spoke more emphatically: "I do not subscribe to the viewpoint that the Government of Canada is in the nature of a hired servant whose duty is to obey the directions, the orders, the mandates of the representatives in Parliament who support it, of Parliament as a whole, and of the populace of the country. I do not subscribe to the theory that the Government is in the relation of a hired man to this House."[12]

Government should be free to go to the people when it chooses to do so: an inflammatory sentiment for some, but in this instance with bi-partisan approbation. Where does authority lie – in or outside Parliament? It is a question as alive in 2016 as in 1923, and much earlier. Writing at the time of the Second Reform Act (1867), George Eliot placed her "political" novel *Felix Holt* in the setting of debate surrounding the First Reform Act (1832), and posed this question through a character, "impetuous young Joyce, a farmer of superior information":

> "Have you ever heard of the king's prerogative?"
>
> "I don't say but what I have," said Rose. "I've nothing against it – nothing at all."
>
> "No, but the Radicals have," said young Joyce, winking. "The prerogative is what they want to clip close. They want us to be governed by delegates from the trade-unions, who are to dictate to everybody, and make everything square to their mastery."[13]

Artistic, but the point is made: who governs or should govern? Yet in the parliamentary system, there is a second, equally important question, which is: how to govern? In Great Britain and in Canada, as in many countries, the answer is through the organization and activities of political parties. Of the first, it has been written that "party was the mould in which parliamentary ambition had to set"; and of the second, one of the progenitors of responsible government (Robert Baldwin), observed that "only through the instrumentality of party ... could 'popular' government be successfully worked."[14] Only through party was any permanent political objective achievable. Demonstrations on the lawn of the centre block of the Parliament Buildings were permissible but politically impracticable unless a member or members in the House of Commons took up the cause of the protestors. Uniquely, in 1910, Sir Wilfrid Laurier invited western grain farmers who were laying siege to Ottawa to sit in the Commons for four hours and read statements and memorials to government ministers. No other interest group (nor farmers since) was ever accorded such a reception.[15] It is sometimes forgotten when the subject is political parties that the great national party organizations in the Atlantic parliamentary democracies are of approximately the same age. "Gladstone was the first major statesman to stump the country."[16] Until then, which really meant until the extension of trunk-line railways north and west of London, governments were made and unmade in Parliament. Politicians did not campaign in the constituencies, and in the absence of campaigns, volunteer workers – the staff of political life over the next century – were not needed. All of this and more, the introduction of the secret ballot, for example, changed in the 1870s. With the lag of perhaps a decade, the same transformation occurred in Canada, with Macdonald the Tory playing Gladstone the Liberals' galvanizing role.[17] Party and not the individual MP bridged the distance separating the borderlands from Parliament. With this extra-parliamentary transformation came fundamental change in the intra-parliamentary assumptions that informed the operation of the House of Commons, among them heightened party discipline and the disappearance of what Macdonald called the "loose fish," those members of unpredictable loyalty when called upon to take a stand.[18]

The difference between the two countries is that while in each of them parties acted as constitutional agencies, unifying and democratizing the institutions of government, in Canada they also functioned as instruments of incorporation, bringing the vast northern reaches of the continent into a national political community. Canadians are not born, they are made; and political parties, directly and indirectly, have wielded a large influence in that process.[19] Political parties incorporate the federal dimension into their own operation, as for instance when they use delegate conventions to select leaders, and in turn inject a neglected federal perspective into Parliament's elected institution. In Canada, representation is divided into three parts: First, as a constitutional matter (consider, for example, the previously noted Constitution Act, 1915 and, even before Confederation, the Act of Union, 1840, which required a majority of the whole legislative assembly of United Canada to alter the provision for equal representation between Canada East and Canada West). Second, as a political matter, when it is recalled that each colony bargained its own terms of entry into the union. And, finally, as a cultural matter, for every major defining event in the country's history – reciprocity, free trade, patriation of the constitution with the accompanying Canadian Charter of Rights and Freedoms, declarations of war, medicare, official language legislation, English-French relations, definitions and redefinitions of divorce, abortion, same-sex marriage, and the legalization of assisted suicide – always depended upon parliamentary enactment or resolution, and thus the participation of the political parties that then sat to the right and left of Mr Speaker. A caveat to that statement acknowledges the same prominence held by political parties in the provinces, who, acting within their constitutional jurisdiction, influence the economic and social well-being of their residents, be it the consequence of actions by the Parti Québécois, the Co-operative Commonwealth Federation in Saskatchewan, the United Farmers of Alberta, or any other provincial government at any time.

With an issue such as one of the foregoing subjects before it, Parliament's main task is not to represent opinion so much as it is to mobilize assent in support (or against) legislation and change. In this capacity, the House is a deliberative as well as representative body, and deliberation is more than an aggregation of individual constituency demands, as the work of the Senate continuously demonstrates. In other words, the burden of government is to persuade opponents sitting across the aisle certainly, but also the unconvinced sitting in its own ranks frequently. What might be called the parliamentary method was enunciated by Sir John A. Macdonald in 1861. Taking as his precept the British House of Commons in its treatment of legislation of great moment, such as Catholic Emancipation, Repeal of the Corn Laws, and the abolition of Slave Trade, he observed that

> every great question had been removed from the arena of party struggle and strife, and had worked their way upon their own merits. (Hear, hear) So must this question [the nature of representation in the Parliament of United Canada]; and after it had fairly worked its way by discussion at the polls, by discussion in the Press, they could fairly assume that the public mind had been educated upon it, and that it was ripe for a verdict to be passed upon it one way or the other.[20]

Metaphorically, and if the opinion of observers is to be believed, the House of Commons (or "Parliament," since the terms are often used interchangeably) is a mirror cracked from side to side: "Parliamentary Democracy Is 'Sick,' 'Tattered, and Needs Help'"; "Time to Worry about the State of Democracy"; "Who Killed Question Period?"; "Ignatieff: It's Time to Fix Parliament."[21] Invariably, the subject of these lamentations is the individual member of Parliament, their cause party discipline. More than distress is evident, however; there is destruction too. It is the latter consequence that explains the use of the word *tragedy* to describe the fall, from what might have been to what is.[22] The implication of the dark attribution is that the Commons and its members could be so much more if it, and they, were left to realize their institutional and individual potential. From the nomination contest, to the caucus, to the chamber and its committees, the MP is treated as a pawn, with the result that "human resources" are wasted. Lacking opportunity to succeed, members feel themselves failures and hold the occupation of legislator responsible for their low self-regard. The used-car salesmen as the comparative measure of society's negative esteem makes a

predictable appearance. In the absence of a "job description" or definition of what an MP is expected to do, neither the member nor his (or
her) constituents understand what is expected of him or satisfied with
his performance. Although they quote him, it is of more significance
than the authors acknowledge that thirty years ago C.E.S. Franks, in
his study *The Parliament of Canada*, observed that "the themes of reform
have not changed."[23]

The continuity is rooted in Parliament's being a unique institution,
with contradictory expectations and interpretations of its purpose held
by those inside and outside its walls. Turnover of MPs at elections, as
a result of electoral defeat in a constituency as well as voluntary retirement, is unusually high in Canada compared to countries such as Australia and Great Britain; two months before the October 2015 election,
"sixty-one current members of Parliament ha[d] already announced
they [would] not run again."[24] This contrast is often cited to Canada's
disadvantage, with the implication being that the "job" is unsatisfying
and unsatisfactorily done. That Canada is a country quite different, in its
linguistic and partisan complexion, for instance, from the other "Anglo"
democracies, goes unremarked, as does the influence of these factors, as
well as federalism, the contrast in size of legislatures, the varied career
paths of party leaders in each country – even, perhaps, the different
relationship that obtains between lower and upper chambers in each
Parliament. Plurality elections have the capacity in Canada to remake
the country politically, an outcome in no way leavened by events in
the upper chamber. There is no electoral double standard – federally or
provincially – for Canadians to interpret. Yet, turnover notwithstanding, politics is less an occupation and rather a temporary calling: "a tool,
not a life," in the words of one former MP.[25]

Representation is a laden concept. This is particularly true in a political system whose central tenet is responsible government, where service to the constituency must be shared with the making of laws and
the scrutiny of administration as the multiple functions of the MP.
Nonetheless, constituency service bulks large in the interpretation MPs
offer of their duties and in the grievances they assign to its conduct.
Essentially, the complaint is that party discipline interferes with fulfilment of their constituency obligations. In colonial days members of the
legislature were officials of the body to which they were elected; in time
they came to view themselves as representatives of the constituency
from which they are chosen. Generally, MPs like doing constituency
work; they find it personally rewarding. Few join Alan Clark, a former

minister in the government of Margaret Thatcher, in begrudging the time and resources devoted to the home front and away from the parliamentary arena as a cost, nor give it his description as "democratic overhead."[26] For MPs of the more-frequently cited persuasion, it is the party whip who is party scold, since partisan calculation surpasses all other considerations. It is against this backdrop that members are described as sheep or automatons. Few caught in the snare of party view it as benignly as the seventh Earl of Romney, a peer, who dispassionately explained his interpretation of legislative politics as follows: "The bright ones are supposed to speak and the others are supposed to support them. That's how it works here ... [The party high command] were not interested in what I've got to say, but they like to have my vote ... [I opposed] consulting everybody, and then doing what nobody wants." Instead, he favoured "a benevolent dictatorship of the well-informed."[27]

Discipline, which all independent-minded people say they abhor, is one means of reconciling the tension that inevitably arises between pressures from localism, on the one hand, and the need to speak nationally, on the other. Nevertheless, thwarted purpose and ambition on the part of MPs is the familiar refrain heard from critics of party discipline, so much so that "it has become a cliché to say that the party machine now dominates government and that the individual Member of Parliament has become a mere cipher."[28] Is there a counterargument to be made? Certainly a more systemic answer is required. In the conclusion to his edited work, *Representatives of the People?: Parliamentarians and Constituents in Western Democracies*, Vernon Bogdanor posits a binary conundrum: on the one hand, "a strong party system will militate against constituency being the focus of the parliamentarian's activity"; but, on the other hand, "responsiveness at the level of the individual constituency leads to collective irresponsibility at the level of the political system."[29] In sum, legislators experience a conflict of allegiances. In parliamentary systems, the struggle is usually resolved in favour of the party; in the congressional system, the winner more often is the constituency. Nowhere is the contrast between the Anglo and the American practice more starkly on view than in Robert Caro's magisterial biography of Lyndon Johnson, whose political prowess and influence over his fellow congressmen, on behalf of the parched districts of northwest Texas (and later the South generally), prevailed for decades in the chamber, committee rooms, and halls of Congress from the moment he arrived.[30]

How to theorize the role of Parliament? The premise that an MP's primary responsibility is to speak for or be an ambassador of his or her constituents abdicates any attempt to provide a theory of the institution. "Members rule" is both an unsatisfactory and unworkable guide to behaviour. With 338 members, a 150-year history, for the past century more than two parties sitting in the chamber, and since 1970 bilingual administration and simultaneous translation, the House of Commons is entwined with the essential characteristics of Canada. Whatever the metaphysics of the concept, the House of Commons is a corporate entity, the only one of its kind in Canada. Every study of parliamentary institutions confirms the dimension of time that members experience on entering the Commons, although few so dramatically as Harold Nicolson writing in his *Diaries and Letters*: "Younger members felt that they had been carried back through Lloyd George to Gladstone away to the battlers of the Reform Bill and the administration of the Duke of Wellington."[31] In Ottawa, too, it is impossible to talk of North American or Trans-Pacific trade without invoking the memory of the reciprocity debates before Confederation or in 1911; or about Truth and Reconciliation and relations with First Nations today, without acknowledgment of treaties concluded and respected, or not; or the absence of treaty; or ISIL, Bill C-51 (the anti-terrorism bill), and Canada, the United Nations and peacekeeping. In *Requiem for a Nun* (1951), William Faulkner wrote that "the past is never dead. It's not even past." Nowhere in Canada is the past as present as it is in the House of Commons (and the Senate). A constituency "mirror" of representation is as inadequate a metaphor as it is an impoverished description of the role of the member of Parliament. Political life in a parliamentary democracy is not a reflection of local, or any other, opinion; it is an autonomous realm ready and required to respond to the unexpected and, sometimes, the unwelcome. Within its constitutionally defined jurisdiction, the House of Commons is the centre of Canada's political universe, its collective prince.

One of the challenges of leadership, Bob Rae has written, is that "moods and desires change, opinions and feelings shift when people are presented with different realities and facts." In this context, he cites a well-known reply by Harold Macmillan to the question, "What happened to some of your plans when you first became prime minister?" "Events, dear boy, events," Macmillan said.[32] The reason is plain – politics is a kaleidoscopic activity, whose essence supports Anthony Birch's claim that traditional doctrines of representation "emerged in the course of debate about relatively specific issues."[33] That sense of mutability quickly pervaded the debate occasioned by Justin Trudeau's promise to reform Canada's plurality electoral system before the next general election, following that of 2015. The argument was strongly advanced from myriad quarters that reform of this magnitude required resort to a referendum to assure its legitimacy. That debate will be examined in more detail below, but its appearance and the energy with which participants in it advanced their respective positions support Macmillan's insight into politics and leadership, and help to explain why it is difficult to be categorical about either, and therefore why a theory about the role of Parliament, and its members, is so elusive. George Étienne Cartier may or may not have had Parliament in mind when he said, "There are a great many things which cannot be defended in theory but which work well in practice."[34] But Parliament does work well in practice, as the history of the country – acknowledging that there are warts – bears witness and as Canada's reputation in the world as a free and democratic society testifies. It is the theory that poses problems.

An example that makes the point was private member's bill C-586, introduced in 2013 by Michael Chong, an Ontario MP, initially cited as C-559, An Act to Amend the Canada Elections Act and the Parliament of Canada Act (reforms) and later colloquially referred to as Reform Act, 2013. The object of the Bill was to put Parliament and the MP back at the centre of decision-making by doing the following: remove from the party leader the power to veto local constituency nominations of candidates; give each party caucus the power to remove its party leader; and strip the party leader of the power to expel an MP from caucus. In an editorial titled "The Way Home to Westminster," the *Globe and Mail* supported the initiative on the grounds it would restore "a certain equilibrium between executive and legislative" long lost in Canada but evident still in Australia, New Zealand, other Commonwealth countries and the mother of Parliaments in London.[35] Several months later, the bill had been amended to give final say over nominations to "a person designated by each registered political party"; to let each caucus after a general election vote to determine whether to give themselves the power to remove a party leader; and to give each party caucus (rather than the leader) power to decide whether to remove or reinstate MPs. Further details of the Bill and the wide-ranging debate as to the wisdom and implications of its provisions are not central to this discussion.

What requires notice is that, as with concern expressed over the exercise of the prerogative powers of prorogation and dissolution in 2008 and 2009 (see chapter one), concern over the power of the prime minister and the Prime Minister's Office manifested itself in a similar way: a desire to codify the rules. Yet, as in the earlier instance, agreement on what that object embraced was less than clear. For example, Duff Conacher, who had spearheaded the unsuccessful court challenge to the Harper government's failure to abide by its own amendment to the Canada Elections Act, expressed disappointment that the Reform Act did not "redefine non-confidence votes ... [so that] a non-confidence vote should only be called when the actual confidence of the government is being questioned, and not by aligning the vote with another act or bill."[36] Here, of course, is the substance of William Irving's resolution of ninety-three years ago, and here another demonstration of the continuity of Canadian politics, especially when the subject is Parliament. Paradoxically, the power of the leader to veto a local constituency candidate had its origin fifty years ago in an attempt to regularize Canadian elections, in this instance with legislation to implement recommendations made in the Report of the Committee on Election Expenses (Barbeau), which in the 1960s studied ways of curtailing election expenses and of instituting financial reimbursement to parties. By whatever manner this object was to be accomplished, it was necessary to specify the individual who was the party's official candidate.[37] The most famous case of a leader refusing to sign the nomination papers of a local candidate occurred in the 1974 general election in Moncton, New Brunswick, when Robert Stanfield, the leader of the Progressive Conservative Party, declined to sign the nomination papers of PC candidate Leonhard Jones, a former mayor of Moncton, and a vocal and controversial opponent of the party's support of official bilingualism.

The Reform Bill of Michael Chong stimulated public and media discussion over the eighteen months it was before MPs and senators. A single question informed nearly every assessment, regardless of which section of the Bill was under review: "Who gets to choose?" If the issue was the local candidate, then should the party leader have a veto? If the matter was the review of the party leader, then should the MPs (of whatever proportion of caucus) decide? It was ironic, and indicative of the uncertainty that often envelopes Canadian political debate, that an initiative intended to limit the power of party leaders and, in the case of one of them, the Prime Minister's Office, should have led to a philo- sophical conundrum posited by two (in this instance, unlikely) allies: Tom Flanagan and Stéphane Dion, the former of whom had argued strenuously against the putative Liberal-NDP coalition in 2008 (on the premise that "only voters have the right to decide on the coalition"), and the latter, one of the project's most prominent proponents. According to Flanagan, "empowering party members to choose the leader builds popular support, thus giving the leader not just legal but also political authority to lead the party and the elected caucus."[38] Dion argued in similar fashion: "C-586 proposes, as a rule, that a leader chosen by tens of thousands of party members can be expelled at the whim of only half the caucus ... The net effect of C-586 would be to dispossess members of every party of their Constitution."[39]

The Chong initiative was anti-leader in its motivation, and while the terms of the Bill spoke of all parties, the public debate centred on the then-ruling Conservatives and "the problem with the PMO," which the *Globe and Mail* described as "a parasite on the body of Parliament."[40] In its amended version, the Reform Act still empowered the parliamentary caucus of a party, if it so chose, to remove its leader. The process for selecting the leader continued unchanged, remaining at the discretion of the party association, usually in a delegate convention or with party members voting at large. In other words, the Reform Act institutionalized a potential asymmetry between selection and removal. It remains to be seen if, and in what situations, the respective caucuses will use their new power. Uncertainty may be justified in light of the fact that in the past caucus members might have taken such votes but did not do so for a complex set of personal, political, and logistical reasons, most of which remain cogent. From the perspective of the present discussion, the asymmetry that results from the change introduced by C-586 is immaterial to the subject at hand, except for the context in which the discussion takes place. What is a political party; does it include the extra-parliamentary party, the intra-parliamentary party, or both? The answer to that question affects one's perception of party and of its mechanics, most crucially the role of discipline.

It is germane to this inquiry to review the origin of leadership conventions in Canada. The Liberals held the first, in 1919; the Conservatives followed in 1927. Prior to 1919, leaders had been selected by party caucuses in the Commons, as was the practice (in proximate fashion) in the United Kingdom. The arrival of leadership conventions followed Canada's only experience with a coalition-like (in fact, a Union) government. That occurred in 1917, at the time of the tumult over introduction of military conscription, the formation of the Union government (which included some prominent Liberals but not the leader, Sir Wilfrid Laurier) and the general election of 1917, held under the terms of the War-time Elections Act and its discriminatory franchise, which gave the vote to women whose male relatives were serving overseas, and took the vote from men who had earlier held it but who came from areas then at war with the King. In light of prairie settlement patterns, with large numbers of central European immigrants arriving before 1914, the incidence of disenfranchisement was heavily regional in its impact. The split between pro- and anti-Unionist Liberals, which mirrored a clear division between English- and French-speaking Canadians, demanded repair in the post-war period, and a policy convention called for 1919 was transformed into a leadership convention following the death of Sir Wilfrid Laurier. The point of this excursion into history is to under-line the reality that on occasion the extra-parliamentary party may be called upon to rescue the parliamentary party, not by making it more representative of constituency opinion – the breach in the Liberal Party in 1917 happened because of that very reason, revealing the split in party ranks over conduct of the First World War – but to unify it.

The events of 1917 have never been repeated, even during the most difficult moments of the struggle to maintain Canadian unity during the last quarter of the last century. The Liberals returned (united) to office in 1921 and under six leaders held power for a total of sixty of the remaining eighty years of that century. Two of the six occupied the leadership for two-thirds of that period. Of course, long arcs of leader-ship are not explained by the mechanism of convention selection alone, as the earlier careers of Macdonald, Laurier, and Borden, each chosen by his respective party caucus, illustrate. Still, for a very long time lead-ership conventions were identified as an important contributing fac-tor to a successful party's organizational and electoral strength, as, for instance, in establishing a claim to speak on behalf of the people, in the sense of a substantial cross-section of the public. In this regard, parties in Canada and the United Kingdom are similar but in another quite different. The split-self of federalism, whether speaking of the divided jurisdictions established by the constitution or the loyalties of citizens, is a dualism that affects the operation of the House of Commons. This is particularly evident in matters of criminal law: Canada has a single criminal code whose provisions in regard to issues of personal moral-ity, such as abortion, same-sex marriage, and physician-assisted death, bring these subjects, most often with the intent of removing existing penalties for behaviour related to them, before Parliament. While the present discussion focuses on the Commons, it needs to be noted that on occasion joint committees of the two chambers may be the investi-gating vehicle, and in such instances members of the Senate participate as actively as members of the Commons. An illustration is the Special Joint Committee on Physician-Assisted Death to advise the government with proposals addressing issues raised in the Supreme Court's *Carter v Canada* decision of February 2015.[41] It should be said, however, that recommendations of a joint committee may not bind the Senate in fulfilling the constitutional role the Supreme Court set down in its ruling in 2014; nor with regard to Liberal senators, whom the leader of the party has severed from the parliamentary caucus, may the party whip be applied. Whether it is applied to members of the lower house is another matter, although the claim that MPs have "Charter rights to freedom of conscience" is open to dispute.[42]

As opposed to the simple characterization that party discipline is autocratic or oppressive, an alternative position may be posited: "We need to recognize the genuine contribution of Parliament and build on its strengths rather than continuing in thralldom to a nostalgic view of Parliament that is in conflict with the obvious facts. We need to reform our thinking about Parliament in order to reform Parliament."[43] With that different image in mind, it is beneficial to recognize how often Parliament and the courts, for instance, work in tandem rather than in conflict on matters mentioned in the preceding paragraph. While American precedent in these subject areas may be no precedent, the contrast in practice is striking. In June 2015, the United States Supreme Court ruled that same-sex marriages were lawful. Later that year in Kentucky, a county clerk refused to issue a same-sex marriage licence. In 2016, the Senate of the state legislature approved a bill to create separate marriage licence forms for same-sex couples, while a separate version of the Bill was expected from the state House of Representatives later that year. By contrast, in a reference case, that is, where the government asked the judiciary for its opinion on a question of law, the Saskatchewan Court of Appeal in 2011 rejected two possible amendments to the province's Marriage Act, each of which would have permitted a provincially appointed marriage commissioner "to decline to solemnize a marriage if performing the ceremony would be contrary to his or her religious beliefs." The basis for the Court's ruling was that "the possible amendments offend the Canadian Charter of Rights and Freedoms. Either of them, if enacted, would violate the equality rights of gay and lesbian individuals."[44]

Several comments may be made about the contrasting fates of same-sex marriage legislation in the two countries, beginning with the close rapport of Parliament and the Supreme Court of Canada in the period between court rulings (usually on a reference question) in 2003 and Parliament's passage of the Civil Marriage Act in 2005. Three Parliaments under three prime ministers (Chrétien, Martin, and Harper) in three different years voted to support same-sex marriage. Equally significant in this example is the fact that the government of Saskatchewan did not appeal the Court of Appeal finding. One reason not to pursue the matter may rest in the composition of the senior courts, which are appointed by the federal government (the governor-in-council). This is not to say they invariably find for federal plaintiffs; they do not. It is to say that although Canada is a federation and although it is by now a cliché to describe it as one of the most decentralized such systems in the world, there are centripetal forces at work nonetheless.

In chapter one, when discussing the role of the Crown in determining who should be invited to form a government, following an election where no party holds an absolute majority of seats in the House of Commons, it was said that interpreting the results in that instance involved weighing rather than counting. In a parliamentary system, government must always be based on public opinion, but that is not to be estimated by the mere counting of heads. Similarly, to maintain the pre-eminence of the constituency in such circumstances is to employ a one-way mirror that may mislead as much as it guides, for the national or public interest is not identical to the sum of individual or constituency interests. These last are problematic to determine, not just because the average size of a constituency is large, even in less populous provinces like Saskatchewan between seventy and eighty thousand inhabitants, but also because intra-party and intra-constituency democracy may easily merge into "the democracy of the fervent few," which is no guide at all.[45]

In a parliamentary system with a constitutional monarchy, what powers are reserved to the people, and who can claim to speak for them? Enough has been said already to suggest answers to both questions. The Crown-in-Parliament (with the adjective *Canadian* attached to both nouns) is the sovereign federally and, with the emendation *legislature* for Parliament, provincially, too. There is no constitutional provision for participation by the public in the making of law; at best, any such exercise is consultative. Legislative attempts to alter that arrangement, so as to deprive the Crown of its discretion to exercise its prerogative powers, are ultra vires, as found, for instance, by the Judicial Committee of the Privy Council (noted above) in the Manitoba Initiative and Referendum reference in 1919. The referendum held in

1995 on the Charlottetown Accord, an agreement reached by federal and provincial leaders on items of intergovernmental discord, was a rare example of resort to this mechanism. It failed to obtain the level of public and provincial support deemed necessary prior to holding the vote. The advantage of that referendum, and of the mechanism generally in the eyes of proponents, is that it eludes what is seen to be the straitjacket of party discipline in a legislature. In an act of political transubstantiation, it makes the normally invisible visible by allowing entry of citizens into the metaphorical agora. Yet the referendum has not acted as the reformer's friend, if Canadian experience is the basis of judgment. In the first half of the last decade, electorates in three provinces, Ontario, British Columbia, and Prince Edward Island, rejected proposals to replace their plurality-based system for counting votes with proportional or preferential alternatives, even though in the first two provinces, the question had been exhaustively studied by citizens' assemblies over a matter of some months. "Paradoxically," as John Courtney has observed, "one of the institutional reforms credited with helping to reduce Canada's democratic deficit (the referendum) may, in turn, have created an unintended hurdle to bringing about change to another institution that too has also been faulted for its contribution to the democratic deficit – First Past The Post [plurality system]."[46] In Canada, and on limited data admittedly, one might be forgiven for seeing the referendum as a sonar for measuring the false depths of public opinion.

The subject of this book is not the comparative merits of electoral systems, although the issue seems never to arise except in a comparative framework. In this regard, the electoral system shares a feature with the upper house. Moreover, both are judged by critics as oppressive of democracy because they are seen to distort the popular will. At its most basic, the complaint is that a party with less than a majority of the popular vote may, under a regime where candidates win individual constituency seats with the largest number but not a majority of votes, form a government. If the percentage of seats were allocated in proportion to percentage of votes won, or if voters were asked to rank constituency candidates in preferential order, it is said that legislatures and governments would be more representative of popular will. This is a claim to be debated and studied in the context of the pledge by the Liberal leader, now prime minister, Justin Trudeau to introduce a new, non-plurality voting system before the next general election, required under the fixed election law in 2019.

Election returns lend themselves to analysis from the perspective of mirrors. Indeed, that is the principal perspective that informs the reformers' case. Still there is another way of viewing the plurality system, one captured in W.E. Gladstone's response to the election returns from Ireland in 1885, when the Irish rejected overwhelmingly his scheme of Home Rule: "Expectation was one thing and the reality of counted votes another, and the clarity with which the Irish constituencies had spoken was unmistakable."[47] Here was a dispassionate summation of a momentous result: living a world away in time and space, Canadians need to be reminded that in the late nineteenth century the Irish Question was as profound and perplexing to politicians at Westminster as slavery had been half-a-century before to politicians in Washington. Clarity may be an open concept, but there is no doubt that it is the foundation of the findings of a poll of Canadians that asked them for their "top goals of a voting system": "The respondents at large said they wanted simple ballots, strong stable government, the ability to directly elect the MPs who represent their constituency, and assurances that the government has MPs from each region of the country."[48] However that description might be summarized, the caption would have to pay attention to the "personal stake [of legislators] in protecting voters' interests"[49] – a stake that includes the interests of the opposition as well as of government. In the grammar of reform it is sometimes overlooked, when advocating non-plural electoral systems, that opposition in Westminster-style Parliaments is a protected and privileged position: "Political opposition, far from being the proverbial discrete and insular minority, can – if they want to speak collectively – actually lay claim to the moral status of a majority."[50] There is irony in that claim, for there is a disposition to see those sitting to Mr Speaker's left as the "losers" in the political contest. And they are, for in the matter of results, there is no ambiguity in the plurality system, nor tolerance for ambiguity among voters either. In that respect plurality elections are the great leveller because the results are clear: all are members of Parliament; some are in the executive, some support that group, and the rest oppose the executive and its supporters. Over time parliamentary opposition is of immense importance to the electorate as sentiment hostile to government accrues. Not representation of people or limitation of power but concentration of responsibility is the quintessential feature of parliamentary government. Among the beneficiaries of this system are the voters. At the next election they know who held the key to responsibility, and thus whom to reward with their votes and whom to penalize by withholding their support.

In his magisterial article, "The Electoral System and the Party System in Canada, 1921–1965," Alan Cairns dispelled the haze that surrounded the subject of the electoral system, one so opaque that it obscured both its origin and its operation. More than anything else, this might be considered the principal achievement of his article: it raised the electoral system to academic consciousness.[51] Like so much else inherited from Britain, the conduct of elections had been accepted with remarkably little comment. Those questions that had traditionally exercised opinion had to do with the ballot, its form and secrecy, and the administration of the count, but never with the principle of what constituted victory at the polls. It needs to be emphasized that modern ideas on the subject are just that – modern.[52] The electoral system was another manifestation (like candidate selection) of the strength of localism in the political life of the vast country. Moreover, until there were more than two parties in a contest, such a question seldom arose, and even when third parties appeared it still might go unheard if the electoral base of the protest party was concentrated (as it often was) in solidly agrarian or nationalistic territory. In this latter situation, the two old parties might have been expected to ponder the implications of the plurality electoral system, but there is scant evidence that they did.

In British Columbia, Liberals and Conservatives had manipulated the electoral system in 1952 to keep the CCF out of office and had gotten a Social Credit government as reward.[53] Alberta had experimented with alternative methods of counting the vote and had then gone back to a plurality system province-wide with no one paying much attention to either result, since the United Farmers of Alberta and then Social Credit seemed invincible. Finally, in Manitoba, a fluid but always moderate coalition of partisans maintained proportional representation for decades "to help break the hold which Eastern-dominated Liberal and Conservative parties had on the province."[54]

What the Cairns article did was elaborate on the matter of "fairness" in the context of national elections and, even more important, demonstrate what had never been an issue in the provinces but was an issue nationally – the regional implications of the system's operation. Its territorial dimension was now made plain. At the time it appeared, the exclusion of the Tories from Quebec extended back more than a half-century; the retreat of the Liberals from the West was more recent. So much was obvious from the reports of the chief electoral officer. What had not been and what was now graphically depicted was that there were two worlds to elections – that of the popular vote and that of parliamentary representation.

The Cairns study was presented at the annual meeting of the Canadian Political Science Association in centennial year 1967. Time has not withered the perception of its analysis, but the intervening half-century has embedded it in the country's history (as it was then). This is another way of saying that Cairns is pre–Constitution Act, 1982 and pre-Charter, with the amending formula and the rights and freedoms those seminal documents entrench. The question is open to debate whether the plurality electoral system may be altered by statute or whether such change requires an amendment to the constitution. In other words, what happened to the Harper government's legislation to introduce consultative elections in the provinces, to produce possible nominees for appointment to the Senate, may happen to forthcoming legislation that seeks to alter the present electoral system. That is to say, such legislation may be found by the Supreme Court of Canada to be beyond the competence of the Parliament of Canada. Then again, perhaps not; perhaps, as Dennis Pilon, a scholar on electoral matters, argues, "the constitution is no barrier to reform."[55] At this point, in the absence not only of a court decision but a court challenge, it is impossible to know the accepted route to electoral reform of the magnitude proposed. Certainly, if the Senate reference becomes a precedent, thereby limiting statutory change to the electoral system, then decades of Commons autonomy in extending the franchise, altering electoral boundaries and the mechanisms for determining electoral boundaries, introducing an election expense regime that limits contributions and expenditures, will themselves constitute no precedent in resolving this contentious question. Senator Serge Joyal, an acknowledged constitutional authority, suggests one reason why the past may prove no guide to the future:

> Adopting some form of proportional representation could make majority governments less likely and require two or more parties to come together to form less stable minority or coalition governments. That in turn could necessitate clarification of the Governor General's prerogative to decide which party leader becomes prime minister and, if a coalition collapses, when to dissolve Parliament ... Any change to the Governor General's powers would require a constitutional amendment approved by all 10 provinces.[56]

Comparisons are invidious in politics, as in other activities, no more so than when the subjects in question are the world's second-largest country (Canada) and one of the smallest (Belgium). Although here too there are precedents: Belgium, along with the Netherlands and Switzerland (because of their linguistic and/or religious diversity), made frequent appearance in the research and report of the Royal Commission on Bilingualism and Biculturalism in the 1960s, as Canada set out to establish its own language regime. In the context of elections and government formation, Belgium has become synonymous as well with the difficulties PR presents a constitutional monarch, who is responsible to see that a government is in place following a general election: "King Baudouin today asked Wilfred Martens, the caretaker Prime Minister, to form a new government, ending a 144-day political stalemate in Belgium."[57] Belgium is the extreme case of a country whose electoral system appears to reinforce its political and administrative challenges: "Negotiation and compromise are Belgian arts, but the accords are often little more than collections of deliberate ambiguities."[58] Here is one explanation for Tony Judt's satiric question: "Is There a Belgium?"[59]

Arguably, it is gratuitous (or worse) to introduce, in critical fashion, the politics of another country when discussing one's own. The excuse lies in the germaneness of the Belgian example from the perspective of a matter historically given little attention in Canada: the formation of government. As opposed to the dissolution or prorogation of Parliament – for example, King-Byng or Harper-Jean – the selection of a first minister has occasioned noticeably less controversy. In anticipation of the 2015 general election, however, lack of agreement on the options facing the governor general suggests that where no party secures a majority, the conventions surrounding this exercise of prerogative power may be in jeopardy of disintegrating, if only because of the multiple streams of advice on offer.[60]

Uncertainty of electoral outcome is not new – that is to be expected; uncertainty of response in light of different interpretations of the outcome is new. The individual political party and its location in the array of choices confronting a governor general – where no party has a majority of seats – is immaterial to this discussion. It is the introduction of a conflict of choice following an election, or, as Senator Joyal noted, "if a coalition collapses, when to dissolve Parliament," that bring new possibilities for action (or more bleakly, inaction) by the Crown, the political parties, and the voters.[61] It is unnecessary and unhelpful to introduce apocalyptic scenarios to provide backdrop for a change in the electoral system. At the same time, an electoral system that makes majorities less likely than in the past, places a premium on political negotiations and those who carry them out to an extent equally unprecedented. Clearly, the implications of such changes for the operation of the House of Commons and for the conduct of the Crown in Canada are significant. So too are they for public understanding of the constitution and public expectations of government. What they would mean for the Senate, the country's continuously sitting second chamber, has gone unremarked to date. That they would have repercussions for a bicameral Parliament of Canada's distinctive characteristics seems inevitable.

At the time of Canada's centennial, the federation was experiencing strain, a condition that would continue for some decades. By the date of the sesquicentennial, those tensions had abated and were replaced by a projected transformation in the institutions at the heart of the country's parliamentary democracy – institutions that, except for endemic criticism of the Senate, had customarily attracted scant reformist interest. In the past half century, that has altered – in part because of societal and demographic change; in part because of adoption of the Constitution Act, 1982, and the Canadian Charter of Rights and Freedoms. Nor are these Canadian phenomena alone. Great Britain, the country that is reputed to provide the mirror for Canada's constitution, has witnessed a constitutional transformation that has gone largely unacknowledged by others and itself.[62] Still, as this and earlier chapters have demonstrated, there are uniquely Canadian forces at work influencing Crown, Commons, and Senate. The challenge these fissiparous forces present to interpreting their course and consequence is that they seem diverse or disparate. It is only by thinking of leadership and discipline, the cardinal features of Canadian parliamentary democracy from Confederation onward, that it is possible to comprehend how the system itself works or how it is thought to work. In that context, how do institutions influence the answer to the question? In shorthand, how was it, in 2015, that Stephen Harper, initially deemed politically strong, was shown to be electorally weak; while Justin Trudeau, portrayed as weak, was revealed as strong on election day? Or the question might be reversed: how does leadership affect institutions? Harper *and* Trudeau and the Senate; Harper and the governor general; Trudeau and the Commons?

Chapter Five

Reconsideration

The age of comparison has passed. Federalism aside, Canadian political institutions – the Senate a singular but not sole example – guarantee that Canada's constitution is far from being "similar in Principle" to that of the United Kingdom – at Confederation or now. Of course, a transformation of a different kind could be said to have occurred in Great Britain itself. In *The New British Constitution*, Oxford scholar Vernon Bogdanor writes, "Formally, the doctrine of the sovereignty of Parliament has been maintained, and no explicit attack has been made upon it; but, nevertheless, all the reforms have served to limit the power of what had hitherto been an omnicompetent government."[1] The magnitude of constitutional change appears to be matched only by lack of public appreciation for what has happened.

The implications of devolution (Gladstone's Home Rule under another name) in Scotland, Wales, and Northern Ireland since 1998 tend to be treated as peripheral to Westminster politics. Yet the individual legislatures at Edinburgh, Cardiff, and Stormont are strikingly distinct from that in London. Elections, for instance, involve an element of proportional representation of one variant or another, and except for the period 2003–5 in Wales, no election has delivered a secure single-party majority. In consequence, "Scotland and Wales have been governed by coalition or minority administrations"; and for this reason, "the government [of those jurisdictions] may be chosen not by the voters but by party negotiations *after* the votes have been counted." Furthermore, it is at these moments that confidence and supply agreements for the duration of the coalition are determined.[2] Whatever else these arrangements signify, the classic Westminster model of responsible government does not obtain in England's Celtic neighbours.

For the House of Commons, however, plurality voting remains the norm and coalition government is the exception. Yet it was the government at Westminster that carried legislation through Parliament to make devolution and representation more reflective of the popular vote elsewhere in the United Kingdom possible. More than that, the devolution legislation was preceded by referendums in each of the three non-English parts of the kingdom. In a system that reputedly sets a high price on precedent, and that until 2011 – when there was a referendum (defeated) on adopting the alternative vote system in parliamentary elections – had held only one national referendum – in 1975 on the question whether the United Kingdom should maintain its membership in the European Economic Community – this surely is unprecedented. In 2016, in a third referendum, a majority of British voters chose to leave the European Union. More than that, these innovations, along with the introduction of a Human Rights Act whose guarantees challenge – and may even override – Parliament's historic claim of sovereignty, constitute change in the character of fundamental law, so much so that one constitutional order is being replaced by another, a development that leads scholars to foresee a new constitutional settlement.

The implications of these adjustments in Great Britain are of immense importance – for Great Britain. Far less so are they important to Canada, except in two indirect ways: first, they demonstrate that institutions, even those celebrated for their slow, imperceptible adaptation to change, can be recreated and reconnected to serve new civic and democratic purposes; and second, they illustrate that the language of parliamentary politics is infinitely malleable. That second observation is useful, but even more than that, it is timely. In 2016 Canada embarked upon self-consciously modern ways of thinking about Parliament – in all its parts. The foregoing chapters of this book indicate the breadth and complexity of the issues such exploration entails. Wherever this enterprise leads, there can be little doubt that the second decade of the twenty-first century – the decade that embraces the country's sesqui-centennial – has established the sense of a new political beginning: a Senate that promises to be independent in its selection and, more so than in the past, in its conduct; a House of Commons, whose members no longer are selected through plurality voting but rather whose numbers reflect preferential or proportional voting choices; and a governor general, who continues to symbolize the sovereign, but whose constitutional duties as a result of alterations to the composition of the chambers of Parliament appear destined to become more public and more central to the daily operation of government. The speed and scope of constitutional change lend support to the view that Canadians are now experiencing what previously they accepted. In the last half of the twentieth century, federalism dominated discussion. Today, debate centres on institutional – even systemic – change, the limits of which at the present time are unknown but open to wide speculation.

Canada and the United Kingdom may be experiencing uncertainty with regard to the lineaments of their constitutional futures, but the cause of that uncertainty in each instance is different. Beginning in the 1970s, European economic relations, Scottish and Welsh nationalism, and civil unrest in Northern Ireland drove the British government to seek political and economic mechanisms to accommodate the tensions and conflicting objectives it confronted at home and across the Channel. In that respect, it could be said that the stimulus was external or peripheral to Westminster. The reverse is the case in Canada, where the impetus for constitutional change has originated with the central authority, whether it was a Conservative government led by Stephen Harper, seeking through parliamentary statute (seven bills in all) to transform the Senate into an indirectly elected body of members with terms, as opposed to a maximum age limit; or whether it was a Liberal government led by Justin Trudeau, seeking through parliamentary statute to alter the electoral system of the House of Commons from one that uses plurality voting to one that embraces a proportional or alternative ballot.

Anyone familiar with the history of the Reform Party and of the movement for a Triple-E Senate, both identified as western Canadian, and more particularly Albertan, in origin, might dispute the claim that Senate reform is a central rather than a peripheral endeavour. Yet the cause of Senate reform, of the Triple-E kind or any other variety (abolition, for example), is not uniquely western Canadian in its provenance or era. Here is Sir Wilfrid Laurier in 1908 in one of the episodic debates on Senate reform: "There is no absolute power under the British system ... The Crown is not absolute because the Commons can refuse supply. The Commons are not absolute because the Commons can be dissolved. The Lords are not absolute because the Lords can have their membership increased, and thereby their power can be destroyed."[3] This assessment predated the Parliament Act of 1911, which gave the Lords a suspensive veto. The point of Laurier's encomium, however, was to draw a contrast between the flexibility inherent in the mother of Parliaments and the rigidity that characterized her Canadian offspring – a contrast that explains why a strong bicameral legislature did not develop at West-minster and why, a century later, stronger bicameralism than in the past is the projection for the future of Canada's Parliament. Nor, in Laurier's view, was the contrast to the disadvantage of Canada's second chamber, the institution that made Confederation possible because of the political compensation it provided provinces, other than Ontario, for the intro-duction of the principle of representation-by-population in the lower house.

The asymmetry of British constitutional development lies in Brit-ain's being "a territorially differentiated union state as opposed to a unitary state." As a consequence, it did not experience the rigidity of a "federal" arrangement of power, which would have insisted upon England's sharing in the devolution initiative.[4] It will be recalled (from chapter three) that in the Confederation Debates, John A. Macdonald saw this matter differently: "The union [of Scotland and England], in matters of legislation, is of a federal character ... Thus, we have, in Great Britain, to a limited extent, an example of the working effects of a Federal Union."[5] Which of these assessments is correct is immaterial. The relevant matter for the present discussion is that territorial expan-sion in each country took a different form. In Britain, it was the union of the Crowns in 1603 (followed a century later by the Act of Union lead-ing to the creation of the United Kingdom), which, according to some interpreters, was imperfect from the outset: "The dream of unity – an abstract, intellectualised, Scottish and hence European ideal of political togetherness – would within a year fall foul of an English conservatism which valued its own hard-won freedoms far above any high-falutin' ideas of political unity."[6] In Canada, Confederation (1867) preceded acquisition and incorporation of Rupert's Land and the Northwest Territories (1870), and the later admission of British Columbia (1871), Prince Edward Island (1873), and Newfoundland (1949).

The United States and Canada were countries of European settle-ment, each of which possessed a moving frontier. The history of these North American democracies is to an important extent the story of the respective frontiers and their relationship to federal authority. One dimension of that story is that after 1783, the United States was a repub-lic and Canada a colony, then a dominion in the British Empire, and after the Statute of Westminster, an independent constitutional mon-archy whose sovereign is the sovereign of the United Kingdom. The importance of that contrast lies less in constitutional form than it does in a feature flowing from the form that continues to set the politics of the two neighbours apart: the place of election and its association with republican sentiment. There has never been strong republican feeling in Canada, except before the achievement of responsible government, when the American elective principle appeared, to some Upper and Lower Canadian colonists, to offer control of local affairs. Yet, to the extent that this interpretation was seen as valid, it brought with it distinctive criticism too, as witness a debate in the Legislative Assembly of United Canada in 1852: "Instead of conceiving this a question between republicanism and monarchy, he [W.H. Merritt] considered it was really a question between centralization and decentralization."[7] When speaking of American politics, non-centralization rather than decentralization might be considered the more accurate descriptor. In any case, the contrast with Canada remains, and continues, because of the institutional persistence of the Crown with its centralizing influence.

Notwithstanding the compound monarchies of Canadian federalism, whose influence in their respective provinces has been extensive, the territorial consolidation of the country and the quest for constitutional autonomy elevated the stature of the Canadian Crown in important respects. For this reason, its centrality in defining modern Canada – in its reach, it was a model of linearity – should not be underestimated, although this is easy to do because there is more than one voice to monarchy – and the one heard closest to home comes from seriatim term-appointees of the sovereign. Compared to the United Kingdom, the continuous narrative of royal government in Canada has grown fainter with the passing years. Taking the longer view from colonial times to the present, it could be said that monarchy's function has oscillated: at one time autocratic, now symbolic, it remains at the heart of administration. Even today, monarchy's significance is open to interpretation – either as hard (to grant or withhold assent to requests for legislative dissolution) or relaxed (the fount of honours). Caught between Parliament and the people, the Crown pervades Canadian life in familiar but often unacknowledged ways, such as in policing, relations with First Nations, and the administration of justice.

Writing about multiculturalism and language policy some decades ago, Canadian scholar Raymond Bréton observed that "language is perhaps the most effective symbolic medium for assuring a mutual reflection of the public world of institutions and the private world in individuals."[8] The context of that remark in no way spoke to the Crown or matters related to it; yet the import of its claim is highly relevant to this topic. In a British-styled constitutional monarchy, there is, outside of the general election, no space for the people as a constituent power. Here is parliamentary supremacy by another description. The walls of the constitution are (or were) deemed impervious to outside opinion. That was accepted constitutional doctrine in the United Kingdom until the 1970s, when the national referendum on continued membership in the European Economic Community was held, followed by a series of referendums on devolution of legislative power to assemblies in the British Isles other than in England. As a consequence of these developments, "there is little doubt that the referendum has now become an accepted part of the constitution" – in Britain but not in Canada.[9]

The same impermeability has been attributed to Canadian legislative institutions but with a distinctive alteration in emphasis, one most visible in the opinion of the Judicial Committee of the Privy Council (JCPC) in 1919 on the validity of Manitoba's Initiative and Referendum Act. The Act in question would have compelled the lieutenant governor "to submit proposed laws to a body of voters instead of to the Legislature of which he is the constitutional head, and render him powerless to prevent such proposed laws, if approved by such voters, from coming into effect." In his opinion, Lord Haldane wrote, "The Lieutenant-Governor is as much the representative of His Majesty for all purposes of Provincial Government as is the Governor-General for all purposes of Dominion Government ... [D]irectly representing the Sovereign in the province, renders natural the exclusion of his office from the power conferred on the Provincial Legislature to amend the constitution of the Province."[10]

Neither then, nor today, might it be said in Canada that the referendum is "an accepted part of the constitution." Whether the explanation lies in Canada's being a federation with jurisdiction divided among eleven legislatures, or in the long-standing tensions that characterize federal-provincial relations, or in consequence of the evolution from imperial colony to independent country, the Crown in Canada stands apart from the daily spectacle that envelopes the sovereign in London, while maintaining an identity distinct from Parliament. The prominence of the Crown in the rationale offered by the JCPC in the Manitoba referendum opinion in 1919; in the conflict between Mackenzie King and Lord Byng over a request for a dissolution of Parliament (denied) in 1926; in the prorogation crisis of 2008, which this time saw the governor general acquiesce in a request by the prime minister of a minority government to prorogue Parliament, thereby avoiding a threatened opposition vote hostile to the government – these and other instances, such as the gubernatorial granting of dissolution outside the terms of the fixed election-date legislation earlier the same year, illustrate the distinctive nature of the prominence garnered by the Crown in Canada.

That continuing prominence, the circumscribed debate on the topic of republicanism, the longevity of the Senate-reform cause – however it is formulated – are such persistent features of Canadian politics that it is open to speculation whether (and if so, in what way) they are related. For instance, is continuing debate over Senate reform an instance of sub-limated republicanism? Lord Elgin thought so: "An elective Legislative Council has been at all times a standing dish with revolutionary parties in Canada."[11] Is republicanism as a constitutional objective softened into obscurity because no one dare speak its name? As infrequent as it may be, is the call for a national referendum, as in the growing debate over electoral reform discussed in chapter four (or to bring about abolition of the Senate), the resistance act of silent populism in Canada?[12] Is the Crown, as it operates in Canada, a near-republican substitute? Among the claims advanced for "a republican option" by constitutional scholar John Whyte, are first, that "civic republican theory captures better than monarchy the overarching concepts of the Canadian state as expressed in the Canadian Constitution," and second, that "civic republicanism, better than a political structure based on monarchy, matches the chief moral imperatives governing the Canadian political community life in this age, this time and place, with the social and political implica-tions of the pluralism that now defines us."[13] Clearly, this is not the time or place to discuss the putative claims of republicanism on Canadian sentiment – but when is the right occasion, since it seems never to arise in other circumstances?

Bogdanor, among other scholars, argues that because the British con-stitution is uncodified, and therefore lacking a criterion for deciding what is constitutional and what is not, there is a lack of interest among the British in constitutional matters. The implication of that comment is that a written constitution makes all the difference. It might, but that does not help further understanding of the Canadian constitution, since it is both written and unwritten. And it is in reference to the latter component that Canadian political scientist Nelson Wiseman, speaking of the controversy over the law to establish fixed election dates, echoes his English counterpart: "Canadians are woefully ignorant about their parliamentary system. The political class contributes to this illiteracy, as many of them are ill-informed, too."[14] In Canada, as in Britain, the "system," at least as far as it extends to the Crown (the Senate may be another matter), is deemed to work. When in 1995, this author was writing *The Invisible Crown: The First Principle of Canadian Government*, he was told on numerous occasions by his fellow citizens, "Don't fix it if it isn't broken." While there is much ambiguity in the pronouns, the sense of contentment with the institutions of constitutional monarchy seemed clear enough then and still does today. Yet when the subject turned to the political executive, criticism of what was perceived to be an all-powerful but weakly controlled executive, conducive to (in Whyte's words) "executive tyranny," was equally forthcoming.

What is to be done? Should something be done? Certainly, the thesis that "the centralization of Canada's political system means that our prime ministers have become far more than 'first among equals' ... [and that] the PMO functions as the 'real cabinet,'" is familiar. "Misalignment of responsibility" feeds "uncodified standards of accountability and transparency [which] are inconsistent with the demands of a modern democracy."[15] There is a great deal of echo in this and similar analysis, which is not to say that the problems being dissected are imaginary or the remedies offered implausible. It is to say that the very familiarity – the repetition – of the complaint demands attention. The reason why there is no progress, or so little of it, in rectifying the problem lies in the persistence of the institutions that critics claim to be at fault. Writing of Robert Baldwin, Michael Cross has said that the great reformer

did not need to uproot the basic institutions to accomplish the reforms he contemplated; indeed, the colonial political structure is still apparent in Canada's governance. The Governor General and provincial Lieutenant-Governors are recognizable descendants of the colonial administrator. The federal Senate, like its colonial predecessor, the Legislative Council, is an appointed body with legislative functions. The House of Commons mirrors the former House of Assembly. The structure remains, up to the head of state, the English monarch.[16]

The institutions Baldwin did not change are with us still; and while the houses of Parliament and the representatives of the Crown may be identified and described with some facility, the practices of constitutional monarchy and responsible government are less easily agreed upon because they are uncodified (arguably, defy codification) and subject to multiple interpretation.

In 1839, in a dispatch to Lord Sydenham, lieutenant governor of Upper Canada and then governor general of United Canada, the colonial secretary Lord Russell remarked that he had "little or [no objection] to the practical views of colonial government recommended by Lord Durham," following the rebellions a few years previously. At the same time, he added, "It does not appear ... that any very definite meaning is generally agreed upon by those who call themselves the advocates of this principle [responsible government] ... It may be said that I have not drawn any specific line beyond which the power of the Governor on the one hand, and the privileges of the Assembly on the other, ought not to extend. But this must be the case in any mixed government."[17]

The colonial secretary's reticence to elaborate on a theory of government, which then – and from the perspective of history – could be termed without exaggeration as the keystone of Canada's democracy, is remarkable. Lest it be overlooked, the means of communication was a dispatch like any other, in no way singular in its presentation. This momentous first step to self-government was underwhelming in form, a sentiment Louis-Joseph Papineau subsequently echoed: "The honourable member had talked about Responsible Government, but it did not come from any part of the constitution, it was only to be found in the Ministerial instructions."[18] Workaday instructions of another kind preceded the formation of the first government of the Dominion of Canada. On 24 May 1867, from London, the governor general Lord Monck wrote to John A. Macdonald, informing him that

> the proclamation appointing the Union to come into operation on July 1 ... had appeared in the Gazette ... so that our work so far has been finished ... It now remains for us to take the necessary steps to put into motion the machinery which has been created, and I write to you to take the needful measures so as to have a ministry ready to be sworn into office and to commence the performance of their usual functions on the 1st July ... I adopt this test for my guidance in consequence of the impossibility, under the circumstances, of ascertaining, in the ordinary constitutional manner, who possesses the confidence of a parliament which does not yet exist.[19]

It is important to observe that the constitutional directives noted in the preceding paragraph are just that – directives that embody understood ways of thinking and talking. How else to explain general phrases like "necessary steps," "needful measures," and "ordinary constitutional manner"?[20] How else to explain the inexplicit injunction, found in the Preamble to the Constitution Act, 1867, that Canada's constitution is to be "similar in Principle to that of the United Kingdom"? "This [it is claimed] has always been understood as a reference to constitutional conventions, in particular those of responsible government. Indeed, it is because of this understanding that it was not necessary for the drafters of the *Constitution Act, 1867* to elaborate the principle of responsible government, and to describe the institutions through which it is implemented, more than they did."[21] Borrowing from the earlier references to republicanism in Canada, one may turn this subject around and say that the elliptical language of constitutional monarchy – whose institution and operation the immediate discussion concerns – helps, because of its vagueness, to undermine the promotion of republican values. At the same time, such economy of expression contributes to a poverty of understanding among the Canadian public about how their own government and constitution work. George Orwell said that the English language becomes "inaccurate because our thoughts are foolish."[22] "Slovenly" language (the adjective is Orwell's) corrupts thought and, when the subject is the operation of parliamentary democracy in a constitutional monarchy, deflects citizens from asking fundamental questions about its operation. Here is why institutional reform is so difficult to achieve and why debate about the topic is often incoherent.

To the extent that there is a long-running consensus on the condition of governing in Canada, its central concern is that Parliament is unacceptably weak and the political executive unduly strong. The following comments deal with federal rather than provincial institutions; yet the thrust of the argument could apply equally well to the latter, although there is less documentation to support an indictment from that perspective. Forever fresh, the complaint may be treated as comparatively new. It is not. Here is Nicholas Flood Davin, a journalist and a Conservative speaking in the final months of the Conservative ascendancy that began at Confederation: "I must emphasize my opinion and enter a protest against the tendency that is noticeable in parliamentary life in Canada for Parliament to efface itself before the Government of the day." Speaking in the same debate, David Mills (Liberal) protested the government's permissive exercise of its appointment power by making selected MPs senators or public servants: "We know not whether this House is composed of members representing the constituencies whose electors sent us here, or whether it is composed of place-men of the Administration."[23] Davin and Mills were speaking at a time of governmental disintegration that accompanied turmoil associated with the federal government's ineffectual response to provincial legislation in Manitoba overturning denominational schools and equal status for the French language, as understood to be provided for in the Manitoba Act of 1870. Yet the rise of party control and especially government dominance of the House was of established lineage even by then.[24] The contrast between then and now is that the reach of government domination is much greater, a phenomenon political scientist Donald Savoie has pungently labelled "court government," where effective power has come to rest with the prime minister and a small group of carefully selected courtiers.[25]

Savoie's scholarly dissection of court government preceded a revelatory illustration of its malpractice. During the trial of Senator Mike Duffy, in relation to charges of breach of trust allegations, fraudulent practices, and accepting a bribe (on all counts of which he was acquitted), the role played by the prime minister's chief of staff, Nigel Wright, in directing Senator Duffy's actions before and after the laying of charges, became a central and publicized dimension of the court case. In the course of summarizing his judgment, Mr Justice Charles Vaillancourt of the Ontario Court of Justice posed the following questions:

> Did I actually have the opportunity to see the inner workings of the PMO? Was Nigel Wright actually ordering senior members of the Senate around as if they were mere pawns on a chessboard? Were those same members of the Senate meekly acquiescing to Mr Wright's orders? Were those same senior members of the Senate robotically marching forth to recite their provided scripted lines? ... Does the reading of these emails give the impression that Senator Duffy was going to do as he was told or face the consequences? The answers to the aforementioned questions are: YES; YES; YES; YES; and YES. The political, covert, relentless, unfolding of events is mindboggling and shocking.[26]

The financial administration of the Senate, as it relates to senators' expenses, is not at issue here. Rather, it is the disequilibrium in the relationship between one house of Parliament and the political executive, which the judgment in the Duffy case reveals, and which may be taken as a Canadian illustration of a long-standing concern in the Anglo-American world about "executive dictatorship." Very long-standing, if it is remembered that (among others) Thomas Jefferson warned of "despotic government"; Lord Acton of the corrupting effects of power; and John Stuart Mill "of the evil effect produced upon the mind of any holder of power."[27] The pre-eminent and much quoted variation on the theme is by Lord Hailsham (Lord Chancellor in the government of

Edward Heath) in the BBC Richard Dimbleby Lecture (1976): "I have reached the conclusion that our constitution is wearing out. Its central defects are gradually coming to outweigh its merits, and its central defects consist in the absolute powers we confer on our sovereign body, and the concentration of those powers in an executive government formed out of the one party which does not always represent the popular will." His solution to the problem was a written constitution for the United Kingdom: "one which limits the powers of Parliament and provides a means of enforcing these limitations by both political and legal means." Significantly, in light of the subject of this book, Lord Hailsham said nothing about the Crown, "because it seems to me that our monarchy is the one part of our constitution which is still working more or less as it was designed to do."[28]

Quite how a written constitution in itself would resolve the problem set down in the preceding paragraph is not immediately apparent, partly because the problem as enunciated comprises several parts: parliamentary supremacy, single party government (usually), and a plurality electoral system that often translates a minority of votes into a majority of seats. Canada of course has a written constitution, but only as it provides for a division of jurisdiction between federal and provincial spheres; in addition, since 1982, there is a domestic amending formula, the Canadian Charter of Rights and Freedoms, and section 35. Responsible government, as a principle, is secured by reference, and it is the intangible quality of that association that feeds the quest for control and oversight of the political executive – all the more so since one lesson drawn from the verdict in the Duffy trial was, in the words of Stephen Harper's lawyer, that "his acquittal should be [a] wake-up call to hold politicians to account."[29] In this analysis, "the authorities that can hold individuals to account" appeared to be a reference to officers of Parliament, the oldest of which is the auditor general, established in 1878 following the Pacific Scandal, with the appointment of John McDougall. It should be noted, as McDougall did in his first report, that "so far as circumstances permit, it is advisable in such contingencies as are not provided for in our own statute, to follow the system which has grown up under the English act." Once again, the preambular reference to the British constitution, found in the Constitution Act, 1867, proved to be a phrase of multiple application, this time in the field of administration.[30]

Despite the attention that officers of Parliament garner today, published studies of their activities remain infrequent. The word *activities* is narrow and deceptive when the subject is officers and their parliamentary world. As agents of a principal, their joint concern, despite the varied terms of reference that frame their mandates, is to promote accountability by restraining the exercise of executive power. Beyond that commonality and the designation "independent," officers reflect diverse characteristics, as regards roles and functions, standards for measuring achievement in meeting the objects that gave them birth, conditions that influenced their creation and – even more – dissolution (when, for instance, was an officer of Parliament last dissolved?). Norman Ward's half-century-old examination of the office of auditor general is a rare exception in this dearth of attention.[31] In 1920, almost a half-century after the creation of the office of the auditor general, a second officer of Parliament appeared – the chief electoral officer. As with the first, scandal – this time the Union government's manipulation of the conduct of the wartime election in 1917 – preceded its creation. The commissioner of official languages, whose essential role is to assure that language equality remains a defining principle of the constitutional architecture of Canada, its Parliament, and its government, was created by the Official Languages Act in 1969. Privacy and information commissioners appeared in the 1980s, ethics commissioners (for the two chambers of Parliament) after that, and then with the election of the Conservative government in 2006 and its subsequent Federal Accountability Act, several officers in areas such as lobbying and integrity. While scandal did not presage the later officers' creation, there was the common belief that the subject of their responsibilities was too sensitive to be left to the partisan and parliamentary forum. "Retroactively Shielding RCMP 'Perilous' Precedent: Watchdog"; "Information Czar Takes Ottawa to Court over Long-Gun Data"; "Ottawa, Privacy Watchdog at Odds over Information Ruling": these newspaper headlines communicate the shared sense of surveillance and protection that envelopes the activities of the parliamentary officer corps.[32]

Officers of Parliament have attracted less scholarly attention than their prominence might appear to warrant. Moreover, when they are the subject of study, it is usually from the perspective of an individual office. Comparisons, whether in terms of influences leading to their creation or with regard to their purpose – for instance, to promote, or defend, or advocate – are rare. So infrequent as to prompt the question, why? One answer is that they do not fit into any theory of parliamentary government. Parliament is a non-specialized institution; by contrast, officers of Parliament lay claim to expert knowledge, the auditor general being the striking example of professional training. According to legal scholar John Whyte, officers are unlike public servants, who may be apolitical and non-partisan, but who are not independent; and it is that last adjective that distinguishes officers – to a degree that some students of Parliament find disturbing.

> The growth of independent legislative officers from one perspective might be seen as the refinement of legislative oversight of government but, in reality, it represents a significant shift in how political accountability is achieved under our constitutional system. This system of specialist review of government represents a new form of separation of powers – one that has acquired constitutional weight, at least in the sense of constitutional practice. Insofar as these new officers find it difficult to sustain an effective role in ensuring accountability in the face of governmental assaults on both their functionality and their neutrality, it is likely that their position will increasingly be seen as needing formal protection through the establishment of constitutional conventional rules ...
>
> [I]t could be said that the focus of political competition has moved away from parliamentary contestation to the conflict between executive government and the more neutral, more specialist and more normatively driven agencies of accountability – the courts, regulatory agencies and oversight officers and commissions.[33]

The creation of officers of Parliament in the United Kingdom has become, in the view of one scholar, "a tactic in political conflict."[34] The veracity of that statement may require substantiation, but it is clear – both in Canada and the United Kingdom – that despite the singular circumstances surrounding the creation of individual officers of Parliament, a theme common to each innovation is the desire to forego legislative supervision in favour of supplementary, and thus deemed independent, oversight of whatever problem or policy area demands attention. From the perspective of the argument advanced in earlier chapters of this book, with regard to rising tension between the comparative appeals of prerogative power versus statute law, a significant feature about the expansion of the corps of officers of Parliament is that it represents a further retreat from discretionary modes of governing.[35] Could one go so far as to say that every officer of Parliament is an indication of Parliament's own decline? Are officers another example, like citizens' assemblies, of a supplementary institution? Is the pendulum, if that is the chosen metaphor, swinging away from partisan to audience democracy? Is this further evidence to explain the finding by Ipsos-Reid, that Sheila Fraser, auditor-general, was "immensely trusted by Canadians *because* 'she ... [was] viewed by Canadians as being above politics.'" In the lexicon of audit accountability, election becomes a positive disqualification for gaining trust, rule by the non-elected expert the preferred option.[36] Rarely has conflict between the two approaches been on display as publicly as in 2014, when, in the absence of prior public or partisan consultation, the government of Stephen Harper proposed changes to electoral regulations and practices (Bill C-23), ultimately passed by Parliament as the Fair Elections Act, which were opposed for what was deemed their suppressive effect on voter activity, by officials in Elections Canada as well as provincial counterparts, such as Ontario's chief electoral officer. The minister of democratic reform (Pierre Poilievre) dismissed opposition to the bill from the general public as ill-informed and from Canada's chief electoral officer as indication of "a desire for 'more power, a bigger budget and less accountability.'"[37]

Has the public become so pluralistic in its interests and loyalties, and the political parties in the House of Commons so polarized, that escape from the conventions of responsible government has become a realistic alternative to be sought? This interpretation sounds extreme, yet there are extreme manifestations to support the claim.

Stop PM/Premier Power Abuses

There is an elite club running Canada – the SuPremos. They are almost all powerful ... Even the *Constitution* doesn't stop them from abusing many of their powers. Most watchdogs can't stop them, and their actions often strike fear in the hearts of Canadians ...

Their abuses of power can only be stopped if thousands and thousands of people act right now!

Please click here and send your letter now calling on politicians across Canada to make key changes to Stop the SuPremos.[38]

The unarticulated premise supporting this injunction – that the people must act to "stop" the politicians – presumably is to that advanced epigrammatically by Amartya Sen, winner in 1998 of the Nobel Prize in economics: "In a democracy, people tend to get what they demand, and more crucially, do not typically get what they do not demand."[39] The rallying of opposition outside of Parliament, combined with a weakened sense of responsibility among legislators for decisions made within, explains the source of the discontent but it does not provide a guide for action. Populism is not a constitutional principle in Canada. It provides no rationale, say, for proposals that the House of Commons participate in appointments to the Supreme Court or ratify foreign policy decisions made by the executive. These are powers reserved specifically to the Crown, which by convention acts on advice of its first minister. Here, once again, is institutional ambivalence with serious repercussions for public understanding of the constitution, in all its many parts. The process, which the historian Edmund Morgan has described as "inventing the people" in the United States, is now so familiar as not to attract comment.[40] Separate and superior – a constituent power – the American people were located not "inside" the legislature, sharing in government, but "outside," watching, limiting, checking government. The corporate idea of government disappeared altogether. The body politic, which took form, as Henry VIII once said, "in the time of Parliament, wherein we as head and you as members are conjoined," had in the United States become disembodied – and with it, the concept of government as protector, guarantor, and sustainer.[41] "The logic of these developments," as historian Gordon Wood concluded, "was to take the people out of government altogether."[42] In the United States, representation is the crucial criterion, and election the mechanism for its realization. In contrast to Canada and other parliamentary democracies, there are no grounds for authority other than numbers. "The classic Westminster theory has it that the Minister (who has sworn to serve the Crown) acts through his subordinate officials and that in law their actions, carried out on his behalf, are his actions, for which he is responsible as if they were his own."[43] Challenges to the political status quo in a constitutional monarchy such as Canada's demand, as a first and necessary step, that the prerogative of the Crown be defended – a requirement that has had the effect of distancing the Canadian system from the people it serves. There is no reserve of legislative power, as in United States, vested in the people.

Officers of Parliament may fit uneasily into the "Westminster theory," but then so does appealing to the demos to pressure political leaders. Whence executive power – from the Crown down or the electorate up? The question has been alluded to earlier in this study, but it is not one that arises very often in Canadian politics. The referendum that followed the Charlottetown Accord (1992) on amendments to the Canadian constitution (and that failed to garner sufficient public support) is an exception, as was the plebiscite on military conscription in 1942, which won support in all provinces but Quebec. Nonetheless, conscription did not proceed in the Second World War for another two years, thereby underlining one difficulty of public consultation in a double federation. During the First World War, conscription was introduced in the summer of 1917, with a general election following in December. O.D. Skelton, already a confidant of Sir Wilfrid Laurier, advised the leader of the opposition "not to accept [conscription] until an election or referendum had been held."[44] Whatever the influence, Laurier stayed out of the Union government; an election, but no referendum, followed; and the next time the voters had the opportunity to express their opinion on the actions of the government, they wreaked vengeance on the Conservatives. The wartime election and the government's accompanying manipulation of the franchise, which was identified directly with Arthur Meighen, who was to lead the Conservative party through most of the 1920s, exerted, as did the King-Byng constitutional crisis in which Meighen acted as the third-party beneficiary, a determining and negative influence on Tory fortunes for three decades.

Between 1917, when Borden headed the Union government, and 1957, when John Diefenbaker became prime minister, the Conservatives formed only one government following a general election, under R.B. Bennett, after 1930 and until 1935. It would be a misinterpretation, however, for anyone unfamiliar with Canada over the thirty-five years of Liberal rule to think that such stability coincided with quiescent times. Far from it, as witness the rise of the farmers' movement as a partisan force, and with it the end of the pure two-party system; the arrival of what Canadians term "minority government"; a decade of twin scourges of economic depression and prairie drought; the economic, societal, and military challenges presented by the Second World War; the post-war economic and demographic recovery associated with large-scale immigration after 1945. To this could be added the march to Canadian autonomy in relations with the United Kingdom.[45] The excuse for this potted history is to emphasize the importance of context to understanding Canadian politics. No doubt the same might be said of the politics of other countries, but in Canada it is central to note that there is a long-standing disposition to look through or over context – that is, to focus on the actors and not the play itself. This is why, when compared to other dimensions of Canadian politics, party leaders and the parliamentary arena attract disproportionate attention among scholars. This is another illustration of the continuing attraction of the story of the achievement of self-government, which invariably is told from the perspective of personalities. In this respect, no one has secured the pre-eminence of Mackenzie King, whether as seen by a constitutional critic, Eugene Forsey, or by a constitutional scholar and poet, F.R. Scott, who in his poem "W.L.M.K." observed, "He never let his on the one hand / Know what his on the other hand was doing."[46]

King's was (and remains) an elusive personality, whose qualities to his critics might seem duplicitous. Whether that assessment is accurate is immaterial to this discussion. What is germane is that the constitution in which he found himself permitted full expression of his talents for indecision and indirection. Undoubtedly, it was a constitution of whose intangible aspects he was fully aware:

> It is a strange mystical sort of thing, this British Constitution that we love. It is partly unwritten; it is partly written. It finds its beginnings in the lore of the past; it comes into being in the form of custom and tradition; it is founded upon the common law. It is made up of precedents, of magna chartas [sic]. Of petitions and bills of rights; it is to be found partly in statutes and partly in the usages and practices of Parliament. It represents the highest achievement of British genius at its best.[47]

The preceding remarks come from a speech, titled "The British Constitution," given at the time of the constitutional crisis of 1926, five days before Arthur Meighen was to assume office (following King's resignation), and after Viscount Byng refused the Liberal prime minister's request for a dissolution of Parliament.

It may be a simplification but it is not an over-simplification to say that it is impossible to speak of conventions of the constitution in Canada and not talk about Mackenzie King. Of course, conventions are the essence of parliamentary government in a constitutional monarchy. That surely is one indisputable meaning to be attributed to the statement that in 1867 the founding provinces "desire[d] ... a Constitution similar in Principle to that of the United Kingdom." But it is the practice that establishes the context for understanding individual conventions. More particularly, it is the language enveloping the practice that conveys the meaning.[48] This is why, notwithstanding their scholarly eminence, works such as Sir Ivor Jenning's *The Law and the Constitution* or A.V. Dicey's *Law of the Constitution* are inadequate alone, and certainly eighty or a hundred and some years after they were first published, to establish the substance of constitutional conventions in Canada.[49] For a quarter of a century after 1921, the metre of Parliament was set by the actions of Mackenzie King. Whether, for instance, the matter was political party or parliamentary leadership; or the formation of a government where no party held a majority of seats in the House of Commons; or the role of the governor general in Canada and, more specifically, the relationship between him and his first minister; the conventions that guided and informed actions at the time they occurred – but more important still, after the fact – originated with, or in reaction to, King. Eugene Forsey's redoubtable treatise *The Royal Power of Dissolution of Parliament in the British Commonwealth* was occasioned, the author said in the book's Preface, as a dissent from "most previous writers on the case [who] have concluded that Lord Byng's refusal of dissolution to Mr King and/or his subsequent grant of dissolution to Mr Meighen were unconstitutional."[50]

Whatever the consensus in 1943 when Forsey's book was first published, today the author commands the constitutional ramparts, at least those parts of it in possession of the scholarly legions. That much was made clear in the controversy over Mr Harper's request to the governor general in 2008 for prorogation of Parliament. But where Forsey saw himself a member of a small minority who upheld Byng and criticized King, in 2008 the academic community strongly supported the premise that it was within the discretion of the governor general to refuse to exercise the prerogative in a manner to enable a prime minister to escape probable defeat in the House of Commons. (Elsewhere there was dissent: in his biography of Stephen Harper, John Ibbitson wrote that had the governor general refused, she "would have been exercising authority that the governor general ... simply does not have."[51]) In the first instance, the defeat of the Meighen government within days of its appointment and, in the second, the collapse of the putative Liberal-NDP coalition (with promised support from the Bloc Québécois) before Parliament resumed following prorogation, demonstrated the vulnerability of a Canadian governor general – to an extent without parallel in the United Kingdom – in times of parliamentary uncertainty with respect to support for an existing government. In each controversy, the principals and principles were the same: the prerogative, the people, Parliament; the difference was the argument advanced by Harper government supporters that "only voters have the right to decide on the coalition."[52] As discussed more fully elsewhere in this book, in the fall of 2008, and despite a new provision of the Canada Elections Act providing for fixed-date elections, the prime minister sought and

was granted a dissolution of Parliament on grounds (as later enunciated) that to extinguish the prerogative with regard to granting dissolution required an amendment as provided for in section 41 of the
Constitution Act, 1982. On this issue, some of those who supported
the prerogative and were later to challenge the government's populist
position hostile to coalition argued that "the decision should not go
unchallenged because it completely subverts Parliament's intention to
prevent snap elections."[53]

The prerogative controversies of 2008 challenged the conviction of
hitherto strong believers in the efficacy of the unwritten conventions of
constitutional monarchy. Peter Russell, a distinguished scholar of the
subject, admitted his "faith ... ha[d] worn thin." While cautioning that
not every "aspect of the Crown's role in parliamentary government"
could be anticipated and written down, he proposed for Canada an
approximation of the "cabinet manuals" found in the United Kingdom
and New Zealand, which set out "agreed-upon practices of parliamentary and cabinet government and the principles that underlie them."[54]
Speaking on another occasion Russell had elaborated on the topic: "The
political consensus on fundamental principles," which a manual would
embody, was desirable because otherwise "the governor general [is
placed] in the position of refereeing a game without an agreed-upon
set of principles."[55]

As the notes associated with the previous paragraph illustrate, there
is a burgeoning literature on the desirability of codifying the practices
of parliamentary government in a constitutional monarchy. The evident
disposition in this matter to rely on rules and structures is, arguably, of
a piece with a recurring theme in this book – a retreat from reliance on
historic understandings as the foundation of responsible government.
John Whyte perceives as reasons for this occurrence two parallel developments: "collapse of any common understanding of conventions ...
[and] increasing disbelief in the political relevance of elections to select
legislators and the government."[56] The negative relationship posited in
that statement would appear to portend a serious test for the legitimacy of the existing constitution. More than that, its tone is in striking
contrast to the sense of confidence found in the work of classic scholars
of Canadian government, such as Norman Ward and James Mallory.
Nevertheless, this is not a study of the conventions of parliamentary
government in Canada, although there is pressing need for exploration
of the subject, beginning with noting that conventions are anything but
conventional in the sense of being ordinary. On the contrary, they are

singular in their importance to the operation of government. Yet such an enterprise is fraught with difficulty, as may be surmised from one of the "assumptions" articulated by the report of the Joint Committee on Conventions of the United Kingdom Parliament: "We do not offer a definition of 'conventions.' We believe we will know one when we see it."[57] More challenging than recognizing and recording conventions, however, is to envision the purpose of such a compilation. Assuming they – whatever the conventions the corpus comprises – may be collected and codified, how are they to be used?

The analogy employed above speaks of "principles" employed "in refereeing a game." Is the comparison apt; is this what a governor general does? Except for Adrienne Clarkson, who wrote an autobiography that included reflections on her period as governor general, observations about the office and its duties as seen by occupants of the position are exceedingly rare.[58] For that reason, the comment by the Lord Dufferin to Sir John A. Macdonald, on a draft he had received of the speech from the throne in 1873, warrants citing:

> There is one sentence in the Speech which I am afraid I must ask you to omit, namely, that in which I am made to say – "The evidence obtained under the Commission has had my careful consideration."
>
> This refers to [the] personal operation of my mind, and transfers to me consequently a *personal* responsibility. It invests me, in fact, with the character of *arbiter* – which thank God, under the intimation [*sic*] I have received, I am not called upon to be. Moreover, the Crown *acts*, but it does not *consider*, under the advice of its ministers.[59]

More perplexing than drafting a speech or offering advice is requesting that the governor general exercise his or her prerogative power. For those who hold the view that the governor general does not have the authority to refuse a request, then there is no conflict of choice – except when the choice is the paramount one of selecting a first minister. In this instance, the sporting analogy is inapplicable once the combatants in a political contest number three or more, and "sides" become fluid. Who supports whom; and how to determine the answer? The chief constitutional duty of the governor general is to see that there is a government in place that commands the support of the House of Commons. Since Confederation, that duty has been comparatively easy to discharge because the partisan composition of the House has made clear which party commands support of the chamber. It does not require extraordinary perception, however, to envision a post-election distribution of party standings where clarity as to the viceregal response has disappeared, and public and partisan controversies ensue. This is not a necessary consequence of moving from a plurality electoral system to one that promotes proportional representation or institutes a preferential ballot. Still, it is easier to foresee this happening where the electoral system has been chosen for the purpose of arithmetically translating the distribution of partisan votes into a similar distribution of parliamentary seats rather than under the existing plurality elections regime. As noted in chapter four, the debate engendered by the Trudeau government's pledge to change the electoral system sparked strong arguments from those in favour and those opposed. The outcome of the debate and of such a change, if that occurs, remains unknown at the time of writing. Nonetheless, it is important to appreciate the potential implications of an alteration in the electoral system for the governor general and his or her interpretation of the office and its responsibilities.

The governor general is not a figurehead but rather the embodiment of the Crown in Canada. That capacity must neither be forgotten nor treated as politically unimportant, for the reason Sir David Smith, official secretary to five governors general of Australia and the man who in November 1975 informed Buckingham Palace of the governor general's dismissal of Gough Whitlam as prime minister and who read from the steps of Parliament in Canberra the governor general's dissolution of the two houses of Parliament, perceptively summarizes: "The real question is not at all how much power does the Governor-General himself have or exercise, but rather how much absolute power does his presence in our [Canada's as well as Australia's] system of government deny to those who are in government and who must first seek to advise and persuade him."[60]

Chapter Six

Recapitulation

One underappreciated advantage of possessing the Crown is that Canada has never had to create or decide upon its own executive. In light of disagreement for decades before 1982 on a domestic amending formula for the constitution, as well as failure ever to cohere on Senate reform, the inherited Crown is surely an institution deserving support from Canadians. Irrespective of what periodic polls might reveal about fluctuating support for the Crown, Canada is indisputably a monarchy in the sense that there is no organized republican sentiment of any significance. Compared to Australia, where sentiment for a republic has been and remains strong but agreement to date on a non-monarchical alternative unachievable, Canadians must deem themselves fortunate to have avoided this constitutional quest, especially given the national unity challenges that preoccupied their governments and the public generally for much of the last decades of the twentieth century.[1]

While it is true that there is (and has been) no republican movement in Canada, it would be more accurate and informative to turn that statement around and say that support for monarchy has remained exceedingly strong from the beginning of European settlement. Authority in the form of the Crown has rarely been questioned, and as court cases from the first decade of the twenty-first century, such as *O'Donohue, McAteer, Motard,* and *Conacher* demonstrate, law today actually enhances the Crown.[2] In the language James Boyd White uses when discussing authority in Shakespeare's *Richard II,* Canadians "acquiesce" (and have for a very long time) in the "narrative" and "understandings" of the Crown and, as a consequence, accept what these mean for how they are governed.[3]

One result is a high regard for law and its enforcement. Although unnecessary to substantiating the point, comparative evidence from the United States is frequently offered to demonstrate it. Seymour Martin Lipset is one commentator who has cited the contrast in legal values and respect for the law between the two societies. In *Continental Divide: The Values and Institutions of the United States and Canada*, he posited the "due process model" in the former and the "crime control model" in the latter.[4] Canada, he says, was a country of "generalized deference" and "diffuse elitism" and, as a consequence, was less aggressive and more law-abiding than its neighbour. It is at this point that the Royal Canadian Mounted Police and their predecessor, the North-West Mounted Police created within a decade of Confederation (in 1873), are usually invoked to illustrate the societal respect policing in Canada has, historically and in modern times. Few (if any) other countries choose to claim the national police as their national symbol. A propos the subject of the paragraph, they are the *royal* mounted police, and contrary to film and television portrayals, the RCMP are very much a real (not a ceremonial) police force, federally and in eight of the ten provinces. According to Richard Gwyn, in his biography of Sir John A. Macdonald, the North-West Mounted Police was the first "distinctively Canadian" institution.[5]

One contrast in the matter of the Crown between the United Kingdom and Canada lies in the different time perspectives employed to analyse it. In the first, monarch succeeds monarch for close on to a thousand years, during which eon Parliament and the common law emerge and themselves evolve. The interweaving of the story of the Crown and of Britain is treated as indistinguishable. In the second, the Crown in right of the federal union of Canada begins on a specific date (1 July 1867) and is identified irrevocably with the territorial and jurisdictional expansion of the country thereafter, whether through the alienation or retention of land and resources to individuals or to provinces. The Crown is an index both of the history of Canadian development as a federation and as an autonomous member of the Commonwealth. One aspect to note of the different time perspectives is the contrasting weight accorded law and convention as each touches the Crown in the two countries. In the United Kingdom, the weight of convention in determining the conduct and stature of the Crown is explained by the uninterrupted succession of sovereigns. As noted in chapter two, in the 106 years that separate the beginning of George V's reign in 1910 and that of his granddaughter, Elizabeth II, in 2016, significant change has occurred in understandings of the Crown's discretion in accepting or rejecting advice from first ministers. In Canada, with the conflict between Viscount Byng and Mackenzie King in 1926 as referent, one might echo that sentiment, but the more crucial constitutional point to draw, in 2016 and as discussed in chapters one and two, is the emerging primacy of law rather than convention as a determinative influence on the behaviour of the Crown. Whatever the situation is in Britain, any tendency in Canada to underestimate the importance of strict law and overemphasize the importance of convention needs correction. At the same time, there is reason to approach schemes for codifying conventions with caution: convention can be liberating, written rules less so.[6]

In the Preface of this book, Charles II is quoted declaring his devotion to Parliament as the vital element of constitution. Against the background of a different set of circumstances, more than a century and a half later, the imperial government in London was to profess by way of action, through the colonial governors in British North America, a similar commitment. In these instances, the result was the achievement of responsible government, a story often told in Canadian history texts but with an emphasis different from the present account. As central as Baldwin, Lafontaine, and Howe, for example, were to securing this constitutional object, it is equally important to recognize that the principle of responsible government was achieved and its practice assured by the cooperation of the Crown and its representatives. Within this constitutional architecture, the colonial reflection of the principle of the Crown-in-Parliament appeared – and remains. It is the governor general (or lieutenant governor in a province) whose paramount duty is to see that a government responsible to and drawn from the legislative body is in place, and that this government commands the support of the elected assembly. Where a political party secures a majority of seats, the governor general's choice is clear. Where there is no party with a majority, his or her task requires an exercise of discretion. As noted in chapter one, counting does not offer a dependable guide for action, since there are precedents where a party with more votes and seats (but not a majority in the last instance) has failed to form a government.

Even though, as previous discussion has shown, numbers exert an attraction for those who seek to clarify or authenticate the use of prerogative powers, there has been since Confederation a reluctance to return to such pre-1867 practices in the Province of Canada as supermajorities or double-majorities (which, it needs be said, had nothing to do with the exercise of the prerogative). Notwithstanding a succession of proposals over the past century or more to reform the Senate, the only one to broach the subject by means of numbers was that advanced by Sir Wilfrid Laurier in 1899. Frustrated by having proposed legislation blocked by a Conservative majority in the Senate, but himself opposed to abolishing the Senate or making it elective, he suggested that "when there is a conflict between the Senate and the popular House, then there should be a joint vote, and the majority should carry."[7] Here, a year before the adoption of the Commonwealth of Australia Constitution Act, 1900, but reflecting long discussion already underway among the country's founding fathers, was a weak version of what became section 57 of the Constitution of Australia, that is provision for "double dissolution" of the two (upper and lower) houses of Parliament followed by a joint sitting on the occasion of inter-cameral gridlock.

The pledge by Justin Trudeau, to move Canada's electoral system for the House of Commons from one based on pluralities to a proportional or preferential scheme, prompted vigorous discussion about the system to be adopted and the mechanism whereby to make that choice. Combined, the two questions elevated the subject of voting and the Commons to an unprecedented degree. Still, the act of voting and the interpretation assigned it may, absent other considerations, distort understanding of the role of Parliament. The Oxford philosopher A.D. Lindsay, who stood for Parliament in the Oxford by-election of 1938, solely in opposition to the Munich Agreement, passionately promoted the importance of parliamentary discussion: "Able and critical opposition is seen least," he maintained, "in the division lists." Where that proves insufficient, then "in the alternation in power of political parties there is often worked out in practical dialectic what discussion could not discover."[8] Parliament, which includes the Senate as well as the Commons, is about talk. One could say the same of cabinet, as Allan Blakeney, Saskatchewan senior public servant, cabinet minister, and premier, once did:

> The major decisions [in cabinet] were collegial decisions and ... therefore it was desirable, and sometimes necessary, for all ministers not only to acquiesce in decisions but also to understand them and why they were made. I wanted all the ministers to be able to explain cabinet decisions and defend them with caucus and the public ...
>
> Getting consensus is sometimes not easy. If it was a contentious issue, I usually asked each minister to give a brief opinion. The classic method is to ask the most junior ministers to speak first so that they are not intimidated by the expressed views of the senior people.[9]

If talk is the currency of parliamentary government, then the Senate, before and more particularly since the Supreme Court ruling in 2014, is a major beneficiary. Independence and reduced partisanship are among the characteristics the Court singled out for favourable comment about the activities of the upper chamber. For reasons made clear in chapter three, until the Supreme Court opinion on the Harper government's legislation to reform the Senate, there was no theory of bicameralism in Canadian political thought. Australia, which has an elected Senate (using three different voting systems since 1901), was, especially during Canada's unity debates in the 1970s and 1980s, regularly invoked by Canadian scholars as a model worthy of emulation.[10] Yet comparisons may mislead, as an Australian political scientist John Uhr warns: "Theories of bicameralism tend to have more to say about the added value of the second chamber than about the limited value of the first chamber, which is either taken as a given or simply assumed as undesirable ... [M]any unicameral assemblies also rest on concepts of balance. What appears as 'balance' to advocates of bicameralism might in fact upset prior constitutional balances dependent on the primacy of the first chamber."[11]

The analogy Uhr uses to describe a bicameral legislature is "of a camera with two lenses." For this reason, he contrasts bicameralism, which "is about constructing a balanced view from two perspectives," with "unicameral assemblies [which] work more like telescopes in providing a simplified and unified vision."[12] Uhr, and the editors of the book in which his piece appears and whose title *Restraining Elective Dictatorship* echoes Lord Hailsham's 1976 BBC lecture, perceive two functions of bicameralism: one negative – to act against the vices of majoritarianism – and the other positive – to promote the virtues of an effective deliberative assembly. Both of these objects may be discerned in the Supreme Court ruling on the Senate, but the public sense of a dual "theoretical" mandate along such lines for Canada's upper chamber is only slowly emerging. In this balance of aims, and certainly when compared to the pre-Charter past, one may see support for the proposition that "modern constitutional doctrine offers an overwhelmingly negative, inertial view of the state."[13] Assuming that this assessment of an emerging theoretical concept for at least one house of Parliament has weight, how will it be affected by the promised change in the electoral system of the other house? Will a lower house whose members are no longer selected using plurality voting but rather some form of ranked ballots or proportional representation system be more or less acquiescent in its relations with the Senate?

Even before that, if it could be argued that a move to reform the electoral system towards ranked ballots or a proportional representative system would favour the governing party, would the Senate be justified for that reason in blocking such legislation? Indeed, when might the Senate obstruct the government or the House? No "manual" exists or has been proposed to answer to these questions.

Nor should it be assumed that the trajectory of the Senate after the Supreme Court opinion and after the introduction of a less-overtly partisan selection mechanism will not deviate in some unexpected direction. Antipathy towards an unelected (indeed, perhaps any) second chamber remains a significant feature of political sentiment in Canada, one that emerges in unexpected guises. An example is provided by a *Globe and Mail* editorial (after the first round of "independent" appointments in March 2016 and after appointment of a government representative in the Senate, each of whom sit separately from the Independent Liberal Caucus formed in 2014) which advocated that "the Canadian Senate draft a resolution modelled on or at least influenced by the British statute of 1911 [the Parliament Act of that year, which reduced the House of Lords' power to a suspensive veto] – to make it clear that, as an unelected house, it is not co-equal with the democratically elected house."[14] Writing hours after the 1911 event, Sir Joseph Pope concluded that by their action in passing what he called the Veto Bill, the Lords had "extinguished themselves."[15] The pungency of the reflexive verb confirms why it is safe to predict that, in this matter, Canada will forever renounce emulation of its United Kingdom counterpart. As a second chamber of Parliament, the Senate may live in a shadow, but, unlike the Lords, it is constitutionally empowered in extraordinary circumstances to escape that condition and do more than delay. The Crown too stands distinct, abjuring the ornamentalism of monarchy, acting because of the amending formula (section 41 of the Constitution Act, 1982) more as a constitutional pillar than a personal one, than at any time in its history. Notwithstanding Canada's being a federation, the Commons part of Parliament appears most like its counterpart at Westminster. Yet that similarity appears (in the spring of 2016) about to change with a new electoral system possible and Canada finding itself following a path blazed by Scotland and Wales over the last quarter century. Arguably, however, Canada is a very different country from those sections of the British Isles, and for this reason it is open to question whether electoral equipment, of whatever design, can carry the weight of what its advocates here desire.

Even after the Supreme Court opinion in 2014, which found legislation providing for indirect election of senators beyond Parliament's power, criticism of the upper chamber's manner of selection continued to be heard. In the eyes of some, the Senate is profoundly handicapped because it is appointed, while the governor general, by contrast, appears to secure advantages because of the same "handicap." The contradiction is curious and explicable only if one adopts the interpretation that the office of governor general is a ceremonial position and the actions of its occupant superfluous to the interests and concerns of daily governing. There is a pressing need for a close study of the office of governor general as well as the activities of its occupants, because of a void in knowledge generally and a want of understanding of the office's potential involvement in the intricacies of government formation, if party alignments and loyalties were to cease to be as predictable as they have been in the past.[16]

One of the most recognized paintings of the eighteenth century and one that relates to Canada is *The Death of General Wolfe* (1770). The artist was Benjamin West, an Anglo-American painter whose subjects were drawn from the Seven Years' War and the American War of Independence. The painting itself was revolutionary because "it elevated a contemporary event to the highest realms of classical history."[17] It was controversial, too: both George Washington and George III disapproved when they first saw it, on the grounds that while the composition might be classical, the subjects wore modern dress. As a result, it was believed the painting – and its meaning – would "date" rather than be "timeless." At one level, the controversy that ensued between the painter, academicians, and politicians would seem far removed from a study of the Canadian constitution, and it is. Yet there is a connection. Canadians are not attracted to abstract thought, or to political passion. As the writer Hugh Hood once critically phrased it, "Canadians don't go for Byronism or Bonapartism. A Canadian Bonaparte is a contradiction in terms."[18] Regrettable or not, that disposition towards pragmatism explains the course of events leading to Confederation as well as the content of the agreement reached. In the decades after 1867, the disputes over federal and provincial jurisdiction deflected attention from the almost unanimous support among the Fathers of Confederation for the need to establish strong national institutions. For example, at the Quebec conference Macdonald championed "one statutory law, one system of courts, one judiciary and eventually one bar." While matters did not work out quite as he or the other Fathers may have envisioned, the thrust of their intention was clear – one in which even Oliver Mowat, a later prominent advocate of provincial rights, said, he "concurred," because "it would weld us into a nation."[19] It was, to be sure, a new beginning.

West's painting of Wolfe remained prominent in Great Britain and North America after 1770, but it received renewed attention in Canada early in the twenty-first century when it reappeared in a work by Canadian artist Charles Pachter. That second picture, titled *History Lesson*, is in two parts: on the viewer's right is a photograph of Mackenzie King, garbed in a Ruritanian-like uniform, standing next to the present Queen's mother, when she and George VI visited Canada in 1939. Framed by the arch of the Peace Tower, the prime minister and her majesty gaze to the right. The object of their attention, at the top left side of the Pachter picture, is a colour photograph of West's painting. Below that iconic depiction of Canada's passage from French to British rule on the Plains of Abraham three solitary words visually vibrate: "Kill," "Conquer," "Rule." Here West's commemorative art is given new, retrospective meaning in light of the knowledge the modern viewer brings to it.

Like mirrors, painting is another form of reflection but with this distinction: it incorporates time as a fourth dimension. Through West, and particularly Pachter, Canada is confirmed by its history. Here, in the latter and with the Parliament Buildings as backdrop, are symbolized monarchy, responsible government, national autonomy, First Nations (one of the subjects present in the West painting), and more. In this depiction, the Canadian community possesses a clear sense of itself. From the time-perspective of a viewer of *History Lesson*, the national pageants of Canada Day and Remembrance Day have come to replace Victoria Day – and have done so in the span of the life of an average three-score-and-ten Canadian. This is not to say that the pictures do not attract criticism – the depiction of the First Nations individual as a "noble savage" is a case in point. Of course paintings, just as mirrors, may distort reality. Nonetheless, in this instance they communicate, and with the more recent work, reinforce the continuous narrative of the effective power of government, which in the case of Canada has always been royal.

This book begins and ends with references to Parliament: the first invokes Charles II, the absent monarch, declaring to the Speaker of the House of Commons at Westminster his loyalty to Parliament; the second depicts a royal consort next to the prime minister on the steps of a lineally related Parliament more than two and a half centuries later. The attributions are appropriate in a study of Canadian politics, because here, as in the United Kingdom, Parliament – and it alone – speaks for the people, who in themselves are not a source of political legitimacy. It is fitting too, because the story of Canada's constitution is the story of legislatures, whether the subject is responsible government, or federalism, or the achievement of constitutional autonomy. In the last half-century the egalitarian intent of the Canadian Charter of Rights and Freedoms and official policies of bilingualism and multiculturalism have transformed the law and politics of the country formed at Confederation, while at the same time they have fed visible societal differences. In the thick of the constitutional debate of the 1990s, political scientist Reginald Whitaker observed that "retention [in Canada] of the trappings of the traditional constitutional structure tends to mystify and confuse the real political issues involved."[20] A quarter century on, it could equally be said that it is the multiple mirrors of the three elements of Parliament – and the mists of misunderstanding about the function, structure, and interrelationship of the parts that persist and thicken over time – that confound debate and complicate efforts to conceive reform.

Notes

Preface

1 Caption accompanying a portrait of Charles II in the Scottish National Portrait Gallery, Edinburgh. See, too, letter written by Charles to the Speaker of the House of Commons, at the time of the Declaration of Breda, in which were outlined the King's terms for the restoration of the monarchy. Godfrey Davies, *The Restoration of Charles II: 1658–1660* (London: Oxford University Press, 1955), 341.

Chapter One

1 Helliwell, J., R. Layard, and J. Sachs, *World Happiness Report 2016, Update*, vol. 1. (New York: Sustainable Development Solutions Network, 2016).

2 *Saskatchewan Federation of Labour v Saskatchewan (Attorney General)*, 2010 SKCA 27(CanLII), para 63.

3 Liam Stack, "Long-Serving PM Championed Multiculturalism," *Globe and Mail*, 21 March 2015, S12.

4 Tim Naumetz, "Conservatives 'Lay Track' to Attack Media, Real Opposition in New Parliament," *Hill Times*, 13 June 2011, 6; CBC News, "Tories Begin Battle against Coalition," 2 December 2008. http://www.cbc.ca/news/canada/tories-begin-battle-against-coalition-1.735525.

5 Michael Bliss, "Playing Footsie with the Enemy," *National Post*, 4 December 2008, A23.

6 *AmericasBarometer: Citizens across the Americas Speak on Democracy and Governance, Canada 2014: Final Report* (Ottawa: Environics Institute and Institute on Governance), 36.

7 The Saskatchewan precedent of 1929 had several distinguishing features, not least that the "outgoing" Liberal leader was J.G. Gardiner, who by 1957 was in the federal cabinet and who on election night pressed the federal Liberal leader, Louis St Laurent, to follow the Saskatchewan example, resist resignation, and force a vote onto the floor of the Commons. St Laurent declined the advice. During the tumult before the vote in Regina in 1929, Gardiner sought and received counsel on alternative strategies from Winston Churchill, then in the city on a lecture tour. See Norman Ward and David Smith, *Jimmy Gardiner: Relentless Liberal* (Toronto: University of Toronto Press, 1990), 107–17.
8 Patricia Cline Cohen, *A Calculating People: The Spread of Numeracy in Early America* (Chicago: University of Chicago Press, 1982).
9 David M. Brock, "The Independence of Election Administration from Government," in special issue, "The Informed Citizen's Guide to Elections: Electioneering Based on the Rule of Law," ed. Greg Tardi and Richard Balasko, *Journal of Parliamentary and Political Law* (Toronto: Carswell, 2015), 93–106.
10 Peter Aucoin, Mark D. Jarvis, and Lori Turnbull, *Democratizing the Constitution: Reforming Responsible Government* (Toronto: Emond Montgomery Publications, 2011).
11 Ibid., 24.
12 Ibid., 24–5.
13 Eugene A. Forsey, *The Royal Power of Dissolution of Parliament in the British Commonwealth* (Toronto: Oxford University Press, 1943); Margaret A. Banks, *Sir John George Bourinot, Victorian Canadian: His Life, Times, and Legacy* (Montreal and Kingston: McGill-Queen's University Press, 2001); H.V. Evatt, *The King and His Dominion Governors* (Oxford: Oxford University Press, 1936); A.V. Dicey, *Introduction to the Study of the Law of the Constitution*, 10th ed., intro. E.C.S. Wade (London: Macmillan, 1962); Walter Bagehot, *The English Constitution* (London: Oxford University Press, 1961).
14 Ryan A. Vieira, *Time and Politics: Parliament and the Culture of Modernity and the British World* (Oxford: Oxford University Press, 2015).
15 In 1884, John A. Macdonald confidently pronounced that "the absolute, uncontrolled right to choose a Premier is, according to Bagehot … the only *personal* prerogative remaining to the Sovereign." Macdonald to Lieutenant Governor of Nova Scotia, 29 July 1884, cited in Sir Joseph Pope, *Correspondence of John A. Macdonald: Selections from the Correspondence of the Rt Hon. Sir John A. Macdonald, GCB* (Toronto: Oxford University Press, 1921), 316–17.
16 Library and Archives Canada (LAC), MG26A, John A. Macdonald Papers. Alexander Campbell to Macdonald, 7 March 1888, 83495–8.

17 David M. Craig, "Bagehot's Republicanism," in *The Monarchy and the British Nation, 1780 to the Present*, ed. Andrzej Olechnowicz (New York: Cambridge University Press, 2007), 141.
18 Richard Crossman, *The Diaries of a Cabinet Minister* (London: Hamilton Cape, 1975).
19 Andrew Coyne, "Canada's Potemkin Parliament: On the Surface, It Looks Almost like Westminster," *National Post*, 26 February 2015, A4.
20 David Cannadine, *Ornamentalism: How the British Saw Their Empire* (New York: Oxford University Press, 2001).
21 *Aniz Alani and the Prime Minister of Canada and the Governor General of Canada*, 2015 FC 649. A second, unsuccessful, motion, brought by Mr Alani, sought to expedite the proceedings by setting a pre-election (that is, pre–19 October 2015) hearing date. 2015 FC 859.
22 *Conacher v Canada (Prime Minister)*, 2009 FC 920, [2010] 3 FCR 411, para 53. For a contemporary discussion of convention and the constitution, see Aucoin et al., *Democratizing the Constitution*, 86–102; for a classic statement, see Sir Ivor Jennings, *The Law and the Constitution*, 5th ed. (London: University of London Press, 1959); and for a new, comparative treatment of the subject, see Brian Galligan and Scott Brenton, eds., *Constitutional Conventions in Westminster Systems: Controversies, Changes and Challenges* (Cambridge: Cambridge University Press, 2015).
23 Aucoin et al., *Democratizing the Constitution*, 65 (emphasis added).
24 *Reference re Senate Reform*, 2014 SCC 32.
25 W.P.M. Kennedy, "Law and Custom of the Canadian Constitution," *The Round Table* (December 1929), in *Constitutional Issues in Canada, 1900–1931*, ed. Robert MacGregor Dawson (London: Oxford University Press, 1933), 57.
26 *Maritime Bank v Receiver General of New Brunswick* (1892) AC 437.
27 Donald Horne, "Who Rules Australia?" *Daedalus* 114, no. 1 (Winter 1985), 177. See, too, Nicholas Aroney, Scott Prasser, and J.R. Nethercote, *Restraining Elective Dictatorship: The Upper House Solution?* (Crawley: University of Western Australia Press, 2008).
28 H. McD. Clokie, "Judicial Review, Federalism, and the Canadian Constitution," *Canadian Journal of Economics and Political Science* 8, no. 4 (November 1942): 553.
29 K.C. Wheare, *Federal Government*, 3rd ed. (London: Oxford University Press, 1953), 12 and 21.
30 LAC, Papers of Eugene Alfred Forsey, typed sheet headed, "Saskatchewan Brief," [1945] file 57/58 Disallowance of Provincial Acts (2), 1945, 1948.
31 Preston King, *Federalism and the Federation* (Baltimore, MD: Johns Hopkins University Press, 1982), 121.

32 Goldwin Smith, "The Political Destiny of Canada," *Canadian Monthly*, February 1880, 598.
33 R. Douglas Francis, "The Anatomy of Power: A Theme in the Writings of Harold Innis," in *Nation, Ideas, Identities*, ed. Michael D. Behiels and Marcel Martel (Don Mills, ON: Oxford University Press, 2000), 27.
34 Jean-Charles Falardeau, "Roots and Values in Canadian Lives," in *Visions of Canada: The Alan B. Plaunt Memorial Lectures, 1958–1992*, ed. Bernard Ostry and Janice Yalden (Montreal and Kingston: McGill-Queen's University Press, 2004), 91.
35 Marianne White, "Happy 400th Birthday Quebec City," *Leader-Post* (Regina), 4 July 2008, B12.
36 Michael James, "The Constitution in Australian Political Thought," in *The Constitutional Challenge: Essays on the Australian Constitution, Constitutionalism and Parliamentary Practice*, ed. James (St Leonards, NSW: Centre for Independent Studies, 1982), 16.
37 1 SCR 319, at para 106. For a discussion of this case, see David E. Smith, *The People's House of Commons: Theories of Democracy in Perspective* (Toronto: University of Toronto Press, 2007), 22 and 62.
38 Senate, "A Matter of Privilege: A Discussion Paper on Canadian Parliamentary Privilege in the 21st Century," interim report of the Standing Committee on Rules, Regulations, and the Rights of Parliament, June 2015, 1. See too, Warren J. Newman, "Parliamentary Privilege, the Canadian Constitution and the Courts," *Ottawa Law Review* 39, no. 3 (2008): 575–609.
39 1 SCR 667, para 41.
40 The quotation is from *Kielley v Carson* (1841), 4 Moore PC 63, cited in Norman Ward, "Called to the Bar of the House of Commons," *Canadian Bar Review* (May 1957), 530–1.
41 Daniel Leblanc, "RCMP Needs Time to Get Ready for New Duties," *Globe and Mail*, 6 February 2015, A4; Laura Ryckewaert, "MPs and Senators Unclear on Details of RCMP Security Takeover," *Hill Times*, 16 March 2015, 19.
42 Neil Nevitte, *The Decline of Deference: Canadian Value Change in Cross-National Perspective* (Peterborough, ON: Broadview, 1994). See, by contrast, Henry Fairlie, who writes that "the habits and concerns of politics are in the grain of British intellectual and professional life," and as a result power is exercised socially, through connection. *The Life in Politics* (London: Methuen, 1968), 249.
43 Alison Loat and Michael MacMillan, *Tragedy in the Commons: Former Members of Parliament Speak Out about Canada's Failing Democracy* (Toronto: Random House Canada, 2014), 7.

44 Quoted in Kate Malloy, "Politicians Should Reclaim Themselves," *Hill Times*, 5 May 2014, http://www.hilltimes.com/2014/05/03/politicians-should-reclaim-themselves-say-authors-of-new-book-tragedy-in-the-commons/28381.

45 W.L. Morton, "The Extension of the Franchise in Canada: A Study in Democratic Nationalism," *Canadian Historical Association Report* 22 (1943): 79.

46 *Re Initiative and Referendum Act*, (1919) AC 935 at 943.

47 A.H.F. Lefroy, *A Short Treatise on Canadian Constitutional Law* (Toronto: Carswell, 1918), 233.

48 S.D. Clark, *Movements of Social Protest in Canada, 1640–1840* (Toronto: University of Toronto Press, 1959), 4.

49 Ian Lumsden, ed., *Closing the 49th Parallel Etc: The Americanization of Canada* (Toronto: University of Toronto Press, 1970).

50 The paper appeared in Thomas A. Hockin, ed., *Apex of Power: The Prime Minister and Political Leadership in Canada*, 2nd ed. (Scarborough, ON: Prentice-Hall, 1977). The setting in which it was presented is discussed by Tom McMillan, "Robert L. Stanfield and Tom Symons: A Public Policy Partnership," in *Tom Symons: A Canadian Life*, ed. Ralph Heintzman, 117–68 (Ottawa: University of Ottawa Press, 2011). A more recent and extended analysis of the same phenomenon is offered by Donald Savoie, *Governing from the Centre: The Concentration of Power in Canadian Politics* (Toronto: University of Toronto Press, 1999).

51 In 1929, the *Report of the Royal Commission on Radio Broadcasting* (chaired by Sir John Aird) noted that "at present the majority of programs heard are from sources outside of Canada. It has been emphasized to us that the continued reception of these has a tendency to mould the minds of young people in the home to ideals and opinions that are not Canadian." *Report of the Royal Commission on Radio Broadcasting* (Ottawa: King's Printer, 1929), 6.

52 David E. Smith, "The Reforms of Keith Davey and Walter Gordon," in *The Regional Decline of a National Party: Liberals on the Prairies*, ed. Smith, 56–62 (Toronto: University of Toronto Press, 1981). Several decades after Aird, Davey, and Gordon chaired their own major inquiries, whose concerns reflected the exposure of Canada to US influence: Report of the Special Senate Committee on Mass Media, *The Uncertain Mirror* (Ottawa: Queen's Printer, 1970); Royal Commission on Canada's Economic Prospects, *Preliminary Report* (Ottawa: King's Printer, 1956); and Royal Commission on Canada's Economic Prospects, *Final Report* (Ottawa: King's Printer, 1957). Whatever the source of the anxiety, the response was eminently Canadian: appoint a royal commission to study the matter. For a thorough canvass of this topic, see Joy St John, "Americanization: Analysis of a Concept," MA thesis, University of Saskatchewan, 1999.

53 In his autobiography *Public Servant*, Sir Joseph Pope, in succession Private Secretary to Sir John A. Macdonald, assistant clerk to the Privy Council, and first permanent under-secretary of state for external affairs, commented, "It was, however, when His Excellency [Lord Aberdeen] proceeded to give reasons for his actions that he exposed the weakness and partiality of his course." Sir Joseph Pope, *Public Servant: The Memoirs of Sir Joseph Pope*, ed. Maurice Pope (Toronto: Oxford University Press, 1960), 110.

54 See Robert E. Hawkins, "Written Reasons and Codified Conventions in Matters of Prorogation and Dissolution," in *The Evolving Canadian Crown*, ed. Jennifer Smith and D. Michael Jackson, 99–116 (Montreal and Kingston: McGill-Queen's University Press, 2012).

55 Janet Ajzenstat, "Are Canadians Deferential?" The Idea File, https://janetajzenstat.wordpress.com/2008/11/21/are-canadians-deferential/. In British Columbia, the Constitution Act 1996 is a regular Act of the legislature and can be amended by normal majority vote. Campbell Sharman, "The Strange Case of a Provincial Constitution: The British Columbia Constitution Act," *Canadian Journal of Political Science*, 17, no. 1 (March 1984), 87–108.

56 Christopher Moore, "Our Canadian Republic," *Literary Review of Canada* (November 2008), http://reviewcanada.ca/magazine/2008/11/our-canadian-republic/.

57 Christopher Moore, *Three Weeks in Quebec City: The Meeting That Made Canada* (Toronto: Allen Lane, 2015), 100.

58 Donald S. Lutz, "The Purposes of American State Constitutions," *Publius* 12 (Winter 1982): 27–44.

59 Reginald George Trotter, *Canadian Federation: Its Origins and Achievement; A Study of Nation Building* (Toronto: J.M. Dent and Sons, 1924), 109.

60 Peter C. Oliver, *The Constitution of Independence: The Development of Constitutional Theory in Australia, Canada, and New Zealand* (Oxford: Oxford University Press, 2005), 143–7.

61 Douglas Cole, "The Problem of 'Nationalism' and 'Imperialism' in British Settlement Colonies," *Journal of British Studies* 10, no. 2 (May 1971): 165.

62 Robert C. Vipond, *Liberty and Community: Canadian Federalism and the Failure of the Constitution* (Albany: State University of New York Press, 1991), 72; David E. Smith, "A Period of Waiting Over: The Prairies in 1939," in *A Country of Limitations: Canada and the World in 1939*, ed. Norman Hillmer, Robert Bothwell, Roger Sarty, and Claude Beauregard, 94–108 (Ottawa: Canadian Committee for the History of the Second World War; National Defence, Directorate of History, 1996).

63 See Simcoe dispatch to Lord Portland in W.P.M. Kennedy, ed., *Statutes, Treaties and Documents of the Canadian Constitution, 1713–1929*, 2nd ed. (Toronto: Oxford University Press, 1930), 215.

64 John Graves Simcoe to the Duke of Portland, 21 December 1794, 3 Simcoe Papers, 235, cited in F.C. Buckley, *The Once and Future King: The Rise of Crown Government in America* (New York: Encounter Books, 2014), 94.
65 Frank Underhill, "The Cabinet and Leadership," *Canadian Forum*, January 1950, 116–17, in *Constitutional Issues in Canada, 1900–1931*, ed. Robert MacGregor Dawson (London: Oxford University Press, 1933), 135; J.R. Mallory, *The Structure of Canadian Government*. Rev. ed. (Toronto: Gage, 1984), 135.
66 Falardeau, "Roots and Values," 85.
67 Moore, "Our Canadian Republic."
68 D.J. Heasman, "Queen's Prerogative," *The Times*, 24 October 1985.
69 Michael Asch, *On Being Here to Stay: Treaties and Aboriginal Rights in Canada* (Toronto: University of Toronto Press, 2014); Nathan Tidridge, *The Queen at the Council Fire: The Treaty of Niagara, Reconciliation and the Dignified Crown of Canada* (Toronto: Dundurn, 2015).
70 Northrop Frye, *The Bush Garden: Essays on the Canadian Imagination* (Toronto: House of Anansi, 1995), x.

Chapter Two

1 Frank MacKinnon, *The Crown in Canada* (Calgary: McClelland and Stewart West, 1976), 76.
2 John Conway, "Politics, Culture, and Constitutions," in *Empire and Nations: Essays in Honour of Frederic H. Soward*, ed. Harvey L. Dyck and H. Peter Krosby (Toronto: University of Toronto Press, ca 1969), 15.
3 Michael Jackson, "Crown and Constitution," presentation to the Public Law Divisional Conference, Saskatchewan Ministry of Justice, Regina, 12 June 2014, 3. See too Philippe Lagassé, "The Crown and Prime Ministerial Power," *Canadian Parliamentary Review* 39, no. 2 (Summer 2016): 17–23.
4 Philippe Lagassé, "Parliamentary and Judicial Ambivalence toward Executive Prerogative Powers in Canada," *Canadian Public Administration* 55, no. 2 (June 2012): 157.
5 The literature discussing the exercise of prorogation in 2008 is extensive: a summary of interpretations is offered by Peter H. Russell and Lorne Sossin, eds., *Parliamentary Democracy in Crisis* (Toronto: University of Toronto Press, 2009); a critique of views expressed in that volume, which according to the critic were mainly opposed to the position of the government, is found in Andrew Potter, "Unbalanced Thoughts," *Literary Review of Canada*, July/August 2009, 3–4; and in Potter, "Letters and Responses" of the same issue, 30–1.

6 Tom Flanagan, "Only Voters Have a Right to Decide on the Coalition,"
   Globe and Mail, 9 January 2009, A13.
7 Forsey, *Royal Power of Dissolution of Parliament*.
8 Peter Neary, "The Morning after a General Election: The Vice-Regal Prerogative," *Canadian Parliamentary Review* 35 (Autumn 2012): 23–9.
9 "May Says Harper Minority Doesn't Make Him PM," 12 September 2015,
   http://thestarphoenix.com/news/local-news/may-says-harper-minority-
   doesnt-make-him-pm.
10 Carissima Mathen, Vanessa MacDonnell, Adam Dodek, Errol Mendes, Peter
   Oliver, and Michael Pal, "Who Governs in a Minority Is about More Than
   Just Politics," *National Post*, 15 October 2015, A10; John Ibbitson, "Johnston
   Could Play Crucial Role on Oct. 20," *Globe and Mail*, 13 October 2015, A6.
   Constitutional scholars cited in the latter article were Bruce Ryder, Adam
   Dodek, and David Schneiderman.
11 *McAteer v Canada (Attorney General)*, 2014 ONCA 578; and *McAteer et al v
   Attorney General of Canada*, 2013 ONSC 5895; *Geneviève Motard et al c Procureur
   générale du Canada et al*, CSQ 200-17-018455-139; *Aniz Alani and the Prime Minister of Canada and the Governor General of Canada*. The contrasting influence
   of oral and written communication on political and legal understanding is
   discussed by Maxwell Cameron, *Strong Constitutions: Social-Cognitive Origins
   of the Separation of Powers* (New York: Oxford University Press, 2013), 19–31.
12 Jennifer Smith and D. Michael Jackson, eds., *The Evolving Canadian Crown*
   (Montreal and Kingston: McGill-Queen's University Press, 2012); D.
   Michael Jackson and Philippe Lagassé, eds., *Canada and the Crown: Essays on
   Constitutional Monarchy* (Montreal and Kingston: McGill-Queen's University
   Press, 2013); and Michel Bédard and Philippe Lagassé, eds., *The Crown and
   Parliament* (Montreal: Éditions Yvon Blais, 2015). In addition to the edited
   works, a fourth volume on the Crown appeared in this period: D. Michael
   Jackson, *The Crown and Canadian Federalism* (Toronto: Dundurn, 2013).
13 A rare instance of a Canadian approximation to the political intimacy
   Morgan offers is found in Martin L. Friedland, *The Case of Valentine Shortis:
   A True Story of Crime and Politics in Canada* (Toronto: University of Toronto
   Press, 1986), in which Lord and Lady Aberdeen and two prime ministers
   (Tupper and Bowell) make crucial appearances.
14 Homepage, Constitution Unit, https://www.ucl.ac.uk/constitution-unit/;
   and "Monarchy, Church, and State," Constitution Unit, https://www.ucl.
   ac.uk/constitution-unit/research/monarchy-church-state.
15 David Schneiderman, *Red, White, and Kind of Blue: The Conservatives and the
   Americanization of Canadian Constitutional Culture* (Toronto: University of
   Toronto Press, 2015).

16 LAC, MG31, E46, Escott Reid Papers, vol. 28 (Constitutional Issues and Royal Title, 1942–1960), Robertson comment in reply to Reid, 27 July 1949.

17 Carolyn J. Tuohy, *Policy and Politics in Canada: Institutionalized Ambivalence* (Philadelphia, PA: Temple University Press, 1992).

18 John Fraser and D. Michael Jackson, "Foreword," in *The Evolving Canadian Crown*, ed. Jennifer Smith and D. Michael Jackson (Montreal and Kingston, McGill-Queen's University Press, 2012), viii.

19 John Fraser, *The Secret of the Crown: Canada's Affair with Royalty* (Toronto: House of Anansi, 2012), 70–1.

20 J. William Galbraith, *John Buchan: Model Governor General* (Toronto: Dundurn, 2013), 161.

21 *Guerin v The Queen*, [1984] 2 SCR 335 at 376.

22 Christopher McCreery, *The Order of Canada: Its Origins, History and Development* (Toronto: University of Toronto Press, 2005); and McCreery, *The Canadian Honours System* (Toronto: Dundurn, 2005).

23 Jackson, *Crown and Canadian Federalism*, 82.

24 Fang Lizhi, *The Most Wanted Man in China: My Journey from Scientist to Enemy of the State* (New York: Henry Holt, 2016), 63.

25 Andrew Marr, "Your Most Disobedient Servant Ma'am," *Sunday Times*, 18 October 2015, 4:2; see Tony Benn, *Free Radical Essays: New Century Essays* (New York: Continuum, 2003), chapter seven, "The Crown versus the People?"

26 Philippe Lagassé, "Accountability for National Defence: Ministerial Responsibility, Military Command and Parliamentary Oversight," IRPP Study no. 4 (March 2010).

27 Ibid., 6.

28 Earl Grey to Sir John Harvey, 31 March 1847, British House of Commons Papers (621), xiii, 1847–8, 79, quoted in R. MacGregor Dawson, *The Government of Canada*, 5th ed., rev. by Norman Ward (Toronto: University of Toronto Press, 1970), 236.

29 Lagassé, "Accountability for National Defence," 8.

30 David E. Smith, "Clarifying the Doctrine of Ministerial Responsibility as It Applies to the Government and Parliament of Canada," in Commission of Inquiry into the Sponsorship Program and Advertising Activities, *Restoring Accountability*, 101–43 (Ottawa: Public Works and Government Services, 2006).

31 LAC, MG 26, L. St Laurent Papers, vol. 253 (Speeches, Canadian Citizenship, Canadian Club Address, Montreal), 6 January 1946. Thereafter, citizenship by design was to be the Canadian way.

32 Sir Robert Herbert, ed., *Speeches on Canadian Affairs by Henry Howard Molyneux, Fourth Earl of Carnarvon* (London: John Murray, 1902), 127.

33 Records of the Governor General's Office, Philip Moore to My dear Prime Minister, 20 June 1978 (1990–91/016, box 13, file 535.1, vol. 1). See Records of the Governor General's Office, Michael Adeane (private secretary to the Queen) to Esmond Butler, 6 February 1970 (1990–91/016, box 14, file 535.2, vol.1). For a more complete discussion, see David E. Smith, "Canadianizing the Crown," in *The Invisible Crown: The First Principle of Canadian Government*, chapter three (Toronto: University of Toronto Press, 1995).

34 Mark D. Walters, "Succession to the Throne and the Architecture of the Constitution of Canada," in *The Crown in Parliament*, ed. Michel Bédard and Philippe Lagassé, 263–92 (Montreal: Éditions Yvon Blais, 2015).

35 *O'Donohue v Canada*, [2003] OJ No. 2764 at para 27 cited in ibid., 288.

36 Ibid., 289 at paras 21, 28.

37 See Peter W. Hogg, "Succession to the Throne," *National Journal of Constitutional Law* 33, no. 1 (Sept. 2014): 83–94. The Superior Court of Quebec supported the position of Professor Hogg and the federal government that a constitutional amendment was unnecessary, as Canada shared its monarchy with the United Kingdom. The Queen of the first is Queen of the second (para 126).

38 *Geneviève Motard et al c Procureur générale du Canada et al*, CSQ 200-17-018455-139.

39 This argument is presaged in Senator Joyal's remarks to the Senate on second reading of Bill C-53, "An Act to Assent to Alterations in the Law Touching the Succession to the Throne," 7 March 2013, http://www.parl.gc.ca/Content/Sen/Chamber/411/Debates/144db_2013-03-07-e.htm. Analysis of the legislation and support for the preceding argument are offered by Hogg, "Succession to the Throne," 84–94. In its judgment in February 2016, the Superior Court of Quebec accepted the argument of the government of Canada entirely; see note 38 above.

40 *Delgamuukw v British Columbia*, [1997] 3 SCR 1010, cited in Michael Asch, *On Being Here to Stay: Treaties and Aboriginal Rights in Canada* (Toronto: University of Toronto Press, 2014), 11.

41 Ibid. 111.

42 "New Advisory Committee on Vice-Regal Appointments," news release, 4 November 2012, http://news.gc.ca/web/article-en.do?nid=704959.

43 N. Kulish, "Presidential Vote Tests Merkel's Ailing Coalition in Germany," *New York Times*, 26 June 2010, A5; Kulish, "Merkel's Pick Wins German Presidency," *USA Today*, 1 July 2010, 7A.

44 Bora Laskin, *The British Tradition in Canadian Law* (London: Stevens and Sons, 1969), 118–19.

45 Ben Pimlott, *The Queen: Elizabeth II and the Monarchy* (London: HarperCollins, 1996), 671.

46 David E. Smith, *The Republican Option in Canada, Past and Present* (Toronto: University of Toronto Press, 1999).

47 *Debates of the Legislative Assembly of United Canada,* XI.1.1852–3, 13 September 1852, 397.

48 Simon Leys, "Chesterton: The Poet Who Dances with a Hundred Legs," in *The Hall of Uselessness: Collected Essays* (New York: New York Review of Books, 2013), 109.

49 Fraser, *Secret of the Crown,* 14.

50 Smith, "Political Destiny of Canada," 601.

51 Raphael Samuel, ed., *Patriotism: The Making and Unmaking of British National Identity,* 3 vols. (London: Routledge, 1989), 1:xix. A non-Marxist, Conor Cruise O'Brien, agreed: *On the Eve of the Millennium.* Massey Lectures for 1994 (Toronto: House of Anansi, 1994).

52 Goldwin French, "The Evangelical Creed in Canada," in *The Shield of Achilles: Aspects of Canada in the Victorian Age,* ed. W.L. Morton, 15–35 (Toronto: McClelland and Stewart, 1968).

53 Peter Scott, *Knowledge and Nation* (Edinburgh: Edinburgh University Press, 1990), 168, cited in Linda Colley, *Britons: Forging the Nation, 1707–1837* (New Haven, CT: Yale University Press, 1992), 373; David Malouf, "Made in England: Australia's British Inheritance," *Quarterly Essays* 12 (2003): 27. See too, David Cannadine, "The Context, Performance and Meaning of Ritual: The British Monarchy and the 'Invention of Tradition,' c. 1820–1977," in *The Invention of Tradition,* ed. Eric Hobsbawm and Terence Ranger, 101–64 (New York: Cambridge University Press, 1983).

54 Pimlott, *The Queen,* 39 and 240.

55 Duff Hart-Davis, ed., *King's Counsellor: Abdication and War; The Diaries of Sir Alan Lascelles* (London: Weidenfeld and Nicolson, 2006).

56 Harold Nicolson, *King George V* (London: Constable, 1953), 138, cited in Roy Jenkins, *Mr Balfour's Poodle: An Account of the Struggle between the House of Lords and the Government of Mr Asquith* (London: William Heinemann, 1954), 124.

57 Galbraith, *John Buchan,* 52.

58 Jenkins, *Mr Balfour's Poodle,* 180.

59 Canada, *A Consolidation of the Constitution Acts, 1867 to 1982* (Ottawa: Department of Justice, 2001).

60 Lawrence Martin, "G-G Steps Up on Democracy," *Globe and Mail,* 30 April 2013, A15.

61 Stephanie Levitz, "Governor General Lauds Stability Monarchy Brings," *Toronto Star,* 11 June 2016, A2.

62 Isaiah Berlin, *The Crooked Timber of Humanity: Chapters in the History of Ideas*, ed. Henry Hardy (Princeton, NJ: Princeton University Press, 1990), 41.
63 Andrew Heard, "The Governor General's Decision to Prorogue Parliament: Parliamentary Democracy Defended or Endangered?" Centre for Constitutional Studies, *Points of View, Discussion Paper*, no. 7 (January 2009); Aucoin, Jarvis, and Turnbull, *Democratizing the Constitution*; John Ibbitson, "The Speaker's Ruling – Harper's Headache: Prospect of Contempt Ruling before Election," *Globe and Mail*, 10 March 2011, 1/6.
64 Janice Dickson, "Liberals Announce Advisory Board for Senate Appointments," iPolitics, 19 January 2016, https://ipolitics.ca/2016/01/19/liberals-announce-advisory-board-for-senate-appointments/.
65 John Ibbitson, "Five Ways a Hung Parliament Could Swing in October," *Globe and Mail*, 27 May 2015, http://www.theglobeandmail.com/news/politics/globe-politics-insider/five-ways-a-hung-parliament-could-swing-in-october/article24615741/?from=25348097.
66 Peter Boyce, *The Queen's Other Realms: The Crown and Its Legacy in Australia, Canada and New Zealand* (Sydney: Federation Press, 2008), 180–2.
67 Peter W. Johnston and Stanley D. Hotop, "Patches on an Old Garment or New Wineskins for New Wine? (Constitutional Reform in Western Australia – Evolution or Revolution?)," *University of Western Australia Law Review* 20 (1990), 430.

Chapter Three

1 *Debates of the Legislative Assembly of United Canada*, 27 March 1856 (XIII. 11.1856), 897.
2 William H. Riker, "The Justification of Bicameralism," *International Political Science Review* 13, no. 1 (1992): 101–16.
3 Canada, House of Commons, Canadian Sessional Papers, vol. 28, no. 246 (1914), "Return to an Order of the House of Commons, Dated March 2, 1914," and "Supplementary Return," 15.
4 J. Patrick Boyer, *Our Scandalous Senate* (Toronto: Dundurn, 2014), 181 and 217–18.
5 Joseph Pope, *Confederation: Being a Series of Hitherto Unpublished Documents Bearing on the British North America Act* (Toronto: Carswell, 1895), 117.
6 Wheare, *Federal Government*: "The federal principle has come to mean what it does because the United States has come to be what it is," 12; and, "It seems justifiable to conclude that although the Canadian Constitution is quasi-federal in law, it is predominantly federal in practice," 21.

7 Memorandum on Representation of the Maritime Provinces, *Canadian Sessional Papers, 1914*, no. 118a, reprinted in *Constitutional Issues in Canada, 1900–1931*, ed. R. MacGregor Dawson (London: Oxford University Press, 1933), 173–5.

8 Lefroy, *Short Treatise on Canadian Constitutional Law*, 41–2.

9 *Commons Debates*, 8 March 1868, 280.

10 *Parliamentary Debates on the Subject of the Confederation of the British North American Provinces*, Quebec, 1865 (Ottawa: King's Printer, 1951), 30–1 (Hereafter *PD*).

11 *PD*, 38.

12 *Commons Debates*, 2 May 1870, 1287.

13 *Commons Debates*, 25 April 1870, 1178.

14 Norman Ward, *The Canadian House of Commons: Representation*, 2nd ed. (Toronto: University of Toronto Press, 1963), 23.

15 Kennedy, "Law and Custom in the Canadian Constitution."

16 Richard Simeon, *Political Science and Federalism: Seven Decades of Scholarly Engagement* (Kingston: Institute of Intergovernmental Relations, 2002), x.

17 Peter S. Onuf, *The Origins of the Federal Republic: Jurisdictional Controversies in the United States, 1775–1786* (Philadelphia: University of Pennsylvania Press, 1983), 24.

18 J. Murray Beck, *The Government of Nova Scotia* (Toronto: University of Toronto Press, 1957), 12; Frank MacKinnon, *The Government of Prince Edward Island* (Toronto: University of Toronto Press, 1951), 136.

19 *Commons Debates*, 3 April 1868, 455.

20 Dom Benoit, *La Vie de Monseigneur Taché* (Montreal, 1904), 11:195–96, cited in Ramsay Cook, *Canada and the French Canadian Question* (Toronto: Macmillan, 1971), 183.

21 See Robert A. Dahl, *How Democratic Is the American Constitution?* (New Haven, CT: Yale University Press), 2002; Adam Liptak, "Smaller States Find Outside Clout Growing in Senate," *New York Times*, 11 March 2013, A1/12.

22 F.A. Kunz, *The Modern Senate of Canada, 1925–63: A Re-Appraisal* (Toronto: University of Toronto Press, 1965).

23 A recent interpretation is found in Michael S. Cross, *A Biography of Robert Baldwin: The Morning-Star of Memory* (Don Mills: Oxford University Press, 2012).

24 C.E.S. Franks, "The Canadian Senate in Modern Times," in *Protecting Canadian Democracy: The Senate You Never Knew*, ed. Serge Joyal (Montreal and Kingston: McGill-Queen's University Press, 2003), 170.

25 For an analysis of the relationship between policy and the constitution, see Roderick A. Macdonald and Robert Wolfe, "Canada's Third National

Policy: The Epiphenomenal or the Real Constitution?" *University of Toronto Law Journal* 59 (Fall 2009): 469–523.

26 Moore, *1867: How the Fathers Made a Deal.*

27 Boyer, *Our Scandalous Senate,* 172.

28 *Reference re Resolution to Amend the Constitution,* [1981] 1 SCR 753; *Reference re the Secession of Quebec,* [1998] 2 SCR 217; *Reference re Senate Reform,* 2014 SCC 32.

29 See J.E. Hodgetts, *Pioneer Public Service: An Administrative History of the United Canadas, 1841–1867* (Toronto: University of Toronto Press, 1955).

30 On the emergence of the first feature, see Norman Ward, "The Formative Years of the House of Commons, 1867–91," *Canadian Journal of Economics and Political Science* 18, no. 4 (November 1952): 431–51.

31 Provinces that had legislative councils, with their dates of abolition, were Manitoba 1876, New Brunswick 1891, Prince Edward Island 1893, Nova Scotia 1928, and Quebec 1968.

32 The words belong to J.W. Johnston, leader of the Conservative opposition in the colony of Nova Scotia, writing in the *Nova Scotian,* 3 March 1851, 69–70. They are found in K.G. Pryke, "Balance and Stability: Nova Scotia Considers an Elective Chamber," in *Documentary Problems in Canadian History: Pre-Confederation,* ed. J.M. Bumsted, 185–7 (Georgetown: Irwin-Dorsey, 1969).

33 J.G. Bourinot, "The Canadian Dominion and the Proposed Australian Constitution: A Study in Comparative Politics," *Transactions of the Royal Society of Canada, Section 11,* 2nd ser., vol. 1 (1895): 19.

34 *PD,* 88.

35 *Aniz Alani and the Prime Minister of Canada and the Governor General of Canada.* A second, unsuccessful motion, brought by Mr Alani, sought to expedite the proceedings by setting a pre-election (that is, 19 October 2015) hearing date. Citation 2015 FC 859.

36 *Aniz Alani v The Prime Minister of Canada, The Governor General of Canada, and The Queen's Privy Council for Canada,* 2016 FC 1139.

37 Roy Jenkins, *Mr Balfour's Poodle: An Account of the Struggle between the House of Lords and the Government of Mr Asquith* (London: William Heinemann, 1954). In this study of the parliamentary crisis of 1909 and 1910, the sovereigns (Edward VII and George V) are assigned significant parts, especially as regards their relationship with the prime minister.

38 "The Appointment of Extra Senators under Section 26 of the British North America Act," *Canadian Journal of Economics and Political Science* 12 (May 1946): 159–67.

39 B. Curry, "Secret Committee, Seeking Non-Partisans: How Harper Found the Next G-G," *Globe and Mail,* 12 July 2010, A1.

40 John Ibbitson, "Johnston's Term Will Continue into 2017," *Globe and Mail*, 18 March 2015, A3.
41 Ibid. Convention – in the sense of customary practice – may change abruptly, even when it concerns a subject at the very heart of the constitution, such as gubernatorial selection of a first minister. For example, after nearly a century of delegate conventions selecting party leaders, section 49.5(2) of a private member's bill (C-586) passed through Parliament in June 2015, makes it optional for a caucus to cast a vote on leadership. This change is discussed in further detail in chapter four.
42 Serge Joyal, "Conclusion: The Senate as the Embodiment of the Federal Principle," in *Protecting Canadian Democracy: The Senate You Never Knew*, ed. Joyal (Montreal and Kingston: McGill-Queen's University Press, 2003), 285.
43 Ibid.
44 See Government of Canada, "Backgrounder – Senate Appointments Process," 2015, http://www.democraticinstitutions.gc.ca/eng/content/backgrounder-senate-appointments-process; "Government Announces Immediate Senate Reform," news release, 3 December 2015, http://news.gc.ca/web/article-en.do?nid=1023449; and "Annex: Qualifications and Merit-Based Assessment Criteria," 2015, http://www.democraticinstitutions.gc.ca/eng/content/annex-qualifications-and-merit-based-assessment-criteria.
45 George Dangerfield, *The Strange Death of Liberal England* (New York: Capricorn Books, 1961).
46 See R. MacGregor Dawson, ed., *The Principle of Official Independence: With Particular Reference to the Political History of Canada* (Toronto: S.B. Gundy, 1922); one of its nine chapters is titled, "The Senator."
47 Office of the Commissioner for Federal Judicial Affairs Canada, "Number of Federally Appointed Judges as of February 1, 2017," 2017, http://www.fja-cmf.gc.ca/appointments-nominations/judges-juges-eng.aspx.
48 See "Terms of Reference," Advisory Committee on Vice-Regal Appointments.
49 Oliver, *Constitution of Independence*.
50 Gil Rémillard, with the collaboration of Andrew Turner, "Senate Reform: Back to Basics," in Joyal, *Protecting Canadian Democracy*, 108, emphasis added.
51 *AmericasBarometer*.
52 Brock, "Independence of Election Administration from Government."
53 David E. Smith, "Party Government, Representation and National Integration in Canada," in *Party Government and Regional Representation in Canada,*

ed., Peter Aucoin, 1–68 (Toronto: University of Toronto Press in Cooperation with the Royal Commission on the Economic Union and Development Prospects for Canada, 1985).

54 Auditor General, *Senators' Expenses,* June Report of the Auditor General to the Senate of Canada, 2015, www.oag-bvg.gc.ca/internet/English/parl_otp_201506_e_40494.html.

55 Government of Canada, "The Senate – Report on Activities," 2013, http://publications.gc.ca/site/eng/9.506415/publication.html#.

56 Judith Brett, "Parliament, Meetings and Civil Society," Australia, Senate Occasional Lecture Series, 27 July 2001, http://www.aph.gov.au/About_Parliament/Senate/Powers_practice_n_procedures/pops/~/link.aspx?_id=12EB7F88D50B4A8D828E543A8319A37E&_z=z.

57 George W. Ross, *Getting into Parliament and After* (Toronto: W. Briggs, 1913), 7.

58 *AmericasBarometer*, 38.

59 *Reference re: Legislative Authority of Parliament in Relation to the Upper House,* [1980] 1 SCR 54 at 67, emphasis added.

60 Chantal Hébert, "Quebec Won't Discuss Senate Reform in Isolation," *Chronicle Herald,* 16 June 2015, http://thechronicleherald.ca/opinion/1293447-hébert-quebec-won't-discuss-senate-reform-in-isolation.

61 Louis Massicotte, "Possible Repercussions of an Elected Senate on Official Language Minorities in Canada," Report for the Office of the Commissioner of Official Languages, March 2007, 16.

62 Ibid.

63 See, for example, Office of the Commissioner of Official Languages, *Investigation Report of Complaints concerning the Redistribution of Federal Ridings Proposed by the Electoral Boundaries Commission for the Province of New Brunswick* (Ottawa, July 1996); see too *Raîche v R.,* Federal Court of Canada Trial Division, filed September 2003: file T-1730-03; and John C. Courtney, "Community of Interest and Effective Representation," chapter ten of *Commissioned Ridings: Designing Canada's Electoral Districts* (Montreal and Kingston: McGill-Queen's University Press, 2001).

64 "Working Together" is a twenty-two-page digest of ideas presented at a symposium on Senate reform, organized by the Faculty of Law of the University of Ottawa on 28 January 2015.

65 Campbell Clark, "Ground Shifts with This Week's Red Chamber Rebellion," *Globe and Mail,* 10 June 2016, A3; Jeffrey Simpson, "In Death, New Life for Parliament," *Globe and Mail,* 22 June 2016, B19.

66 Richard Hofstadter, *The Age of Reform: From Bryan to FDR* (New York: Vintage, 1960), 23.

Chapter Four

1 See the Memorandum on Representation of the Maritime Provinces; and Pope, ed., *Confederation*, 69.

2 John D. Fair, "House of Lords Reform, 1917–18," chapter nine, *British Inter-party Conferences: A Study of the Procedure of Conciliation in British Politics, 1867–1921* (Oxford: Clarendon, 1980).

3 Royal Commission on the Reform of the House of Lords in 2000, *A House for the Future* (London: Stationery Office, 2000), Cm. 4534.

4 David E. Smith, "The Westminster Model in Ottawa: A Study in the Absence of Influence," *British Journal of Canadian Studies* 15, nos 1 and 2 (2002): 54–64.

5 A.F. Madden, "'Not for Export': The Westminster Model of Government and British Colonial Practice," *Journal of Imperial and Commonwealth History* 8, no. 1 (October 1979): 16.

6 Robert A. MacKay, *The Unreformed Senate of Canada* (London: Humphrey Milford, for Oxford University Press, 1926); Kunz, *Modern Senate of Canada*; and Colin Campbell, *The Canadian Senate: A Lobby Within* (Toronto: Macmillan, 1978).

7 *Commons Debates*, 1872, 926; and *Commons Debates*, 1892, 3255, quoted in Ward, *Canadian House of Commons*, 30.

8 Saskatchewan Archives Board, James G. Gardiner Papers, address, "The British System of Parliamentary Government," delivered by James G. Gardiner at the Annual Meeting of the Toronto Board of Trade, 14 February 1938. For the origin of this practice, see R. MacGregor Dawson, *The Government of Canada*, 5th ed., rev. Norman Ward (Toronto: University of Toronto Press, 1970), 329–30.

9 *Debates of the Legislative Assembly of United Canada*, XI.11.1852–3, 1105.

10 Mackenzie to Dufferin, 28 May 1877, *Dufferin-Carnarvon Correspondence, 1874–1878*, ed. C.W. de Kiewiet and F.H. Underhill, 355–6 (Toronto: Champlain Society, 1955) (emphasis added).

11 Lord Elgin to Lord Grey, 22 January 1848, in *The Elgin-Grey Papers, 1846–1852*, 4 vols., ed. Sir Arthur G. Doughty, 1:119 (Ottawa: King's Printer, 1937).

12 *Commons Debates*, 12 February 1923, 208–31, repr. in R. MacGregor Dawson, *Constitutional Issues in Canada, 1900–1931* (London: Oxford University Press, 1933), 135–45.

13 George Eliot, *Felix Holt: The Radical*, ed. with intro. by Peter Coveney (Harmondsworth, UK: Penguin Books, 1972), 302–3.

14 Maurice Cowling, *1867: Disraeli, Gladstone and Revolution – The Passing of the Second Reform Bill* (Cambridge: Cambridge University Press, 1967), 4; Cross, *Biography of Robert Baldwin*, 45.

15 Nathan S. Elliott, "'We Have Asked for Bread and You Gave Us a Stone': Western Farmers and the Siege of Ottawa" (MA thesis, University of Saskatchewan, 2004), 87.

16 H.J. Hanham, *Elections and Party Management: Politics in the Time of Disraeli and Gladstone* (London: Longmans Green, 1959), 202.

17 Gordon Stewart, *The Origins of Canadian Politics: A Comparative Approach* (Vancouver: University of British Columbia Press, 1986).

18 Ward, "Formative Years of the House of Commons."

19 Michael Adams and Andrew Griffith, "Take Pride That Parliament Reflects the Face of Canada," *Globe and Mail*, 13 January 2016, A12.

20 Sarah Katherine Gibson and Arthur Milnes, eds., *Canada Transformed: The Speeches of Sir John A. Macdonald; A Bicentennial Celebration* (Toronto: McClelland and Stewart, 2014), 132.

21 Bea Vongdouangchanh, "Parliamentary Democracy Is 'Sick,' 'Tattered, and Needs Help,'" *Hill Times*, 28 October 2013, 1/4; Allan Cutler, "Time to Worry about the State of Democracy," *Hill Times*, 31 March 2014, 13; Dale Smith, "Who Killed Question Period?," *National Post*, 29 May 2015, A13; and John Ibbitson, "Ignatieff: It's Time to Fix Parliament," *Globe and Mail*, 2 February 2013, F3.

22 Loat and MacMillan, *Tragedy in the Commons*.

23 Ibid., 180, 85, and 7.

24 Jane Hilderman and David Campbell, "A Chance to Change the Culture in Ottawa," *National Post*, 11 August 2015, A9.

25 Ken Dryden, "Parliamentary Discontent: Many MPs Leave Politics Disillusioned – But What Does That Really Mean for Our Democracy?," *Literary Review of Canada* (June 2014): 6–7.

26 Alan Clark, *Diaries* (London: Phoenix Giant, 1993), 120.

27 "The Earl of Romney," *Telegraph*, 10 June 2004, http://www.telegraph.co.uk/news/obituaries/1464065/The-Earl-of-Romney.html.

28 Hugh Berrington, "MPs and Their Constituents in Britain: The History of the Relationship," in *Representatives of the People?: Parliamentarians and Constituents in Western Democracies*, ed. Vernon Bogdanor (Brookfield, VT: Gower Publishing, 1985), 15–16.

29 Vernon Bogdanor, "Conclusion," in *Representatives of the People?*, ed. Bogdanor, 295 and 300.

30 Robert A. Caro, *The Years of Lyndon Johnson*, 4 vols. (New York: Vintage Books, 1982, 1990, 2002, 2012).

31 Harold Nicolson, *Diaries and Letters, 1930–1939*, ed. Nigel Nicolson, 3 vols. (London: Collins, 1966–8), 1:296.

32 Bob Rae, *What's Happened to Politics?* (Toronto: Simon and Schuster Canada, 2015), 25–6.

33 Anthony H. Birch, *Representative and Responsible Government: An Essay on the British Constitution* (London: Allen and Unwin, 1964), 23.

34 *Debates of the Legislative Assembly of United Canada,* XI.111.1852–3, March 1853, p. 1832.

35 "The Way Home to Westminster," *Globe and Mail,* 7 December 2013, F9. See as well, Michael Chong, "Reform Act, 2014 Backgrounder," 11 September 2014, http://michaelchong.ca/2014/09/11/reform-act-2014-backgrounder/.

36 Ally Foster, "From PMO to MP: Shifting the Political Power Structure," *Power and Influence* (Fall 2015), 31.

37 F. Leslie Seidle, "The Canada Elections Act: The House of Commons and the Parties," in *The Canadian House of Commons: Essays in Honour of Norman Ward,* ed. John C. Courtney, 113–34 (Calgary: University of Calgary Press, 1985).

38 Tom Flanagan, "This Is No Way to Choose a Leader," *Globe and Mail,* 28 December 2013, F2.

39 Stéphane Dion, "Improving Canadian Democracy," notes for an address delivered in the context of a debate on Bill C-586, University of Ottawa, 25 November 2014.

40 Editorials, *Globe and Mail,* 21 and 25 August 2015, A10 (both); see too, Daniel Leblanc, "PMO Tampering Appalls Ex-House Clerk," *Globe and Mail,* 8 May 2015, A4.

41 2015 SCC 5.

42 Margaret Somerville, "A Charter Issue That Demands a Vote of Conscience," *Globe and Mail,* 24 February 2016, A15.

43 Jack Stilborn, "Reforming Our Thinking: The Key to Real Parliamentary Reform," *Hill Times,* 17 February 2014, 10.

44 In the Matter of Marriage Commissioners Appointed under *The Marriage Act, 1995,* SS 1995, c M-4.1; and in the Matter of a Reference by the Lieutenant Governor to the Court of Appeal under *The Constitutional Questions Act, RSS 1978,* c C-29, 2010 SKCA, paras 2 and 3.

45 Anthony King, *Who Governs Britain?* (Milton Keynes, UK: Penguin Random House, 2015), 55.

46 John C. Courtney, "Can Canada's Past Electoral Reforms Help Us to Understand the Debate over Its Method of Election?" in *Imperfect Democracies: The Democratic Deficit in Canada and the United States,* ed. Patti Tamara Lenard and Richard Simeon (Vancouver: UBC Press, 2012), 132.

47 Roy Jenkins, *Gladstone* (London: Macmillan, 1995), 535.
48 Gloria Galloway, "Poll Sees Mixed Views on Electoral Reform," *Globe and Mail*, 2 December 2015, A6.
49 John Robson, "Save Our Democracy," *National Post*, 2 November 2015, A11.
50 Andrew Stark, "Trudeau's Big Idea and the Art of Compromise," *Globe and Mail*, 19 June 2015, A17.
51 Alan Cairns, "The Electoral System and the Party System, 1921–1965," *Canadian Journal of Political Science* 1 (March 1968): 55–80.
52 See Sir Goronwy Edwards, "The Emergence of Majority Rule in English Parliamentary Elections," *Transactions of the Royal Historical Society*, 5th ser. 14 (1964): 175–96; and Edwards, "The Emergence of Majority Rule in the Procedure of the House of Commons," *Transactions of the Royal Historical Society*, 5th ser. 15 (1965): 165–87. I am indebted to my late colleague Duff Spafford for introducing me to these sources.
53 H.F. Angus, "The British Columbia Election, June, 1952," in *Voting in Canada*, ed. John C. Courtney, 35–8 (Scarborough, ON: Prentice-Hall of Canada, 1967).
54 M.S. Donnelly, *The Government of Manitoba* (Toronto: University of Toronto Press, 1963), 75.
55 Michael Pal, "Why the Top Court Must Weigh In on Electoral Reform," *Globe and Mail*, 15 January 2016, A14; Dennis Pilon, "Constitution No Barrier to Reform," *National Post*, 1 February 2016, A8.
56 Joan Bryden, "Move to Proportional Rep Might Require Constitutional Amendment: Joyal," iPolitics, 3 February 2016, http://ipolitics.ca/2016/02/03/move-to-proportional-rep-might-require-constitutional-amendment-joyal/.
57 Paul L. Montgomery, "Belgian King Asks Prime Minister to End Impasse," *New York Times*, 7 May 1988, http://www.nytimes.com/1988/05/07/world/belgian-king-asks-prime-minister-to-end-impasse.html.
58 Ibid.
59 Tony Judt, "Is There a Belgium?," *New York Review of Books* 46, no. 19 (2 December 1999).
60 Ibbitson, "Five Ways a Hung Parliament Could Swing."
61 Bryden, "Move to Proportional Rep."
62 Vernon Bogdanor, *The New British Constitution* (Oxford: Hart Publishing, 2009).

Chapter Five

1 Bogdanor, *New British Constitution*, 40.
2 Ibid., 123 and 126 (emphasis added).

3 *Commons Debates*, 20 January 1908, col. 1571.
4 Bogdanor, *New British Constitution*, 273.
5 *Parliamentary Debates on the Subject of the Confederation of the British North American Provinces*, 30–1.
6 Adam Nicolson, *God's Secretaries: The Making of the King James Bible* (New York: HarperCollins Publishers, 2003), 13.
7 *Debates of the Legislative Assembly of United Canada*, 13 September 1852 (XI.I.1852–3), 397.
8 Raymond Bréton, "Multiculturalism and Canadian Nation-Building," in *The Politics of Gender, Ethnicity, and Language in Canada*, ed. Alan Cairns and Cynthia Williams (Toronto: University of Toronto Press, in cooperation with the Royal Commission on the Economic Union and Development Prospects for Canada, 1985), 34:31.
9 Bogdanor, *New British Constitution*, 7.
10 *Re Initiative and Referendum Act* (1919) AC 935.
11 Lord Elgin to Lord Grey, 27 August 1849, in Doughty, *Elgin-Grey Papers*, 2:452.
12 Michael Den Tandt, "Duffy Laid the Tories Low: Now Party Can Make Senate Abolition a Winning Proposition," *National Post*, 24 April 2016, http://news.nationalpost.com/news/canada/michael-den-tandt-duffy-laid-the-tories-low-now-party-can-make-senate-abolition-a-winning-proposition.
13 John D. Whyte, "A Case for the Republican Option," in *Canada and the Crown: Essays on Constitutional Monarchy*, ed. D. Michael Jackson and Philippe Lagassé (Montreal and Kingston: McGill-Queen's University Press, 2013), 122–3.
14 Nelson Wiseman, "Phony Laws? Thank Goodness," *Globe and Mail*, 9 July 2014, A9.
15 Bea Vongdouangchanh, "Public Institutions Need 'Reboot' to Restore Trust, PPF Report Says," *Hill Times*, 2 November 2015, 23. The full title of the Public Policy Forum Report is "Time to Reboot: Nine Ways to Restore Trust in Canada's Public Institutions."
16 Cross, *Biography of Robert Baldwin*, 5.
17 Lord Russell to Poulett Thomson (Lord Sydenham), 16 October 1839, repr. in *Statutes, Treaties, and Documents of the Canadian Constitution, 1713–1929*, ed. W.P.M. Kennedy (Toronto: Oxford University Press, 1930), 421 and 422.
18 *Debates of the Legislative Assembly of United Canada*, VIII.III.1849, 2437.
19 LAC, MG 26A, John A. Macdonald Papers, 51:2047–9. I wish to thank Vincent Pouliot for bringing this reference to my attention.

20 For an extended discussion of language and politics, see James Boyd White, *When Words Lose Their Meaning: Constitutions and Reconstitutions of Language, Character and Community* (Chicago: University of Chicago Press, 1984).

21 Fabien Gélinas and Léonid Sirota, "Constitutional Conventions and Senate Reform," *Revue québécoise de droit constitutionnel* 5 (2013): 117.

22 George Orwell, "Politics and the English Language," http://www.orwell.ru/library/essays/politics/english/e_polit/.

23 *Commons Debates*, 9 January 1896, 41 and 39.

24 See Ward, "Formative Years of the House of Commons."

25 Donald Savoie, *Court Government and the Collapse of Accountability in Canada and the United Kingdom* (Toronto: University of Toronto Press, 2008); see as well, Savoie, *Governing from the Centre*.

26 *R v Duffy*, 2016 ONCJ 220, paras 1029–32 and 1034–37, http://canlii.ca/t/gplvk. See as well, Josh Wingrove, "Former MP Describes PMO's Tight Control," *Globe and Mail*, 8 September 2014, A5. A former Conservative MP, Brent Rathgeber wrote *Irresponsible Government: The Decline of Parliamentary Democracy in Canada* (Toronto: Dundurn, 2014).

27 Senate, Parliament of Australia, "What Is Wrong with an Elective Dictatorship?" 1994, http://www.aph.gov.au/sitecore/content/Home/About_Parliament/Senate/Powers_practice_n_procedures/hamer/chap11.

28 Lord Hailsham, "Elective Dictatorship," Richard Dimbleby Lecture, *Listener,* 21 October 1976, 496–500.

29 Canadian Press, "Duffy Acquittal Should be Wake-Up Call to Hold Politicians to Account, Stephen Harper's Lawyer Says," 26 April 2016, https://www.thestar.com/news/canada/2016/04/26/harper-played-no-role-in-rcmp-decision-to-charge-duffy-his-lawyer-argues.html.

30 Maxwell Henderson, *Plain Talk: Memoirs of an Auditor General* (Toronto: McClelland and Stewart, 1984), 162.

31 Norman Ward, *The Public Purse: A Study in Canadian Democracy* (Toronto: University of Toronto Press, 1962). See also Ann Chaplin, *Officers of Parliament: Accountability, Virtue and the Constitution* (Montreal: Éditions Yvon Blais, 2011); and Kevin Page, with Vern Stenlund, *Unaccountable: Truth and Lies on Parliament Hill* (Toronto: Viking, 2015).

32 Gloria Galloway, "Retroactively Shielding RCMP 'Perilous' Precedent: Watchdog," *Globe and Mail*, 15 May 2015, 1/8; Galloway, "Information Czar Takes Ottawa to Court over Long-Gun Data," *Globe and Mail*, 24 June 2015, 1; and Josh Wingrove, "Ottawa, Privacy Watchdog at Odds over Information Ruling," *Globe and Mail*, 18 June 2014, 10.

33 John D. Whyte, "Constitutional Change and Constitutional Durability," *Journal of Parliamentary and Political Law* 5 (2011): 428 and 429.

34 G. Drewry, "Reform of the Legislative Process: Some Neglected Questions," *Parliamentary Affairs* 25, no. 4 (1972): 298–9, quoted in Alexandra Kelso, *Parliamentary Reform at Westminster* (Manchester: Manchester University Press, 2009), 42.

35 David Schneiderman, "How to Tame a PM's Prerogative: In a Showdown with the Crown, Parliament Can Use Statute to Take Matters into Its Own Hands," *Globe and Mail*, 10 March 2010, A15.

36 "Straight-Talking Fraser Strikes Fear on the Hill," *Globe and Mail*, 12 February 2004, 4 (emphasis added).

37 Andrew Coyne, "Elections Act Portends Future Crisis," *National Post*, 10 April 2014, A4.

38 "Democracy Watch Announces Summer Blockbuster Opening across Canada: Stop the SuPremos.ca," news release, Democracy Watch, 18 June 2014, http://democracywatch.ca/20140619-democracy-watch-announces-summer-blockbuster-coming-to-canada-stopthesupremos-ca/.

39 Amartya Sen, *Democracy as Freedom* (New York: Anchor Books, 2000), 156.

40 Edmund S. Morgan, *Inventing the People: The Rise of Popular Sovereignty in England and America* (New York: W.W. Norton, 1988).

41 Ernst H. Kantorowicz, *The King's Two Bodies: A Study in Mediaeval Political Theology* (Princeton, NJ: Princeton University Press, 1957), 382.

42 Gordon S. Wood, *Representation in the American Revolution* (Charlottesville: University Press of Virginia, 1969), 10–11 and 7.

43 P. Weller and D. Jaensch, eds., *Responsible Government in Australia* (Richmond, Victoria: Drummond Publications, 1980), cited in James A. Thomson, "State Constitutional Law: Gathering the Fragments," *Western Australian Law Review* 16 (1985): 95.

44 Norman Hillmer, *O.D. Skelton: A Portrait of Canadian Ambition* (Toronto: University of Toronto Press, 2015), 55.

45 Ibid., esp. chapter eight.

46 F.R. Scott, "W.L.M.K.," in *The Blasted Pine: An Anthology of Satire, Invective and Disrespectful Verse by Canadian Writers*, ed. F.R. Scott and A.J.M. Smith, 27–8 (Toronto: Macmillan Canada, 1962).

47 W.L. Mackenzie King, *The Message of the Carillon and Other Addresses* (Toronto: Macmillan of Canada, 1928), 97.

48 I have taken this idea from the work of James Boyd White, *Acts of Hope: Creating Authority in Literature, Law, and Politics* (Chicago: University of Chicago Press, 1994); see chapter two, "Shakespeare's Richard II: Imagining the Modern World."

49 Jennings, *The Law and the Constitution*; Dicey, *Introduction to the Study of the Law*.

50 Forsey, *Royal Power of Dissolution of Parliament*, xvi.

51 John Ibbitson, *Stephen Harper* (Toronto: McClelland and Stewart, 2015), 285.

52 Flanagan, "Only Voters Have a Right to Decide on the Coalition."

53 Peter H. Russell, "Educating Canadians on the Crown: A Diamond Jubilee Challenge," in *Canada and the Crown: Essays on Constitutional Monarchy*, ed. D. Michael Jackson and Philippe Lagassé (Montreal and Kingston: McGill-Queen's University Press, 2013), 83.

54 Ibid., 81 and 83. An examination of existing practice in regard to cabinet manuals or similar documents is found in James W.J. Bowden and Nicholas A. MacDonald, "Writing the Unwritten: The Officialization of Constitutional Convention in Canada, the United Kingdom, New Zealand and Australia," *Journal of Parliamentary and Political Law* 6 (2012): 365–400. Support for the proposition of reducing conventions to writing may be found in *Public Policy Forum*, "Government Formation in Canada" (Ottawa Roundtable), 21 March 2011.

55 P.H. Russell, "Learning to Live with Minority Parliaments," in *Parliamentary Democracy in Crisis*, ed. P.H. Russell and L. Sossin (Toronto: University of Toronto Press, 2009), quoted in Robert E. Hawkins, "Written Reasons and Codified Conventions in Matters of Prorogation and Dissolution," in *The Evolving Canadian Crown*, ed. Jennifer Smith and D. Michael Jackson (Montreal and Kingston: McGill-Queen's University Press, 2012), 106–7.

56 Whyte, "Constitutional Change and Constitutional Durability," 427.

57 House of Lords and House of Commons (HL Paper 265-1/HC 1212-1), Joint Committee on Conventions, "Conventions of the UK Parliament," Report of Session 2005–6, 1:11.

58 Adrienne Clarkson, *Heart Matters* (Toronto: Viking, 2006).

59 Dufferin to Macdonald, 23 October 1873, in *Correspondence of Sir John Macdonald: Selections from the Correspondence of the Right Honourable Sir John Alexander Macdonald, G.C.B.*, ed. Sir Joseph Pope (Toronto: Doubleday, Page, 1921), 230.

60 Sir David Smith, *Head of State: The Governor-General, the Monarchy, the Republic and the Dismissal* (Sydney: Macleay, 2005), 121.

Chapter Six

1 Smith, *Republican Option in Canada*, chapter eight, "Contexts and Contrasts."

2 *O'Donohue v Canada* [2003] OJ no. 2764; *McAteer v Canada (Attorney General)*, 2014 ONCA 578; and *McAteer et al v Attorney General of Canada*, 2013 ONSC 5895; *Motard et al c Procureur générale du Canada et al*, CSQ 200-17-018455-139; and *Conacher v Canada (Prime Minister)*, 2009 FC 920, [2010] 3 FCR 411.

3 White, *Acts of Hope*, 71.
4 Seymour Martin Lipset, *Continental Divide: The Values and Institutions of the United States and Canada* (New York: Routledge, 1990), 93.
5 Richard Gwyn, *Sir John A. Macdonald: His Life, Our Times* (Toronto: Random House Canada, 2011), 90.
6 Christopher Guly, "Canada's Unwritten Constitutional Conventions Need to Be Written Down, Says GG," *Hill Times*, 8 August 2016, 4.
7 Wilfrid Laurier, *Globe*, 4 January 1899, 1; cited in Margaret Banks, *Sir John George Bourniot: Victorian Canadian: His Life, Times, and Legacy* (Montreal and Kingston: McGill-Queen's University Press, 2001), 136.
8 A.D. Lindsay, *The Essentials of Democracy* (London: Humphrey Milford/ Oxford University Press, 1930), 39 and 47.
9 Allan Blakeney and Sandford Borins, *Political Management in Canada: Conversations on Statecraft*, 2nd ed. (Toronto: University of Toronto Press, 1998), 30 and 31.
10 See, for example, Donald V. Smiley and Ronald L. Watts, *Intrastate Federalism in Canada* (Toronto: University of Toronto Press, in cooperation with the Royal Commission on the Economic Union and Development Prospects for Canada, 1985).
11 John Uhr, "Bicameralism and Democratic Deliberation," in *Restraining Elective Dictatorship: The Upper House Solution?*, ed. Nicholas Aroney, Scott Prasser, and L.R. Nethercote (Crawley, WA: University of Western Australia Press, 2008), 17.
12 Ibid., 16.
13 Cameron, *Strong Constitutions*, 95.
14 "What's It For?" *Globe and Mail*, 6 May 2016, A10 (editorial).
15 Pope, *Public Servant*, 236.
16 In the United Kingdom, see, for example, Jennifer Lees-Marshment, "Marketing the Monarchy," chapter three in *The Political Marketing Revolution: Transforming the Government of the UK* (Manchester: Manchester University Press, 2004).
17 Loyd Grossman, *Benjamin West and the Struggle to Be Modern* (London: Merrell, 2015), 7. The editors of the *Globe and Mail* confirmed the familiarity of the artistic reference to the painting by reproducing it on the editorial page of the publication. *Globe and Mail*, 2 June 2016, A12.
18 Hugh Hood, "Moral Imagination: Canadian Thing," in *The Governor's Bridge Is Closed* ([Ottawa]: Oberon, 1973), 91–2.
19 Pope, *Confederation*, 82.
20 Reginald Whitaker, "Democracy and the Canadian Constitution," chapter seven, *A Sovereign Idea: Essays on Canada as a Democratic Community* (Montreal and Kingston: McGill-Queen's University Press, 1992), 216.

Bibliography

Adams, Michael, and Andrew Griffith. "Take Pride That Parliament Reflects the Face of Canada." *Globe and Mail*, 13 January 2016.

Ajzenstat, Janet. "Are Canadians Deferential?" The Idea File. https://janetajzenstat.wordpress.com/2008/11/21/are-canadians-deferential/.

AmericasBarometer: Citizens across the Americas Speak on Democracy and Governance, Canada 2014: Final Report. Ottawa: Environics Institute and Institute on Governance, 2014.

Angus, H.F. "The British Columbia Election, June, 1952." In *Voting in Canada*, ed. John C. Courtney, 35–8. Scarborough, ON: Prentice-Hall of Canada, 1967.

Aniz Alani and the Prime Minister of Canada and the Governor General of Canada, docket T-2506–14, citation 2015 FC 649; citation 2015 FC 859.

"The Appointment of Extra Senators under Section 26 of the British North America Act." *Canadian Journal of Economics and Political Science* 12 (May 1946): 159–67.

Aroney, Nicholas, Scott Prasser, and J.R. Nethercote. *Restraining Elective Dictatorship: The Upper House Solution?* Crawley: University of Western Australia Press, 2008.

Asch, Michael. *On Being Here to Stay: Treaties and Aboriginal Rights in Canada*. Toronto: University of Toronto Press, 2014.

Aucoin, Peter, Mark D. Jarvis, and Lori Turnbull. *Democratizing the Constitution: Reforming Responsible Government*. Toronto: Emond Montgomery Publications, 2011.

Auditor General. *Senators' Expenses*. June Report of the Auditor General to the Senate of Canada, 2015. www.oag-bvg.gc.ca/internet/English/parl_otp_201506_e_40494.html.

Bagehot, Walter. *The English Constitution*. London: Oxford University Press, 1961.

Banks, Margaret A. *Sir John George Bourinot, Victorian Canadian: His Life, Times, and Legacy*. Montreal and Kingston: McGill-Queen's University Press, 2001.

Beck, J. Murray. *The Government of Nova Scotia*. Toronto: University of Toronto Press, 1957.

Bédard, Michel, and Philippe Lagassé, eds. *The Crown in Parliament*. Montreal: Éditions Yvon Blais, 2015.

Benn, Tony. *Free Radical Essays: New Century Essays*. New York: Continuum, 2003.

Benoit, Dom. *La Vie de Monseigneur Taché* (Montreal, 1904), 11:195–6. Cited in Ramsay Cook, *Canada and the French Canadian Question*. Toronto: Macmillan, 1971.

Berlin, Isaiah. *The Crooked Timber of Humanity: Chapters in the History of Ideas*. Edited by Henry Hardy. Princeton, NJ: Princeton University Press, 1990.

Berrington, Hugh. "MPs and Their Constituents in Britain: The History of the Relationship." In *Representatives of the People?: Parliamentarians and Constituents in Western Democracies*, ed. Vernon Bogdanor, 15–43. Brookfield, VT: Gower Publishing, 1985.

Birch, Anthony H. *Representative and Responsible Government: An Essay on the British Constitution*. London: Allen and Unwin, 1964.

Blakeney, Allan, and Sandford Borins. *Political Management in Canada: Conversations on Statecraft*. 2nd ed. Toronto: University of Toronto Press, 1998.

Bliss, Michael. "Playing Footsie with the Enemy." *National Post*, 4 December 2008, A23.

Bogdanor, Vernon. *The New British Constitution*. Oxford: Hart Publishing, 2009.

– *Representatives of the People?: Parliamentarians and Constituents in Western Democracies*. Brookfield, VT: Gower Publishing, 1985.

Bourinot, J.G. "The Canadian Dominion and the Proposed Australian Constitution: A Study in Comparative Politics." *Transactions of the Royal Society of Canada, Section 11*, 2nd ser., vol. 1 (1895): 3–43.

Bowden, James W.J., and Nicholas A. MacDonald. "Writing the Unwritten: The Officialization of Constitutional Convention in Canada, the United Kingdom, New Zealand and Australia." *Journal of Parliamentary and Political Law* 6 (2012): 365–400.

Boyce, Peter. *The Queen's Other Realms: The Crown and Its Legacy in Australia, Canada and New Zealand*. Sydney: Federation Press, 2008.

Boyer, J. Patrick. *Our Scandalous Senate*. Toronto: Dundurn, 2014.

Bréton, Raymond. "Multiculturalism and Canadian Nation-Building." In *The Politics of Gender, Ethnicity, and Language in Canada*, ed. Alan Cairns and Cynthia Williams, 34:27–66. Toronto: University of Toronto Press, in cooperation with the Royal Commission on the Economic Union and Development Prospects for Canada, 1985.

Brett, Judith. "Parliament, Meetings and Civil Society." Australia, Senate
    Occasional Lecture Series, 27 July 2001. http://www.aph.gov.au/About_
    Parliament/Senate/Powers_practice_n_procedures/pops/~/link.aspx?_
    id=12EB7F88D50B4A8D828E543A8319A37E&_z=z.
Brock, David M. "The Independence of Election Administration from
    Government." In Special Issue, "The Informed Citizen's Guide to Elections:
    Electioneering Based on the Rule of Law," ed. Greg Tardi and Richard
    Balasko, special issue, *Journal of Parliamentary and Political Law*, 93–106.
    Toronto: Carswell, 2015.
Bryden, Joan. "Move to Proportional Rep Might Require Constitutional
    Amendment: Joyal." 3 February 2016. http://ipolitics.ca/2016/02/03/
    move-to-proportional-rep-might-require-constitutional-amendment-joyal/.
Cairns, Alan. "The Electoral System and the Party System, 1921–1965."
    Canadian Journal of Political Science 1 (March 1968): 55–80.
Cameron, Maxwell A. *Strong Constitutions: Social-Cognitive Origins of the
    Separation of Powers*. New York: Oxford University Press, 2013.
Campbell, Colin. *The Canadian Senate: A Lobby Within*. Toronto: Macmillan, 1978.
Canada (House of Commons) v Vaid, 1 SCR 667, para 41.
Canada. *A Consolidation of the Constitution Acts, 1867 to 1982*. Ottawa:
    Department of Justice, 2001.
Canada. House of Commons, Sessional Papers, vol. 28, no. 246 (1914):
    "Return to an Order of the House of Commons, Dated March 2, 1914," and
    "Supplementary Return."
Canadian Press. "Duffy Acquittal Should Be Wake-up Call to Hold Politicians
    to Account, Stephen Harper's Lawyer Says." 26 April 2016. https://www.
    thestar.com/news/canada/2016/04/26/harper-played-no-role-in-rcmp-
    decision-to-charge-duffy-his-lawyer-argues.html.
Cannadine, David. "The Context, Performance and Meaning of Ritual: The
    British Monarchy and the 'Invention of Tradition,' c. 1820–1977." In *The
    Invention of Tradition*, ed. Eric Hobsbawm and Terence Ranger, 101–64. New
    York: Cambridge University Press, 1983.
– *Ornamentalism: How the British Saw Their Empire*. New York: Oxford
    University Press, 2001.
Caro, Robert A. *The Years of Lyndon Johnson*. 4 vols. New York: Vintage Books,
    1982, 1990, 2002, 2012.
Carter v Canada, 2016 SCC 4.
CBC News. "Tories Begin Battle against Coalition," 2 December 2008. http://
    www.cbc.ca/news/canada/tories-begin-battle-against-coalition-1.735525.
Chaplin, Ann. *Officers of Parliament: Accountability, Virtue and the Constitution*.
    Montreal: Éditions Yvon Blais, 2011.

Chong, Michael. "Reform Act, 2014 Backgrounder." 11 September 2014.
http://michaelchong.ca/2014/09/11/reform-act-2014-backgrounder/.

Clark, Alan. *Diaries*. London: Phoenix Giant, 1993.

Clark, Campbell. "Ground Shifts with This Week's Red Chamber Rebellion."
Globe and Mail, 10 June 2016, A3.

Clark, S.D. *Movements of Social Protest in Canada, 1640–1840*. Toronto:
University of Toronto Press, 1959.

Clarkson, Adrienne. *Heart Matters*. Toronto: Viking, 2006.

Clokie, H. McD. "Judicial Review, Federalism, and the Canadian
Constitution." *Canadian Journal of Economics and Political Science* 8, no. 4
(November 1942): 537–56.

Cohen, Patricia Cline. *A Calculating People: The Spread of Numeracy in Early
America*. Chicago: University of Chicago Press, 1982.

Cole, Douglas. "The Problem of 'Nationalism' 'Imperialism' in British
Settlement Colonies." *Journal of British Studies* 10, no. 2 (May 1971): 165.

Commons Debates, 8 March 1868, 280.

Commons Debates, 3 April 1868, 455.

Commons Debates, 25 April 1870, 1178.

Commons Debates, 2 May 1870, 1287.

Commons Debates, 9 January 1896, 41 and 39.

Commons Debates, 20 January 1908, col. 1571.

Conacher v Canada, Prime Minister, 2009 FC 920, [2010] 3 FCR 411.

The Constitutional Questions Act, RSS 1978, c C-29, 2010 SKCA.

Constitution Unit. University College London. "Homepage." https://www.
ucl.ac.uk/constitution-unit/.

– "Monarchy, Church, and State." https://www.ucl.ac.uk/constitution-unit/
research/monarchy-church-state.

Conway, John. "Politics, Culture, and Constitutions." In *Empire and Nations:
Essays in Honour of Frederic H. Soward*, ed. Harvey L. Dyck and H. Peter
Krosby, 3–17. Toronto: University of Toronto Press, ca 1969.

Courtney, John C. "Can Canada's Past Electoral Reforms Help Us to
Understand the Debate over Its Method of Election?" Chapter ten of
Imperfect Democracies, ed. Patti Tamara Lenard and Richard Simeon, 111–37.
Vancouver: UBC Press, 2012.

– *Commissioned Ridings: Designing Canada's Electoral Districts*. Montreal and
Kingston: McGill-Queen's University Press, 2001.

Cowling, Maurice. *1867: Disraeli, Gladstone and Revolution – The Passing of the
Second Reform Bill*. Cambridge: Cambridge University Press, 1967.

Coyne, Andrew. "Canada's Potemkin Parliament: On the Surface, It Looks
Almost like Westminster." *National Post*, 26 February 2015.

– "Elections Act Portends Future Crisis." *National Post*, 10 April 2014.

Craig, David M. "Bagehot's Republicanism." In *The Monarchy and the British Nation, 1780 to the Present*, ed. Andrzej Olechnowicz, 139–62. New York: Cambridge University Press, 2007.

Cross, Michael. *A Biography of Robert Baldwin: The Morning-Star of Memory.* Toronto: Oxford University Press, 2012.

Crossman, Richard. *The Diaries of a Cabinet Minister.* London: Hamilton Cape, 1975.

Curry, B. "Secret Committee, Seeking Non-Partisans: How Harper Found the Next G-G." *Globe and Mail*, 12 July 2010, A1.

Cutler, Allan. "Time to Worry about the State of Democracy." *Hill Times*, 31 March 2014.

Dahl, Robert A. *How Democratic Is the American Constitution?* New Haven, CT: Yale University Press, 2002.

Dangerfield, George. *The Strange Death of Liberal England.* New York: Capricorn Books, 1961.

Davies, Godfrey. *The Restoration of Charles II: 1658–1660.* London: Oxford University Press, 1955.

Dawson, R. MacGregor, ed. *Constitutional Issues in Canada, 1900–1931.* London: Oxford University Press, 1933.

– *The Government of Canada.* 5th ed., rev. by Norman Ward. Toronto: University of Toronto Press, 1970.

–, ed. *The Principle of Official Independence: With Particular Reference to the Political History of Canada.* Toronto: S.B. Gundy, 1922.

Debates of the Legislative Assembly of United Canada, VIII.III.1849, 2437.

Debates of the Legislative Assembly of United Canada, XI.1.1852–3, 397.

Debates of the Legislative Assembly of United Canada, XI.11.1852–3, 1105.

Debates of the Legislative Assembly of United Canada, XI.111.1852–3, 1832.

Debates of the Legislative Assembly of United Canada, XIII.11.1856, 897.

de Kiewiet, C.W., and F.H. Underhill, eds. *Dufferin-Carnarvon Correspondence, 1874–1878.* Toronto: Champlain Society, 1955.

Delgamuukw v British Columbia, [1997] 3 SCR 1010. Cited in Michael Asch, *On Being Here to Stay: Treaties and Aboriginal Rights in Canada.* Toronto: University of Toronto Press, 2014.

"Democracy Watch Announces Summer Blockbuster Opening across Canada: Stop the SuPremos.ca." http://democracywatch.ca/20140619-democracy-watch-announces-summer-blockbuster-coming-to-canada-stopthesupremos-ca/.

Dicey, A.V. *Introduction to the Study of the Law of the* Constitution. 10th ed., intro. E.C.S. Wade. London: Macmillan, 1962.

Dion, Stéphane. "Improving Canadian Democracy." Notes for an address delivered in the context of a debate on Bill C-586, University of Ottawa, 25 November 2014.

Donnelly, M.S. *The Government of Manitoba.* Toronto: University of Toronto Press, 1963.

Doughty, Sir Arthur G. *The Elgin-Grey Papers, 1848–1852.* 4 vols. Ottawa: King's Printer, 1937.

Drewry, G. "Reform of the Legislative Process: Some Neglected Questions." *Parliamentary Affairs* 25, no. 4 (1972): 286–99. Quoted in Alexandra Kelso, *Parliamentary Reform at Westminster.* Manchester: Manchester University Press, 2009.

Dryden, Ken. "Parliamentary Discontent: Many MPs Leave Politics Disillusioned – But What Does That Really Mean for Our Democracy?" *Literary Review of Canada* (June 2014): 6–7.

Dufferin to Macdonald, 23 October 1873. In *Correspondence of Sir John Macdonald: Selections from the Correspondence of the Right Honourable Sir John Alexander Macdonald, GCB,* ed. Sir Joseph Pope. Toronto: Doubleday, Page, 1921.

"The Earl of Romney." *Telegraph,* 10 June 2004. http://www.telegraph.co.uk/news/obituaries/1464065/The-Earl-of-Romney.html.

Editorial. *Globe and Mail,* 21 and 25 August 2015.

Edwards, Sir Goronwy. "The Emergence of Majority Rule in English Parliamentary Elections." *Transactions of the Royal Historical Society,* 5th ser., 14 (1964): 175–96.

– "The Emergence of Majority Rule in the Procedure of the House of Commons." *Transactions of the Royal Historical Society,* 5th ser., 14 (1964): 165–87.

Elgin, Lord, to Lord Grey, 27 August 1849. In *The Elgin-Grey Papers, 1846–1852,* vol. II, ed. Sir Arthur G. Doughty. Ottawa: King's Printer, 1937.

Eliot, George. *Felix Holt: The Radical,* ed. with intro. by Peter Coveney. Harmondsworth, UK: Penguin Books, 1972.

Elliott, Nathan S. "'We Have Asked for Bread and You Gave Us a Stone': Western Farmers and the Siege of Ottawa." MA thesis, University of Saskatchewan, 2004.

Evatt, H.V. *The King and His Dominion Governors.* Oxford: Oxford University Press, 1936.

Fair, John D. "House of Lords Reform, 1917–18." In *British Interparty Conferences: A Study of the Procedure of Conciliation in British Politics, 1867–1921,* 182–97. Oxford: Clarendon, 1980.

Fairlie, Henry. *The Life in Politics.* London: Methuen, 1968.

Falardeau, Jean-Charles. "Roots and Values in Canadian Lives." In *Visions of Canada: The Alan B. Plaunt Memorial Lectures, 1958–1992,* ed. Bernard

Ostry and Janice Yalden, 75–98. Montreal and Kingston: McGill-Queen's University Press, 2004.

Flanagan, Tom. "Only Voters Have a Right to Decide on the Coalition." *Globe and Mail*, 9 January 2009.

– "This Is No Way to Choose a Leader." *Globe and Mail*, 28 December 2013.

Forsey, Eugene. *The Royal Power of Dissolution of Parliament in the British Commonwealth*, repr. with H.V. Evatt, *The King and His Dominion Governors*. 2nd ed. 1967, as *Evatt and Forsey on the Reserve Power*. Sydney: Legal Books, 1990.

Foster, Ally. "From PMO to MP: Shifting the Political Power Structure." *Power and Influence* (Fall 2015): 26–31.

Francis, R. Douglas. "The Anatomy of Power: A Theme in the Writings of Harold Innis." In *Nation, Ideas, Identities*, ed. Michael D. Behiels and Marcel Martel, 26–40. Don Mills, ON: Oxford University Press, 2000.

Franks, C.E.S. "The Canadian Senate in Modern Times." In *Protecting Canadian Democracy: The Senate You Never Knew*, ed. Serge Joyal, 152–88. Montreal and Kingston: McGill-Queen's University Press, 2003.

Fraser, John. *The Secret of the Crown: Canada's Affair with Royalty*. Toronto: House of Anansi, 2012.

Fraser, John, and D. Michael Jackson. "Foreword." In *The Evolving Canadian Crown*, ed. Jennifer Smith and D. Michael Jackson, vii–viii. Montreal and Kingston: McGill-Queen's University Press, 2012.

French, Goldwin. "The Evangelical Creed in Canada." In *The Shield of Achilles: Aspects of Canada in the Victorian Age*, ed. W.L. Morton, 15–35. Toronto: McClelland and Stewart, 1968.

Friedland, Martin L. *The Case of Valentine Shortis: A True Story of Crime and Politics in Canada*. Toronto: University of Toronto Press, 1986.

Frye, Northrop. *The Bush Garden: Essays on the Canadian Imagination*. Toronto: House of Anansi, 1995.

Galbraith, J. William. *John Buchan: Model Governor General*. Toronto: Dundurn, 2013.

Galligan, Brian, and Scott Brenton, eds. *Constitutional Conventions in Westminster Systems: Controversies, Changes and Challenges*. Cambridge: Cambridge University Press, 2015.

Galloway, Gloria. "Information Czar Takes Ottawa to Court over Long-Gun Data." *Globe and Mail*, 24 June 2015.

– "Poll Sees Mixed Views on Electoral Reform." *Globe and Mail*, 2 December 2015.

– "Retroactively Shielding RCMP 'Perilous' Precedent: Watchdog." *Globe and Mail*, 15 May 2015.

Gélinas, Fabien, and Léonid Sirota. "Constitutional Conventions and Senate Reform." *Revue québécoise de droit constitutionnel* 5 (2013): 107–23.

Gibson, Sarah Katherine, and Arthur Milnes, eds. *Canada Transformed: The Speeches of Sir John A. Macdonald; A Bicentennial Celebration.* Toronto: McClelland and Stewart, 2014.

Government of Canada. "Annex: Qualifications and Merit-Based Assessment Criteria." 2015. http://www.democraticinstitutions.gc.ca/eng/content/annex-qualifications-and-merit-based-assessment-criteria.

– "Backgrounder – Senate Appointments Process." 2015. http://www.democraticinstitutions.gc.ca/eng/content/backgrounder-senate-appointments-process.

– "Government Announces Immediate Senate Reform." 3 December 2015. http://news.gc.ca/web/article-en.do?nid=1023449.

– "The Senate – Report on Activities." 2013. http://publications.gc.ca/site/eng/9.506415/publication.html#.

Grey, Earl, to Sir John Harvey, 31 March 1847. British House of Commons Papers (621), xiii, 1847–48: 79. Quoted in R. MacGregor Dawson, *The Government of Canada*, 5th ed., rev. by Norman Ward. Toronto: University of Toronto Press, 1970.

Grossman, Loyd. *Benjamin West and the Struggle to be Modern.* London: Merrell, 2015.

Guerin v The Queen, [1984] 2 SCR 335 at 376.

Guly, Christopher. "Canada's Unwritten Constitutional Conventions Need to Be Written Down, Says GG." *Hill Times*, 8 August 2016, 4.

Gwyn, Richard. *Sir John A. Macdonald: His Life, Our Times.* Toronto: Random House Canada, 2011.

Hailsham, Lord. "Elective Dictatorship." The Richard Dimbleby Lecture. *Listener*, 21 October 1976, 496–500.

Hanham, H.J. *Elections and Party Management: Politics in the Time of Disraeli and Gladstone.* London: Longmans Green, 1959.

Hart-Davis, Duff, ed. *King's Counsellor: Abdication and War; The Diaries of Sir Alan Lascelles.* London: Weidenfeld and Nicolson, 2006.

Hawkins, Robert E. "Written Reasons and Codified Conventions in Matters of Prorogation and Dissolution." In *The Evolving Canadian Crown*, ed. Jennifer Smith and D. Michael Jackson, 99–116. Montreal and Kingston: McGill-Queen's University Press, 2012.

Heard, Andrew. "The Governor General's Decision to Prorogue Parliament: Parliamentary Democracy Defended or Endangered?" Centre for Constitutional Studies, *Points of View, Discussion Paper*, no. 7 (January 2009).

Heasman, D.J. "Queen's Prerogative." *Times*, 24 October 1985.

Hébert, Chantal. "Quebec Won't Discuss Senate Reform in Isolation." *Chronicle Herald*, 16 June 2015. http://thechronicleherald.ca/opinion/1293447-hébert-quebec-won't-discuss-senate-reform-in-isolation.

Helliwell, J., R. Layard, and J. Sachs. *World Happiness Report 2016, Update*, vol. 1. New York: Sustainable Development Solutions Network, 2016.

Henderson, Maxwell. *Plain Talk: Memoirs of an Auditor General*. Toronto: McClelland and Stewart, 1984.

Herbert, Sir Robert, ed. *Speeches on Canadian Affairs by Henry Howard Molyneux, Fourth Earl of Carnarvon*. London: John Murray, 1902.

Hilderman, Jane, and David Campbell. "A Chance to Change the Culture in Ottawa." *National Post*, 11 August 2015.

Hillmer, Norman. *O.D. Skelton: A Portrait of Canadian Ambition*. Toronto: University of Toronto Press, 2015.

Hockin, Thomas A., ed. *Apex of Power: The Prime Minister and Political Leadership in Canada*. 2nd ed. Scarborough, ON: Prentice-Hall, 1977.

Hodgetts, J.E. *Pioneer Public Service: An Administrative History of the United Canadas, 1841–1867*. Toronto: University of Toronto Press, 1955.

Hofstadter, Richard. *The Age of Reform: From Bryan to FDR*. New York: Vintage, 1960.

Hogg, Peter W. "Succession to the Throne." *National Journal of Constitutional Law* 33, no. 1 (Sept. 2014): 83–94.

Hood, Hugh. "Moral Imagination: Canadian Thing." In *The Governor's Bridge Is Closed*, 91–2. Ottawa: Oberon, 1973.

Horne, Donald. "Who Rules Australia?" *Daedalus* 114, no. 1 (Winter 1985): 171–96.

House of Lords and House of Commons. HL Paper 265-1/HC 1212-1. Joint Committee on Conventions, "Conventions of the UK Parliament." Report of Session 2005–6, vol. 1, 11.

Ibbitson, John. "Five Ways a Hung Parliament Could Swing in October." *Globe and Mail*, 27 May 2015. http://www.theglobeandmail.com/news/politics/globe-politics-insider/five-ways-a-hung-parliament-could-swing-in-october/article24615741/?from=25348097.

– "Ignatieff: It's Time to Fix Parliament." *Globe and Mail*, 2 February 2013.

– "Johnston Could Play Crucial Role on Oct. 20." *Globe and Mail*, 13 October 2015.

– "Johnston's Term Will Continue into 2017." *Globe and Mail*, 18 March 2015, A3.

– "The Speaker's Ruling – Harper's Headache: Prospect of Contempt Ruling before Election." *Globe and Mail*, 10 March 2011, 1/6.

– *Stephen Harper*. Toronto: McClelland and Stewart, 2015.

Jackson, Michael. *The Crown and Canadian Federalism*. Toronto: Dundurn, 2013.

– "Crown and Constitution." Presentation to the Public Law Divisional Conference, Saskatchewan Ministry of Justice, Regina, 12 June 2014.

Jackson, D. Michael, and Philippe Lagassé, eds. *Canada and the Crown: Essays on Constitutional Monarchy*. Montreal and Kingston: McGill-Queen's University Press, 2013.

James, Michael. "The Constitution in Australian Political Thought." In The *Constitutional Challenge: Essays on the Australian Constitution, Constitutionalism and Parliamentary Practice*, ed. Michael James, 7–36. St Leonards, NSW: Centre for Independent Studies, 1982.

Jenkins, Roy. *Gladstone*. London: Macmillan, 1995.

– *Mr Balfour's Poodle: An Account of the Struggle between the House of Lords and the Government of Mr Asquith*. London: William Heinemann, 1954.

Jennings, Sir Ivor. *The Law and the Constitution*. 5th ed. London: University of London Press, 1959.

Johnston, J.W. In the *Nova Scotian*, 3 March 1851, 69–70. Cited in K.G. Pryke, "Balance and Stability: Nova Scotia Considers an Elective Chamber," in *Documentary Problems in Canadian History, Pre-Confederation*, ed. J.M. Bumsted, 185–7. Georgetown: Irwin-Dorsey, 1969.

Johnston, Peter W., and Stanley D. Hotop. "Patched of an Old Garment or New Wineskins for New Wine? (Constitutional Reform in Western Australia – Evolution or Revolution?)." *University of Western Australia Law Review* 20 (1990): 428–44.

Joyal, Serge. "Conclusion: The Senate as the Embodiment of the Federal Principle." In *Protecting Canadian Democracy: The Senate You Never Knew*, ed. Joyal, 271–316. Montreal and Kingston: McGill-Queen's University Press, 2003.

Judt, Tony. "Is There a Belgium?" *New York Review of Books* 46, no. 19 (2 December 1999).

Kantorowicz, Ernst H. *The King's Two Bodies: A Study in Mediaeval Political Theology*. Princeton, NJ: Princeton University Press, 1957.

Kennedy, W.P.M. "Law and Custom of the Canadian Constitution." *The Round Table*, December 1929. In *Constitutional Issues in Canada, 1900–1931*, ed. Robert MacGregor Dawson, 50–62. London: Oxford University Press, 1933.

Kielley v Carson (1841), 4 Moore PC 63. Cited in Norman Ward, "Called to the Bar of the House of Commons." *Canadian Bar Review* (May 1957): 529–46.

King, Anthony. *Who Governs Britain?* Milton Keynes, UK: Penguin Random House, 2015.

King, Preston. *Federalism and the Federation*. Baltimore, MD: Johns Hopkins University Press, 1982.

King, W.L. Mackenzie. *The Message of the Carillon and Other Addresses*. Toronto: Macmillan of Canada, 1928.

Kulish, N. "Merkel's Pick Wins German Presidency." *USA Today*, 1 July 2010, 7A.

– "Presidential Vote Tests Merkel's Ailing Coalition in Germany." *New York Times*, 26 June 2010.

Kunz, F.A. *The Modern Senate of Canada, 1925–1963: A Re-Appraisal.* Toronto: University of Toronto Press, 1965.

Lagassé, Philippe. "Accountability for National Defence: Ministerial Responsibility, Military Command and Parliamentary Oversight." IRPP Study no. 4 (March 2010).

– "The Crown and Prime Ministerial Power." *Canadian Parliamentary Review* 39, no. 2 (Summer 2016): 17–23.

– "Parliamentary and Judicial Ambivalence toward Executive Prerogative Powers in Canada." *Canadian Public Administration* 55, no. 2 (June 2012): 157–80.

Laskin, Bora. *The British Tradition in Canadian Law.* London: Stevens and Sons, 1969.

Laurier, Sir Wilfrid. *The Globe*, 4 January 1899. Cited in Margaret Banks, *Sir John George Bourniot: Victorian Canadian; His Life, Times, and Legacy.* Montreal and Kingston: McGill-Queen's University Press, 2001.

Lawrence Martin. "G-G Steps Up on Democracy." *Globe and Mail*, 30 April 2013, A15.

Leblanc, Daniel. "PMO Tampering Appalls Ex-House Clerk." *Globe and Mail*, 8 May 2015.

– "RCMP Needs Time to Get Ready for New Duties." *Globe and Mail*, 6 February 2015, A4.

Lees-Marshment, Jennifer. "Marketing the Monarchy." In *The Political Marketing Revolution: Transforming the Government of the U.K.* Manchester: Manchester University Press, 2004.

Lefroy, A.H.F. *A Short Treatise on Canadian Constitutional Law.* Toronto: Carswell, 1918.

Levitz, Stephanie. "Governor General Lauds Stability Monarchy Brings." *Toronto Star*, 11 June 2016, A2.

Leys, Simon. "Chesterton: The Poet Who Dances with a Hundred Legs." In *The Hall of Uselessness: Collected Essays*, 101–13. New York: New York Review of Books, 2013.

Library and Archives Canada (LAC), MG26, L. St Laurent Papers, vol. 253 (Speeches, Canadian Citizenship, Canadian Club Address, Montreal), 6 January 1946.

– MG26A, John A. Macdonald Papers. Alexander Campbell to Macdonald, 7 March 1888, 83495–8.

– MG31, E46, Escott Reid Papers, vol. 28 (Constitutional Issues and Royal Title, 1942–1960).

– Papers of Eugene Alfred Forsey, typed sheet headed, "Saskatchewan Brief." [1945] file 57/58 Disallowance of Provincial Acts (2), 1945, 1948.

Lindsay, A.D. *The Essentials of Democracy.* London: Humphrey Milford/Oxford University Press, 1930.

Lipset, Seymour Martin. *Continental Divide: The Values and Institutions of the United States and Canada.* New York: Routledge, 1990.

Liptak, Adam. "Smaller States Find Outside Clout Growing in Senate." *New York Times,* 11 March 2013, A1/12.

Lizhi, Fang. *The Most Wanted Man in China: My Journey from Scientist to Enemy of the State.* New York: Henry Holt, 2016.

Loat, Alison, and Michael MacMillan. *Tragedy in the Commons: Former Members of Parliament Speak Out about Canada's Failing Democracy.* Toronto: Random House Canada, 2014.

Lumsden, Ian, ed. *Closing the 49th Parallel Etc: The Americanization of Canada.* Toronto: University of Toronto Press, 1970.

Lutz, Donald S. "The Purposes of American State Constitutions." *Publius* 12 (Winter 1982): 27–44.

Macdonald, Roderick A., and Robert Wolfe. "Canada's Third National Policy: The Epiphenomenal or the Real Constitution?" *University of Toronto Law Journal* 59 (Fall 2009): 469–523.

MacKay, Robert A. *The Unreformed Senate of Canada.* London: Humphrey Milford, for Oxford University Press, 1926.

MacKinnon, Frank. *The Crown in Canada.* Calgary: McClelland and Stewart West, 1976.

– *The Government of Prince Edward Island.* Toronto: University of Toronto Press, 1951.

Madden, A.F. "'Not for Export': The Westminster Model of Government and British Colonial Practice." *Journal of Imperial and Commonwealth History* 8, no. 1 (Oct. 1979): 10–29.

Mallory, J.R. *The Structure of Canadian Government.* Rev. ed. Toronto: Gage, 1984.

Malloy, Kate. "Politicians Should Reclaim Themselves." *Hill Times,* 5 May 2014. https://www.hilltimes.com/2014/05/03/politicians-should-reclaim-themselves-say-authors-of-new-book-tragedy-in-the-commons/28381.

Malouf, David. "Made in England: Australia's British Inheritance." *Quarterly Essays* 12 (2003): 27.

Maritime Bank v Receiver General of New Brunswick (1892) AC 437.

Marr, Andrew. "Your Most Disobedient Servant Ma'am." *Sunday Times,* 18 October 2015, 4:2.

Martin, Lawrence. "G-G Steps Up on Democracy." *Globe and Mail,* 30 April 2013.

Massicotte, Louis. "Possible Repercussions of an Elected Senate on Official Language Minorities in Canada." Report for the Office of the Commissioner of Official Languages, March 2007.

Mathen, Carissima, Vanessa MacDonnell, Adam Dodek, Errol Mendes, Peter Oliver, and Michael Pal. "Who Governs in a Minority Is about More Than Just Politics." *National Post*, 15 October 2015, A10.

The Marriage Act, 1995, SS 1995, c M-4.1.

"May Says Harper Minority Doesn't Make Him PM." *Saskatoon StarPhoenix*, 12 September 2015. http://thestarphoenix.com/news/local-news/may-says-harper-minority-doesnt-make-him-pm.

McAteer et al v Attorney General of Canada, 2013 ONSC 5895.

McAteer v Canada (Attorney General), 2014 ONCA 578 (Docket C57775).

McCreery, Christopher. *The Canadian Honours System*. Toronto: Dundurn, 2005.

– *The Order of Canada: Its Origins, History and Development*. Toronto: University of Toronto Press, 2005.

McMillan, Tom. "Robert L. Stanfield and Tom Symons: A Public Policy Partnership." In *Tom Symons: A Canadian Life*, ed. Ralph Heintzman, 117–68. Ottawa: University of Ottawa Press, 2011.

Memorandum on Representation of the Maritime Provinces, Canadian Sessional Papers, 1914, no. 118a. Repr. in *Constitutional Issues in Canada, 1900–1931*, ed. R. MacGregor Dawson, 173–5. London: Oxford University Press, 1933.

Montgomery, Paul L. "Belgian King Asks Prime Minister to End Impasse." *New York Times*, 7 May 1988. http://www.nytimes.com/1988/05/07/world/belgian-king-asks-prime-minister-to-end-impasse.html.

Moore, Christopher. *1867: How the Fathers Made a Deal*. Toronto: McClelland and Stewart, 1998.

– "Our Canadian Republic." *Literary Review of Canada*, November 2008. http://www.reviewcanada.ca/magazine/2008/11/our-canadian-republic/.

– *Three Weeks in Quebec City: The Meeting That Made Canada*. Toronto: Allen Lane, 2015.

Morgan, Edmund S. *Inventing the People: The Rise of Popular Sovereignty in England and America*. New York: W.W. Norton, 1988.

Morton, W.L. "The Extension of the Franchise in Canada: A Study in Democratic Nationalism." *Canadian Historical Association Report* 22 (1943): 72–81.

Motard, Geneviève et al c Procureur générale du Canada et al, CSQ 200-17-018455-139.

Naumetz, Tim. "Conservatives 'Lay Track' to Attack Media, Real Opposition in New Parliament." *Hill Times*, 13 June 2011, 1, 6.

Neary, Peter. "The Morning after a General Election: The Vice-Regal Prerogative." *Canadian Parliamentary Review* 35 (Autumn 2012): 23–9.

Nevitte, Neil. *The Decline of Deference: Canadian Value Change in Cross-National Perspective.* Peterborough, ON: Broadview, 1996.

Newman, Warren J. "Parliamentary Privilege, the Canadian Constitution and the Courts." *Ottawa Law Review* 39, no. 3 (2008): 575–609.

Nicolson, Adam. *God's Secretaries: The Making of the King James Bible.* New York: HarperCollins Publishers, 2003.

Nicolson, Harold. *Diaries and Letters, 1930–1939,* ed. Nigel Nicolson. 3 vols. London: Collins, 1966–8.

– *King George V* (London: Constable, 1953), 138. Cited in Roy Jenkins, *Mr Balfour's Poodle: An Account of the Struggle between the House of Lords and the Government of Mr Asquith.* London: William Heinemann, 1954.

O'Brien, Conor Cruise. *On the Eve of the Millennium.* Massey Lectures for 1994. Toronto: House of Anansi, 1994.

O'Donohue v Canada [2003] OJ No. 2764.

Office of the Commissioner for Federal Judicial Affairs Canada. "Number of Federally Appointed Judges as of February 1, 2017." 2017. http://www.fja-cmf.gc.ca/appointments-nominations/judges-juges-eng.aspx.

Office of the Commissioner of Official Languages. *Investigation Report of Complaints concerning the Redistribution of Federal Ridings Proposed by the Electoral Boundaries Commission for the Province of New Brunswick.* Ottawa, July 1996.

Oliver, Peter C. *The Constitution of Independence: The Development of Constitutional Theory in Australia, Canada, and New Zealand.* Oxford: Oxford University Press, 2005.

Onuf, Peter S. *The Origins of the Federal Republic: Jurisdictional Controversies in the United States, 1775–1786.* Philadelphia: University of Pennsylvania Press, 1983.

Orwell, George. "Politics and the English Language." http://www.orwell.ru/library/essays/politics/english/e_polit/.

Page, Kevin, with Vern Stenlund. *Unaccountable: Truth and Lies on Parliament Hill.* Toronto: Viking, 2015.

Pal, Michael. "Why the Top Court Must Weigh In on Electoral Reform." *Globe and Mail,* 15 January 2016.

Parliamentary Debates on the Subject of the Confederation of the British North American Provinces. Quebec, 1865. Ottawa: King's Printer, 1951.

Pilon, Dennis. "Constitution No Barrier to Reform." *National Post,* 1 February 2016.

Pimlott, Ben. *The Queen: Elizabeth II and the Monarchy.* London: HarperCollins, 1996.

Pope, Joseph, ed. *Confederation: Being a Series of Hitherto Unpublished Documents Bearing on the British North America Act.* Toronto: Carswell Law Publishers, 1895.

– *Correspondence of John A. Macdonald: Selections from the Correspondence of the Rt Hon. Sir John A. Macdonald, GCB.* Toronto: Oxford University Press, 1921.

– *Public Servant: The Memoirs of Sir Joseph Pope.* Edited and completed by Maurice Pope. Toronto: Oxford University Press, 1960.

Potter, Andrew. "Letters and Responses." *Literary Review of Canada,* July/August 2009, 30–1.

Public Policy Forum. "Government Formation in Canada." Ottawa Roundtable. 21 March 2011.

Rae, Bob. *What's Happened to Politics?* Toronto: Simon and Schuster Canada, 2015.

Raîche v R. Federal Court of Canada Trial Division, filed September 2003: file T-1730-03.

Rathgeber, Brent. *Irresponsible Government: The Decline of Parliamentary Democracy in Canada.* Toronto: Dundurn, 2014.

Records of the Governor General's Office. Michael Adeane (private secretary to the Queen) to Esmond Butler, 6 February 1970 (1990–91/016, box 14, file 535.2, vol. 1).

– Philip Moore to My dear Prime Minister, 20 June 1978 (1990–91/016, box 13, file 535.1, vol. 1).

Reference re Legislative Authority of Parliament in Relation to the Upper House, [1980] 1 SCR 54.

Reference re Resolution to Amend the Constitution, [1981] 1 SCR 753.

Reference re Senate Reform, 2014 SCC 32.

Reference re the Secession of Quebec, [1998] 2 SCR 217.

Re Initiative and Referendum Act, (1919) AC 935.

Rémillard, Gil, and Andrew Turner. "Senate Reform: Back to Basics." In *Protecting Canadian Democracy: The Senate You Never Knew,* ed. Serge Joyal, 105–32. Montreal and Kingston: McGill-Queen's University Press.

Report of the Royal Commission on Radio Broadcasting. Ottawa: King's Printer, 1929.

Report of the Special Senate Committee on Mass Media. *The Uncertain Mirror.* Ottawa: Queen's Printer, 1970.

Riker, William H. "The Justification of Bicameralism." *International Political Science Review* 13, no. 1 (1992): 101–16.

Robson, John. "Save Our Democracy." *National Post,* 2 November 2015.

Ross, George W. *Getting into Parliament and After.* Toronto: W. Briggs, 1913.

Royal Commission on Canada's Economic Prospects. *Final Report.* Ottawa: King's 1957.

– *Preliminary Report.* Ottawa: King's Printer, 1956.

Royal Commission on the Reform of the House of Lords in 2000. *A House for the Future*. London: Stationery Office, 2000, Cm. 4534.

Russell, Lord, to Poulett Thomson (Lord Sydenham). 16 October 1839. Repr in *Statutes, Treaties, and Documents of the Canadian Constitution, 1713–1929*, ed. W.P.M. Kennedy, 421 and 422. Toronto: Oxford University Press, 1930.

Russell, P.H. "Educating Canadians on the Crown: A Diamond Jubilee Challenge." In *Canada and the Crown: Essays on Constitutional Monarchy*, ed. D. Michael Jackson and Philippe Lagassé, 75–85. Montreal and Kingston: McGill-Queen's University Press, 2013.

– "Learning to Live with Minority Parliaments." In *Parliamentary Democracy in Crisis*, ed. P.H. Russell and L. Sossin. Toronto: University of Toronto Press, 2009. Quoted in Robert E. Hawkins, "Written Reasons and Codified Conventions in Matters of Prorogation and Dissolution." In *The Evolving Canadian Crown*, ed. Jennifer Smith and D. Michael Jackson, 99–116. Montreal and Kingston: McGill-Queen's University Press, 2012.

Russell, Peter H., and Lorne Sossin, eds. *Parliamentary Democracy in Crisis*. Toronto: University of Toronto Press, 2009.

R v Duffy, 2016 ONCJ 220, paras 1029–32 and 1034–37. http://canlii.ca/t/gplvk.

Ryckewaert, Laura. "MPs and Senators Unclear on Details of RCMP Security Takeover." *Hill Times*, 16 March 2015, 19.

Samuel, Raphael, ed. *Patriotism: The Making and Unmaking of British National Identity*. Vol. 1, *History and Politics*. London: Routledge, 1989.

Saskatchewan Archives Board. James G. Gardiner Papers, "The British System of Parliamentary Government," delivered by James G. Gardiner at the Annual Meeting of the Toronto Board of Trade, 14 February 1938.

Saskatchewan Federation of Labour v Saskatchewan (Attorney General), 2010 SKCA 27(CanLII), para 63.

Savoie, Donald. *Court Government and the Collapse of Accountability in Canada and the United Kingdom*. Toronto: University of Toronto Press, 2008.

– *Governing from the Centre: The Concentration of Power in Canadian Politics*. Toronto: University of Toronto Press, 1999.

Schneiderman, David. "How to Tame a PM's Prerogative: In a Showdown with the Crown, Parliament Can Use Statute to Take Matters into Its Own Hands." *Globe and Mail*, 10 March 2010, A15.

– *Red, White, and Kind of Blue: The Conservatives and the Americanization of Canadian Constitutional Culture*. Toronto: University of Toronto Press, 2015.

Scott, F.R. "W.L.M.K." In *The Blasted Pine: An Anthology of Satire, Invective and Disrespectful Verse by Canadian Writers*, ed. F.R. Scott and A.J.M. Smith, 27–8. Toronto: Macmillan Canada, 1962.

Scott, Peter. *Knowledge and Nation*. Edinburgh: Edinburgh University Press, 1990. Cited in Linda Colley, *Britons: Forging the Nation, 1707–1837*. New Haven, CT: Yale University Press, 1992.

Seidle, F. Leslie. "The Canada Elections Act: The House of Commons and the Parties." In *The Canadian House of Commons: Essays in Honour of Norman Ward*, ed. John C. Courtney, 113–34. Calgary: University of Calgary Press, 1985.

Sen, Amartya. *Democracy as Freedom*. New York: Anchor Books, 2000.

Senate. "A Matter of Privilege: A Discussion Paper on Canadian Parliamentary Privilege in the 21st Century." Interim report of the Standing Committee on Rules, Regulations, and the Rights of Parliament. June 2015.

Senate, Parliament of Australia. "What Is Wrong with an Elective Dictatorship?" 1994. http://www.aph.gov.au/sitecore/content/Home/About_Parliament/Senate/Powers_practice_n_procedures/hamer/chap11.

Senate Reform Reference, [2014] 1 SCR 433.

Sharman, Campbell. "The Strange Case of a Provincial Constitution: The British Columbia Constitution Act." *Canadian Journal of Political Science* 17, no. 1 (March 1984): 87–108.

Simcoe, John Graves. Letter to the Duke of Portland, 21 December 1794, 3 Simcoe Papers at 235. Cited in F.C. Buckley, *The Once and Future King: The Rise of Crown Government in America*. New York: Encounter Books, 2014.

Simeon, Richard. *Political Science and Federalism: Seven Decades of Scholarly Engagement*. Kingston: Institute of Intergovernmental Relations, 2002.

Simpson, Jeffrey. "In Death, New Life for Parliament." *Globe and Mail*, 22 June 2016, B19.

Smiley, Donald V., and Ronald L. Watts. *Intrastate Federalism in Canada*. Toronto: University of Toronto Press, in cooperation with the Royal Commission on the Economic Union and Development Prospects for Canada, 1985.

Smith, Dale. "Who Killed Question Period?" *National Post*, 29 May 2015.

Smith, David E. *The Invisible Crown: The First Principle of Canadian Government*, Toronto: University of Toronto Press, 1995.

– "Clarifying the Doctrine of Ministerial Responsibility as It Applies to the Government and Parliament of Canada." In Commission of Inquiry into the Sponsorship Program and Advertising Activities, *Restoring Accountability*, 1:101–43. Ottawa: Public Works and Government Services, 2006.

– "Party Government, Representation and National Integration in Canada." In *Party Government and Regional Representation in Canada*, ed. Peter Aucoin, 1–68. Toronto: University of Toronto Press, in cooperation with the Royal Commission on the Economic Union and Development Prospects for Canada, 1985.

– *The People's House of Commons: Theories of Democracy in Perspective.* Toronto: University of Toronto Press, 2007.
– "A Period of Waiting Over: The Prairies in 1939." In *A Country of Limitations: Canada and the World in 1939*, ed. Norman Hillmer, Robert Bothwell, Roger Sarty, and Claude Beauregard (Canadian Committee for the History of the Second World War), 94–108. Ottawa: National Defence, Directorate of History, 1996.
– "The Reforms of Keith Davey and Walter Gordon." In *The Regional Decline of a National Party: Liberals on the Prairies*, ed. Smith, 56–62. Toronto: University of Toronto Press, 1981.
– *The Republican Option in Canada: Past and Present.* Toronto: University of Toronto Press, 1999.
– "The Westminster Model in Ottawa: A Study in the Absence of Influence." *British Journal of Canadian Studies* 15, nos 1 and 2 (2002): 54–64.
Smith, Sir David. *Head of State: The Governor-General, the Monarchy, the Republic and the Dismissal.* Sydney: Macleay, 2005.
Smith, Denis. "President and Parliament: The Transformation of Parliamentary Government in Canada." Presented to the Priorities for Canada Conference. Reprinted in *The Canadian Political Process*, 3rd ed., ed. Richard Schultz, Orest M. Kruhlak, and John C. Terry, 345–60. Toronto: Holt, Rinehart and Winston of Canada, 1979.
Smith, Goldwin. "The Political Destiny of Canada." *Canadian Monthly*, February 1880, 596–614.
Smith, Jennifer, and D. Michael Jackson, eds. *The Evolving Canadian Crown.* Montreal and Kingston: McGill-Queen's University Press, 2012.
Somerville, Margaret. "A Charter Issue That Demands a Vote of Conscience." *Globe and Mail*, 24 February 2016.
Stack, Liam. "Long-Serving PM Championed Multiculturalism." *Globe and Mail*, 21 March 2015.
Stark, Andrew. "Trudeau's Big Idea and the Art of Compromise." *Globe and Mail*, 19 June 2015.
Stewart, Gordon. *The Origins of Canadian Politics: A Comparative Approach.* Vancouver: University of British Columbia Press, 1986.
Stilborn, Jack. "Reforming Our Thinking: The Key to Real Parliamentary Reform." *Hill Times*, 17 February 2014.
St John, Joy. "Americanization: Analysis of a Concept." MA thesis, University of Saskatchewan, 1999.
"Straight-Talking Fraser Strikes Fear on the Hill." *Globe and Mail*, 12 February 2004.
Tandt, Michael Den. "Duffy Laid the Tories Low: Now Party Can Make Senate Abolition a Winning Proposition." *National Post*, 24 April 2016. http://news.

nationalpost.com/news/canada/michael-den-tandt-duffy-laid-the-
tories-low-now-party-can-make-senate-abolition-a-winning-proposition.

"Terms of Reference." Advisory Committee on Vice-Regal Appointments, 4
November 2012. http://news.gc.ca/web/article-en.do?nid=704959.

Tidridge, Nathan. *The Queen at the Council Fire: The Treaty of Niagara,
Reconciliation and the Dignified Crown of Canada*. Toronto: Dundurn, 2015.

Trotter, Reginald George. *Canadian Federation: Its Origins and Achievement; A
Study of Nation Building*. Toronto: J.M. Dent and Sons, 1924.

Tuohy, Carolyn J. *Policy and Politics in Canada: Institutionalized Ambivalence*.
Philadelphia, PA: Temple University Press, 1992.

Uhr, John. "Bicameralism and Democratic Deliberation." In *Restraining Elective
Dictatorship: The Upper House Solution?*, ed. Nicholas Aroney, Scott Prasser, and
L.R. Nethercote, 11–27. Crawley: University of Western Australia Press, 2008.

Underhill, Frank. "The Cabinet and Leadership." *Canadian Forum*, January
1950, 116–17. Cited in Robert MacGregor Dawson, *Constitutional Issues in
Canada, 1900–1931*. London: Oxford University Press, 1933.

Vieira, Ryan A. *Time and Politics: Parliament and the Culture of Modernity and the
British World*. Oxford: Oxford University Press, 2015.

Vipond, Robert C. *Liberty and Community: Canadian Federalism and the Failure of
the Constitution*. Albany: State University of New York Press, 1991.

Vongdouangchanh, Bea. "Parliamentary Democracy Is 'Sick,' 'Tattered, and
Needs Help.'" *Hill Times*, 28 October 2013.

– "Public Institutions Need 'Reboot' to Restore Trust, PPF Report Says." *Hill
Times*, 2 November 2015.

Walters, Mark D. "Succession to the Throne and the Architecture of the
Constitution of Canada." In *The Crown in Parliament*, ed. Michel Bédard and
Philippe Lagassé, 263–92. Montreal: Éditions Yvon Blais, 2015.

Ward, Norman, ed. *The Canadian House of Commons: Representation*. 2nd ed.
Toronto: University of Toronto Press, 1963.

– "The Formative Years of the House of Commons, 1867–91." *Canadian Journal
of Economics and Political Science* 18, no. 4 (November 1952): 431–51.

– *The Public Purse: A Study in Canadian Democracy*. Toronto: University of
Toronto Press, 1962.

Ward, Norman, and David Smith. *Jimmy Gardiner: Relentless Liberal*. Toronto:
University of Toronto Press, 1990.

"The Way Home to Westminster." *Globe and Mail*, 7 December 2013.

Weller, P., and D. Jaensch, eds. *Responsible Government in Australia*. Richmond,
Victoria: Drummond Publications, 1980. Cited in James A. Thomson, "State
Constitutional Law: Gathering the Fragments." *Western Australian Law
Review* 16 (1985): 90–104.

"What's It For?" *Globe and Mail*, 6 May 2016.

Wheare, K.C. *Federal Government*. 3rd ed. London: Oxford University Press, 1953.

Whitaker, Reginald. *A Sovereign Idea: Essays on Canada as a Democratic Community*. Montreal and Kingston: McGill-Queen's University Press, 1992.

White, James Boyd. *Acts of Hope: Creating Authority in Literature, Law, and Politics*. Chicago: University of Chicago Press, 1994.

– *When Words Lose Their Meaning: Constitutions and Reconstitutions of Language, Character and Community*. Chicago: University of Chicago Press, 1984.

White, Marianne. "Happy 400th Birthday Quebec City." *Leader-Post* (Regina), 4 July 2008, B12.

Whyte, John D. "A Case for the Republican Option." In *Canada and the Crown: Essays on Constitutional Monarchy*, ed. D. Michael Jackson and Philippe Lagassé, 119–37. Montreal and Kingston: McGill-Queen's University Press, 2013.

– "Constitutional Change and Constitutional Durability." *Journal of Parliamentary and Political Law* 5 (2011): 419–36.

Wingrove, Josh. "Former MP Describes PMO's Tight Control." *Globe and Mail*, 8 September 2014.

– "Ottawa, Privacy Watchdog at Odds over Information Ruling." *Globe and Mail*, 18 June 2014.

Wiseman, Nelson. "Phony Laws? Thank Goodness." *Globe and Mail*, 9 July 2014, A9.

Wood, Gordon S. *Representation in the American Revolution*. Charlottesville: University Press of Virginia, 1969.

"Working Together." Symposium on Senate reform. Faculty of Law of the University of Ottawa, 28 January 2015.

Index

Aboriginal and treaty rights, 39–40, 99

abortion, 95, 103

academic and public interest, 123–5, 128; lack of, 18, 42; increasing, 80–1, 82, 86; in monarchy, 27, 30, 43–4

access to information commissioner, 15

accountability, 15, 21, 36, 70–1; executive, 124; of Officers of Parliament, 15–16; political, 35, 91, 125; of the Senate, 80, 81, 84; in UK, 8, 89

Adams, Michael, 5, 78, 81–2

Advisory Committee on Vice-Regal Appointments, 40, 76

advocacy groups, 9

Alberta, 108, 114; creation of, 55

amending formula, 10, 11, 22, 26, 39, 72, 123, 134, 139; in Great Britain, 20

Americanization of Canadian politics, 18–19, 31

appointment: of judges, 75–6, 85; of the Lords, 74–5, 85, 89; prerogative of, 27, 29; to the Supreme Court, 127. *See also* Senate: appointment to

Audience, The, 30–1

auditor general, 15, 123, 124; and senator expenses, 16, 72, 80

Australia, 4, 63; Constitution, 137; direct democracy in, 18; dissolution of Parliament, 133, 137; and the monarchy, 41; republicanism in, 134; upper house, 12, 138

authority: governor general's, 37, 130, 132; executive, 20, 45, 49; governmental, 71, 93

autonomy, 22, 36, 77, 93, 142; Crown as model of, 26, 38–9, 116

Bagehot, Walter, 7–8, 20, 45, 59

Baldwin, Robert, 94, 119

Balfour Declaration, 44

Belgium, 110

bicameralism, xi, xiii, 21, 47, 50, 58–66, 71–2, 75, 77–8, 115

bilingualism, 39, 55, 99, 101, 142; Royal Commission on Bilingualism and Biculturalism, 110

Bill C-14, 86

Bill C-16, Canada Elections Act, 9–10

Bill C-23, 126

Bill C-51, 99

Bill C-60, 37–8
Bill C-586, 100–2
Bill of Rights of 1689, 70
Blair, Tony, 73
Blakeney, Allan, 137
Bliss, Michael, 4, 42
Bloc Québécois, 130
Bogdanor, Vernon, 98, 112, 118
boundaries: electoral, 5–6, 58, 75, 81, 109; provincial, 63
Bourinot, Sir John George, 7, 66
Boyer, Patrick, 51, 62
Bréton, Raymond, 116
Brett, Judith, 82
British Columbia, 55–6, 106, 108, 115
British North America (BNA) Act, 37, 57
Brown, George, 62, 66, 92
by-elections, 91
Byng, Viscount, 24, 28, 30, 44, 110, 117, 128–9, 130, 136

cabinet government, 7, 66, 119, 131, 137; federalized, 56
Cairns, Alan, 108–9
Campbell, Alexander, 7
Campbell, Colin, 90
Canada Elections Act, Bill C-16, 9–10, 91, 100–1
Canada (House of Commons) v Vaid, 15
Cannadine, David, 8
Carnarvon, Earl, 37
Cartier, George-Étienne, 57, 100
CCF (Co-operative Commonwealth Federation), 95, 108
census, 54–6, 81, 87
centralization: of American federalism, 116; of Canadian federalism, 12, 56, 105, 116
Charlottetown Accord, 106, 127–8

Charter of Rights and Freedoms, 11, 15, 18, 56, 95, 111, 123, 142; and courts, 45, 104; section 35, ix
chief electoral officer, 15, 124, 126
Chong, Michael, 100
Chrétien, Jean, 105
churches, 43, 73
Church of England, 74, 89
Citizenship Act, 36–7, 40–1
Civil Marriage Act, 105
Clark, Alan, 97–8
Clark, Joe, 5
Clark, S.D., 18
Clarkson, Adrienne, 32, 42, 132
Clokie, H. McD., 12
coalition government, 18, 28, 69, 92, 101–2, 109–10, 130–1; as legitimate, 4–5; in UK, 112–13
colonial government, 59, 61, 64, 91, 97, 119–20, 136
common law, 23, 35, 56, 126, 135
Commonwealth, 15, 22, 41, 135; Australian, 18, 33, 100, 137; New Zealand, 48
compact theory, 62
Conacher, Duff, 9, 101
Conacher v Canada (Prime Minister), 9–10, 134
Confederation, 51, 54–5, 60–1, 115, 121–2; compact theory of, 62; entry into, 57–8, 63, 64–5; pre-Confederation, 95, 99, 136. See also Fathers of Confederation
Confederation Debates, 54, 84, 115
confidence, 20, 70; loss of, in government, 9–10, 15; non-confidence, 6, 101
confidence chamber, 47, 64, 70–1, 72

Congress, 12, 57–8, 98
constitution, Canadian, 22, 72;
    compared to American, 56–8;
    duality of, 20; patriation of, 95
Constitution Act, 1867, 5, 11–12; on
    the Crown, 45, 49, 66; divided
    jurisdiction, 32, 56–7; Part III, 45;
    preamble, ix, 8, 14–15, 23, 38, 49,
    62, 120, 123; and the provinces, 12;
    on Senate role, 10–11; senatorial
    regions, 56; Section 9, 17, 20, 45,
    49, 56, 57, 75; Section 18, 15;
    Section 23, 73; Section 24, 66;
    Section 50, 9; Section 51A, 53;
    Section 94, 56, 57
Constitution Act, 1915, 53–4, 56, 65,
    88, 95
Constitution Act, 1982: Part I – see
    Charter of Rights and Freedoms;
    Part V, 10–11, 39; Section 35, xi,
    39, 123; Section 41, 8, 9, 10, 24,
    26, 53–4, 72, 131, 139; Subsection
    56.1(1) 9; Section 96, 75
constitutional architecture, 11, 16, 26,
    51, 53, 77, 85, 124, 136
constitutional monarchy, 6, 18,
    19–22, 25, 38, 45, 65–6, 69, 92, 105,
    119, 121; features of, 8, 19, 129,
    131
constitution by association, ix, 38,
    49, 62
Constitution Unit, 31
control, 18, 69, 91, 122–3
Conway, John, 26–7
Couillard, Philippe, 83
court challenge, 101, 109
Courtney, John, 106
Coyne, Andrew, 8
criminal code: Canadian, 15, 103
Crossman, Richard, 7–8

Crown, 21–5, 34, 36–7, 134–6; as
    distinct from monarchy, 26–8, 30,
    32, 40–3, 46–7; historic powers,
    21–2; honours, 33–4; increasingly
    public role, 28–9, role in Canada,
    32–3, 46–7; role in government, 20,
    35; role in selection of Senators,
    11; prerogative powers, 34, 61,
    105–6; vs republicanism, 21–2, 26.
    See also dissolution of Parliament;
    governor general
Crown in Canada, 26–7, 29, 38–9,
    117–18; legal perspective on,
    28–30
crown/monarchy distinction, 26, 30

decentralization of Canadian
    federalism, 12, 56, 105, 116
defence, national, 19, 27, 35–6
deference, 16, 64, 135
Delgamuukw, 39
Democracy Watch, 9
democratic deficit, 16, 25, 106
denominational schools, 55, 121
devolution, 43, 112–13, 115, 117
Dicey, A.V., 7, 129
Diefenbaker, John, 128
Dion, Stéphane, 101–2
direct democracy, 17–18, 36
discipline. See party discipline
discretion, 6, 9–10, 19–20, 28, 105,
    125, 130, 135–6
discrimination, 38, 90, 102–3
dissolution of Parliament, 9, 19, 92,
    93, 117–18, 124, 130–1; in Britain, 8;
    Crown Prerogative, 10, 28, 110–11,
    116. See also Harper government;
    King-Byng conflict
domestic imperialism, 22
double federalism, 14, 50, 57, 128

duality in Canadian politics, 20,
24–5, 32, 37, 45–6, 103; law and
policy, 59–60
Dufferin, Lord, 132
Duffy, Mike, 80, 122, 123
Dunkin, Christopher, 54

electoral boundaries, 5, 58, 75, 81,
109
electoral expenses, 6, 101–2, 109
Elizabeth II, 31, 43–4
equality, 58; in the Charter, 41, 104;
in the Senate, 60, 84
ethics commissioners, 124
Evatt, H.V., 7
expansion: territorial, 51, 88, 115, 135

Fair Elections Act, 82, 126
Falardeau, Jean-Charles, 14
Fathers of Confederation, 42, 49, 52,
56, 60–1, 68–9; diversity, 61; on
Senate, 99
Federal Accountability Act, 124
Federal Court of Appeal, 9
Federal Court of Canada, 9, 67
federalism, 12–14, 16, 51–3, 56, 116;
asymmetry of, 60, 88, 103;
jurisdictional, 12–13, 18, 87–8;
double federalism, 14, 50, 57, 128;
Supreme Court on, 62–3; in US, 12
federal principle, 12, 52, 58
First Canadian, 37
First Nations, 34, 39–40, 99, 116
First Past the Post, 46, 106
fixed election dates, 9, 35, 80, 135–6
Fixed-Term Parliaments Act, 8, 10
Flanagan, Tom, 101–2
foreign affairs, 18, 27
Forsey, Eugene, 7, 13, 20, 28, 67, 129,
130

franchise, 7, 128; female, 102–3;
in UK, 59, 88
Franks, C.E.S., 60, 68, 97
Fraser, John, 32, 42
Fraser, Malcolm, 4
Fraser, Sheila, 126
freedom, 41; in Parliament, 14–15,
70, 78, 104
Frye, Northrop, 25

Galbraith, J. William, 32–3
Galt, Alexander, 51–2
Gardiner, James, 91
Geneviève Motard and Patrick Taillon v
Attorney General of Canada, 39, 93, 134
Germany, 40–1
Gladstone, William, 94–5, 107, 112
Globe and Mail, 100, 139
Glorious Revolution, 23, 65, 91–2
governor general, 8, 35, 37–8, 46–8,
136, 140; acts on advice of the
prime minister, 44–6, 65–7, 71;
discretion, 9–10, 20, 109, 130–1,
135–6; duty of, 132–3; honours,
33–4; non-partisan, 48, 68, 76;
office created, 21; politicization of,
37–8; representative of the Crown,
4, 11, 17, 30, 40, 113, 119, 132–3;
selection of, 40, 67–8. See also
dissolution of Parliament
Great Britain. See United Kingdom
Gwyn, Richard, 135

Hailsham, Lord, 123–3, 138
Haldane, Lord, 117
Harper, Stephen, 111
Harper government, x, 4, 67–8, 101,
105, 109, 114, 126, 138; dissolution
of Parliament, 9–10, 19, 27–8, 42,
46, 110, 130; fixed elections, 9–10

Harrington, Justice, 9, 67
head of state/head of government,
    20, 34
Hincks, Francis, 42
House of Commons, 18, 36;
    allocation of seats, 87; authority,
    93–4; autonomy, 93–4; deliberative
    body, 96; disruptive potential,
    73–4; election, 105–7; independence,
    90–1; members, 96–9, 102, 104, 107;
    opposition to, 107; political life,
    92–3; representation, 15, 96–8; role
    of, 86–7, 99–101, 109–11; seen as
    weak, 121–2
House of Lords, 59, 72–5, 88–9, 114;
    historic, 44, 71, 139; Senate
    compared to, 49–50
House of Representatives, 104

independent members, 79, 124–5
information commissioners, 124
initiative, 17, 91, 105
Innis, Harold, 13
Internet, the: political activity on, 81
Ireland, 54, 74, 107; Irish Free State, 41

James, Michael, 14
Jean, Michaëlle, 19, 27–8, 32, 42, 110
Johnson, Lyndon, 98
Johnston, David, 40, 46, 47, 68
Joyal, Serge, 109, 110
Judicial Committee of the Privy
    Council (JCPC), 12, 17, 52, 105, 117
judiciary, 38, 45, 69, 78, 140

Kennedy, W.P.M., 11–12, 22, 56
King, Preston, 13
King, William Lyon Mackenzie, 5,
    64, 93, 129–30. See also King-Byng
    conflict

King-Byng conflict, 24, 28, 30, 44,
    110, 117, 128–9, 130, 136
Kunz, F.A., 59, 90

Lagassé, Philippe, 29, 35, 36
language, 83–4, 116, 124; and
    federalism, 13–14; Official
    Languages Act, 14, 124. See also
    bilingualism, 39, 55, 99, 101, 110, 142
Lascelles, Sir Alan, 44
Laskin, Bora, 41
Laurier, Sir Wilfrid, 19, 94, 102–3,
    114–15, 128, 137
leadership convention, 19, 102–3
Lefroy, A.H.F., 17, 54
Liberal-NDP coalition, 4, 92, 101, 130
lieutenant governor, 17, 18, 32–3,
    75, 117, 119, 136; appointment of,
    76, 85
Lipset, Seymour Martin, 135
Liquidators of the Maritime Bank, 12
Loat and MacMillan, 17, 18

Macdonald, Sir John A., 54–5, 69,
    95–6; on representation, 55, 90; on
    legislative union, 63, 73, 115
MacKay, Robert A., 90
Mackenzie, Alexander, 92
MacKinnon, Frank, 26
Macmillan, Harold, 99–100
majoritarianism, 56, 60, 62, 70, 71,
    138
Mallory, James, 23, 131
Manitoba, 55–6, 63, 84, 108, 121–2;
    language issues, 13–14; initiative
    and referendum (1919), 17, 105–6,
    117
Manitoba Act, 14, 55, 122
Maritime Provinces, 50, 52–5, 57;
    pre-Confederation, 21–2, 63, 65, 66

marriage, 95, 103–5
Martin, Lawrence, 46
Martin, Paul, 42
Massey, Vincent, 31
Massicotte, Louis, 83
May, Elizabeth, 29
McAteer v Canada (Attorney General),
   41, 134
media, electronic, 25, 81
Meighen, Arthur, 28, 93, 128, 129–30
member of Parliament (MP), 6, 54,
   79, 80, 82–4, 95–101, 104, 107;
   recall of illegal, 91
Mills, David, 55, 121
minorities, 61, 80; interests, 3, 14, 58,
   63, 71, 78; language, 83–4
minority government, 28, 117–18,
   123, 128
monarchy, 21–2, 40–1, 45, 118, 134;
   effect on Canadian identity, 22–3,
   27, 31–2, 38–9; compound, 24,
   32, 37, 116; as distinct from the
   Crown, 26–8, 30, 32, 40–3, 46–7;
   parliamentary, 14; and responsible
   government, 21, 24, 119. See also
   constitutional monarchy
Monck, Lord (governor general),
   120
Moore, Christopher, 20–1, 62
Morgan, Peter, 30–1
Morton, W.L., 17
Mulroney, Brian, 69
multiculturalism, 39, 116, 142

nationalism: in Canada, 22, 27, 36–7,
   40, 43; in Scotland and Wales, 43,
   114
New Brunswick, 50, 63, 84, 101
New Brunswick Broadcasting v Nova
   Scotia, 14

Newfoundland and Labrador, 63,
   65, 115
New Zealand, 41, 48, 100, 131
non-confidence, 6, 101
Northern Ireland, 112, 114
Northwest Territories, 58, 65, 115
Nova Scotia, 49, 50, 57, 63

oath of allegiance, 29, 41
O'Donohue, 38, 134
officers of Parliament, 15, 123–7
Official Languages Act, 14, 124
Oliver, Peter C., 77
Ontario, 22, 49, 52, 57, 63, 66, 76, 84,
   106
opposition, 4, 80, 107; government-
   opposition alignment, 70, 84
Order of Canada, 33
ornamentalism, 8, 139

Parliament Act (1911), 50, 89, 114
parliamentary monarchy, 6, 14
party discipline, 17–18, 64, 70–1, 79,
   80–1, 85, 96–8, 104
patronage, 63, 69, 85
Peerages Act, 89
Pilon, Dennis, 109
Pimlott, Ben, 41
plurality elections, 18, 97, 133, 138;
   Trudeau government to reform,
   47, 100, 106–9, 114, 137; in Great
   Britain, 113, 123
populism, 77, 118, 127, 131
Prairie Provinces, pre-confederation,
   55–6
Prime Minister's Office (PMO), 18,
   46, 101, 102, 119
Prince Edward Island, 57, 63, 64, 106,
   115
Priorities for Canada Conference, 19

private member's bill: C-586, 100–2
Procedure for Amending the
   Constitution of Canada, 11, 39
prorogation, 27–8, 30; controversy,
   15, 24, 42. See also dissolution of
   Parliament; Harper government;
   King-Byng conflict
provincial: constitutions, 57–8;
   court appointments, 75–6; federal–
   provincial relations, 37–9, 53, 117;
   governments, 17–18; jurisdiction,
   88, 123, 140; legislatures, role of,
   8, 9; representation, 66; second
   chambers, 12
public, the: political interest, 20–1,
   46–8, 66, 77, 80–3, 86, 96, 102; and
   the House, 125–9; and the Senate,
   69–70, 78, 80, 84–5, 138; role in
   making law, 105–6
public servants, 32, 121, 125

Quebec, 49–50, 55, 57, 63, 66
Quebec Conference, 64
Québécois, the, 14

Rae, Bob, 99
RCPM, 135
recall, 91
redistribution of seats, 55, 58, 81, 83,
   84
Reference re Senate Reform, 10, 58, 67
Reform Act, 100–2
Reform Party, 114
Reid, Escott, 31
religion, 43; freedom of, 41
representation by population (rep-by-
   pop), 52, 53–5, 58, 63, 66, 88, 90, 115
republicanism, 21–5, 41–2, 116, 118,
   134; in Australia, 41; in US, 22, 57,
   115

responsible government, 18, 35, 42,
   85, 97, 123, 126; achievement of,
   64, 90, 136; and the Crown, 21, 24,
   119; historically, 59, 60, 64–6, 92,
   94, 116, 120–1; and the Senate, 51,
   85
Riel, Louis, 91
Riker, William, 50
Robertson, Gordon, 31–2
Royal Commission on Bilingualism
   and Biculturalism, 110
Rupert's Land, 58, 115
Russell, Peter, 131

same-sex marriage, 95, 103–5
Samuel, Raphael, 43
Saskatchewan: government, 5;
   same-sex marriage, 105; seats in
   the House, 55
Saskatchewan Federation of Labour v
   Saskatchewan (Attorney General), 4
Savoie, Donald, 122
Scotland, 43, 54, 73, 112
Scott, F.R., 129
second chamber, hostility to, 25
sectionalism, 13
self-government, before Confederation,
   12, 24–5, 61, 64, 88, 120, 129
Senate, 51–8, 65, 79, 80–6, 87; civic
   empowerment, 80–3; committees,
   83; to complement the House, 60,
   71, 75, 79–86, 89; criticism of, 50–1,
   64–5, 67, 140; as a "deal," 51–2;
   expenses, 16, 46, 72, 77, 80–1,
   122; and federalism, 51–3, 63;
   history of, 49–57, 63–6; compared
   to House of Lords, 49–50;
   independence, 66–70, 75, 77–9,
   84, 86, 138; legislative body,
   10–11, 60, 65, 70, 79, 86, 89;

party discipline, 70–1; not representative body, 75, 86; retirement, 65, 69, 88; role, 53, 61–3, 65, 78, 83–6, 138–9; senatorial regions, 54–6, 66, 74–5, 82; size, 50, 61, 65, 75, 81, 88; tenure, 60, 77

Senate: appointment to, 10–11, 47, 50, 63, 67–9, 71–2, 83–4, 109, 139; judicial selection model, 75–6, 85

senate reform, 73–5. *See also* Triple-E Senate

Senate Reform Reference, 47

Simcoe, John Graves, 23, 62

Skelton, O.D., 128

Smith, Goldwin, 13, 43

Social Credit party, 108

South Africa, 41–2

Speaker (HOC), 15

Statute of Westminster, 32–3, 41, 44, 93, 115

St Laurent, Louis, 36–7, 69

Succession to the Crown Act, 2013, 38, 73

Succession to the Throne Act, 2013, 38, 93

Supreme Court of Canada (SCC), 53; appointments to, 77, 127; on bicameralism, 47, 59, 72, 85; on the Crown, 26; on federalism, 62; on privilege, 14–15; on the Senate, 51, 58–60, 77–80, 82–3, 104, 138–40; on Senate reform, 10–11, 38–40, 51, 67, 72

Supreme Court of the United Kingdom, 73, 89

Taché, Archbishop, 57

Thatcher, Margaret, 73

transparency, 15, 17, 21, 119

treaties, 99; treaty obligations, 34; rights, 39–40

Triple-E Senate, 13, 58, 75; proposal of, x–xi, 77, 83, 114

Trudeau, Justin, 111; electoral reform, 25, 47, 100, 106, 114, 133, 137; on senatorial appointment, 37, 72

Trudeau, Pierre, 5

Uhr, John, 138

Underhill, Frank, 23

unicameralism, 66, 138; in Canada, 64, 88; in UK, 50, 62

unitary system in Britain, 13, 20, 45, 87, 115

United Kingdom, 31–4, 40, 54, 65–6, 73–4, 88–9, 91–2, 111–17, 128–9, 135; EEC, 113, 117; prerogative power, 61; Second Reform Act, 50; unitary, 50, 87. *See also* House of Lords

United Nations Human Development Index, 3

United States of America, 54, 56–8, 62, 66, 68, 115, 127; Congress, 12, 57–8, 98; same-sex marriage, 104

Valery, Paul, 23–4

veto: of nominations, 100–1; of bills (Canada: Senate), 71; suspensive (UK: House of Lords), 50, 74, 114, 139

voter loyalty, 18; decline in, 86

Wales, 43, 54, 112, 139

war, 27, 35, 36, 95

Ward, Norman, 91, 131

War of Independence, 77

War-time Elections Act, 102

well-being, as international
   standard, 3
West, Benjamin: "Death of General
   Wolfe," 140–1
Wheare, K.C., 12–13
Whyte, John, 118–19, 125, 131
Wiseman, Nelson, 118

women: and franchise, 103; in the
   Lords, 89
Wood, Gordon, 127
world wars: effect on economy, 19;
   First, 103, 128; Second, 128
Wright, Nigel, 122